Government Documents and Reference Services

Forthcoming topics in *The Reference Librarian* series:

• The Bright Side of Reference Services, Number 33

Published:

Reference Services in the 1980s, Numbers 1/2
Reference Services Administration and Management, Number 3
Ethics and Reference Services, Number 4
Video to Online: Reference Services and the New Technology, Numbers 5/6
Reference Services for Children and Young Adults, Numbers 7/8
Reference Services and Technical Services: Interactions in Library Practice, Number 9
Library Instruction and Reference Services, Number 10
Evaluation of Reference Services, Number 11
Conflicts in Reference Services, Number 12
Reference Services in Archives, Number 13
Personnel Issues in Reference Services, Number 14
The Publishing and Review of Reference Sources, Number 15
Reference Services Today: From Interview to Burnout, Number 16
International Aspects of Reference and Information Services, Number 17
Current Trends in Information: Research and Theory, Number 18
Finance, Budget, and Management for Reference Services, Number 19
Reference Services and Public Policy, Number 20
Information and Referral in Reference Services, Number 21
Information Brokers and Reference Services, Number 22
Expert Systems in Reference Services, Number 23
Integrating Library Use Skills into the General Education Curriculum, Number 24
Rothstein on Reference . . . with some help from friends, Numbers 25/26
Serials and Reference Services, Numbers 27/28
Weeding and Maintenance of Reference Collections, Number 29
Continuing Education of Reference Librarians, Number 30
The Reference Library User: Problems and Solutions, Number 31
Government Documents and Reference Services, Number 32

Government Documents and Reference Services

Robin Kinder
Editor

The Haworth Press
New York • London • Sydney

Government Documents and Reference Services has also been published as *The Reference Librarian*, Number 32, 1991.

© 1991 by The Haworth Press, Inc. All rights reserved. No part of this work may be reproduced or utilized in any form or by any means, electronic or mechanical, including photocopying, microfilm and recording, or by any information storage and retrieval system, without permission in writing from the publisher. Printed in the United States of America.

The Haworth Press, Inc. 10 Alice Street, Binghamton, NY 13904-1580
EUROSPAN/Haworth, 3 Henrietta Street, London WC2E 8LU England
ASTAM/Haworth, 162-168 Parramatta Road, Stanmore, Sydney, N.S.W. 2048 Australia

Library of Congress Cataloging-in-Publication Data

Government documents and reference services / Robin Kinder, editor.
p. cm.
ISBN 1-56024-136-5 (alk. paper)
1. Libraries, Depository – Reference services. 2. Libraries – Special collections – Government publications. 3. Reference services (Libraries). 4. Government publications. I. Kinder, Robin.
Z675.D4G68 1991
025.5'2 – dc20

91-28080
CIP

025.52
G721

Government Documents and Reference Services

CONTENTS

THE TECHNICAL DOCUMENT

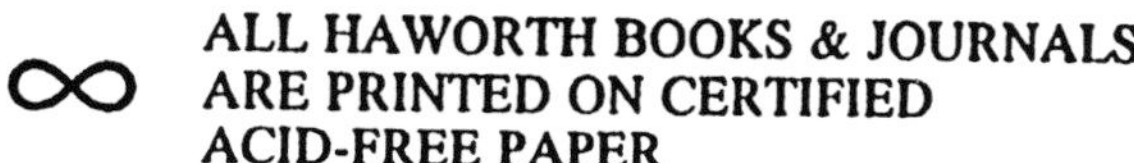
ALL HAWORTH BOOKS & JOURNALS ARE PRINTED ON CERTIFIED ACID-FREE PAPER

ABOUT THE EDITOR

Robin Kinder, MLS, is a reference librarian at William Allan Neilson Library, Smith College, Northhampton, Massachusetts. Her subject interests include literature, government documents, law and women's studies. She is the associate editor of *the Reference Librarian* and *The Acquisitions Librarian*.

Introduction: Access and Advocacy: Government Documents and the Librarian

Access to government documents is the theme of this issue. Whether discussing the merits of CD-roms, or reference sources in specific subject areas, of the usefulness of government documents residing in the online catalog, the contributors knowingly present the dilemmas of accessing federal sources of information.

The infamous unobtrusive testing of reference librarians' use and non-use of public documents revealed a truth most librarians know: consulting a document may well be the last resort. One agrees that document searching can be difficult, perplexing or even impossible to navigate, depending on the circumstances of the library setting. One wonders if these tested librarians simply did not know, were too worldy to even try, or perhaps even had the user's best interest in mind when the question arose. Did the librarian, for instance, determine at any point that the difficulty of information retrieval rendered that information less useful for the client? This last tack obviously smacks of an excuse or at least of a means of escape.

These considerations don't absolve the librarian of responsibility in accessing a document when that document provides the answer. What is illuminated is the dilemma of access and how that impacts on the librarian's ability to provide information in a timely fashion. Given the quality and timeliness of current governmental printed sources, one begins to understand that the librarian would welcome even the crudest CD-rom product over chaos. In many ways, Morehead's brief and nostalgic look at past bibliographic sources in documents show how far we have come and how far we have yet to go.

It would seem, however, that CD-rom products and online public catalogs give us the possibility, for the first time in many libraries, of providing a client with the most relevent answer in the shortest time. This is not every librarian's dream, especially those to whom thoroughness and comprehensiveness are the hallmark of a successful search. Still, as far as

© 1991 by the Haworth Press, Inc. All rights reserved.

documents are concerned, one must consider the argument for or against technology to be a moot point. (Anything approaching bibliographic control over so unweildy a beast must be not only welcomed but celebrated.) Librarians fail to advocate for the user when we argue the fine points of CD-rom access, the bibliographic inconsistencies or searching failures, especially when the market is limited and comparison among access systems suddenly diminishes to a select few when considering documents retrieval.

Most clients, when asking a question, do not even know that the answer they seek lies in the sources of information they pay for annually. Even those who do request a document source generally are seeking a specific statistic, citation, or agency document; only more sophisticated users require comprehensive searching through public documents. When they reach that level, these users know they are in for a process both tedious and, at times, wonderfully serendipitous. In a public library setting, government documents are often the only source that will provide the answer to a necessary question—not a purely academic one—and the librarian cannot and should not provide a secondary source, with apologies. Thus the user determines the level of service, not the librarian. In most instances, the user is unimpressed by depth and more impressed by delivery. Extensive manual searching enervates the user, frustrates the librarian, and rarely makes for a successful reference transaction. If electronic technology in any way bridges the gulf between user and document, then that technology becomes advocate for the user, even if it appears at times purely the devil's advocate to the librarian.

Librarians must know the basic governmental sources. (This involves more than occasionally consulting U.S. statistics or the pertinent hearing on a subject. It involves knowing the structure of government, its agencies and the mandates these agencies carry. Once this is mastered, the librarian is well on his or her way to considering these agencies as possible sources when a question arises. From there, the specific source presents itself.) Librarians have a responsibliity to provide the answer regardless of the level of difficulty in accessing the answer. Beyond these two points, the field remains open, chaotic and at a creative juncture, in the way all reference sources appear as they become transformed into electronic sources. Librarians in general, not only documents librarians, must advocate for any source that increases access to documents for the user. Using CD-roms, criticizing their weaknesses, and arguing for enhancements will insure these products will become more sophisticated. At present, most libraries lack even basic governmental CD-roms, a failure resting equally on librarians and administrators. If the librarian does not advocate from a position of knowing what is best for the library's clientele, the administration will continue to cede documents a low place, clinging to the old belief that documents are the bane of librarians everywhere.

How much librarians advocate in a sense may be directly related to that unobtrusive testing. If we do not care to consult documents to answer a question, then going out on a limb for electronic access is far beyond our meager abilities. The unobtrusive testing perhaps revealed our meagerness all too well, our laxness in playing the role of advocate for the user whenever we are in a reference transaction. This introduction reveals a piece of the mosaic that comprises this collection. The writers here have provided the reader with an array of fascinating objects—from looking at specific catalogs, bibliographic sources, and electronic technology to considering the possibilities of the future, presenting philosophical ideas that are always strongly present when we consider the source. It is no wonder that the topic can evoke the strongest reaction in the American public—the U.S. government—should find its parallel when librarians look to a microcosm of that government—the ubiquitous, maddening, but always impressive government document.

Robin Kinder

Yesterday, Today, Tomorrow

Joe Morehead

SUMMARY. The rapid growth of computer technologies to supplement and eventually supplant print as the dominant medium for the provision of government reference information has profound implications for the role of government and the private sector in the creation, enhancement, and dissemination of these products and services. The reluctance of the federal government to provide full and free access to information in electronic formats precludes society's attainment of the concept of equity that is a touchstone of democracy. A way most certain to insure public access would acknowledge a First Amendment penumbra embodying the right to be informed, but this would require a Supreme Court ruling pursuant to a justiciable controversy. Based upon current official policies, the future holds little promise of an equitable diffusion of government information in non-print formats through the depository library system or related statutory mandates.

For what is time? Who can readily and briefly explain this? Who can even in thought comprehend it, so as to utter a word about it? But what in discourse do we mention more familiarly and knowingly, than time? And, we understand, when we speak of it; we understand

Joe Morehead is Professor at the School of Information Science and Policy, State University of New York at Albany, Albany, NY 12222.

© 1991 by The Haworth Press, Inc. All rights reserved.

also, when we hear it spoken of by another. What then is time? If no one asks me, I know. If I wish to explain it to one that asketh, I know not.

St. Augustine[1]

INTRODUCTION

Compared to the grand philosophical perplexity that troubled the soul of the Bishop of Hippo, this personal reminiscence is a mere exiguity. Over two decades of plashing among the bogs and fens of government reference sources permits me to reflect upon what used to be, acknowledge the present, and gaze, however dimly, into the future. No majestic vistas of the imagination are proffered in this account. The question that puzzled St. Augustine and other eminent thinkers has been co-opted by the cosmologists, who now posture as the metaphysicians of time past and time future. But these imperfect observations, like shadowy ambrotypes, may nonetheless afford some perspective "of what is past, or passing, or to come."[2] If there is a message in this text, it concerns the contrast between the fragmentation of time wrought by the computer and the policies of government which, like the mills of God, grind slow and exceeding small.

YESTERDAY

Weaned on the stately prose and descriptive density of Schmeckebier and guided by the bibliographic lamps of Andriot, Childs, and Leidy, I found my way among the flawed icons of government reference information as it was practiced in the 1960s: the use of Poore's *Descriptive Catalogue*, Greely's *Public Documents of the First Fourteen Congresses*, the 1911 *Checklist*, the *Monthly Checklist of State Publications*, the *United Nations Documents Index*, and other sources too numerous to mention. Conversely, I was delighted with the bibliographic fidelity and amplitude of the renowned *Document Catalog*, the utility of the *Numerical Lists and Schedule of Volumes*, the magisterial integrity of Dubester's *Catalog of United States Census Publications*. Helping patrons search for small craft in a rolling sea of government information became a challenge, an adventure. Effecting a rescue mission engendered a palpable pleasure.

There was actually a time when the pre-1976 *Monthly Catalog* arrived in depository libraries precisely ten days into the new month, bearing the entries of the previous issue. Today we would be astonished at such punctuality, accustomed as we have become to persistent, pernicious delays of *years* in the distribution of important sources like the bound volumes of the *Congressional Record* or the *Treaties and Other International Acts Series* (TIAS) pamphlets. The availability of some of these textual and bibliographic sources in expensive, commercial (but less dilatory) mediums does not absolve governments from timely provision of information in a choice of formats.

Some of the old standbys I used consistently to answer many a reference question still prevail. I am thinking of sources like the quadrennial "Plum Book," which excited a flurry of use until patrons, sated with its pages and pages of wearying schedules, abandoned it to await the next presidential election and the next edition.[3] In 1988 a commercially published "rival," called the "Prune Book," was greeted favorably by the reviewing media. Subtitled *The 100 Toughest Jobs in Washington*, the *Prune Book* is a far more interesting read than the official drupaceous sobriquet.[4]

Memories of other publications with colorful popular names include New York City's *Green Book*, New York State's *Red Book* and *Blue Book*, the *National Reporter Blue Book* set, the *Uniform System of Citation*, known as the *Bluebook*, and, more recently, the University of Chicago Law Review's *Maroon Book*. One amusing aspect of these reference sources is that some no longer bear the color by which they have long been identified.

During my tenure at a large metropolitan public library, I found it necessary to refer again and again to certain federal government sources. Directories like the Department of State's quarterly *Diplomatic List* and annual *Foreign Consular Offices in the United States* proved invaluable. The Naval Observatory's *Astronomical Almanac*, which I knew by its former title, the *American Ephemeris and Nautical Almanac*, was used primarily by astrology aficionados. *Where to Write for Birth and Death Records, United States and Outlying Areas* was one of a trio that I used to answer telephone queries almost daily. Since 1982 it is known by the title *Where to Write for Vital Records*.[5] *Medal of Honor Recipients* cumulates every so often. Issued as a committee print by the Senate Committee on Veterans' Affairs, this publication not only provides the names of those who were awarded this nation's highest military honor but also historical background on the esteemed decoration. The same Senate committee issued a separate monograph for Medal of Honor recipients of the Vietnam conflict.[6] I used the former source frequently, as I used the three-volume *Minerals Yearbook* for its helpful source notes. Last but certainly not least I had at hand a well-thumbed edition of the Secret Service's irregularly issued booklet titled *Know Your Money*, a didactic brochure informing us how to detect counterfeit bills and coins and how to guard against forgery losses.

In addition to the above, there are the basic federal reference materials everyone consults. These include, but are not limited to, the *Official Congressional Directory*, *Statistical Abstract of the United States*, *United States Government Manual*, *Congressional District Atlas*, *Budget of the United States Government*, and its big sister, the *Budget . . . Appendix*. Indeed, so facile did I become at ferreting out information from some of these books that I almost came to believe I had absorbed large particles of data into my circulatory system, with pieces of information lodged even in my Island of Langerhans.

But that was then, this is now.

TODAY

"Now! Now!" cried the Queen. "Faster! Faster!"

Lewis Carroll[7]

While viewing a case on WESTLAW's WALT II terminal recently, I needed to Shepardize a specific headnote. Typing in the requisite command, I awaited the display of citing sources. Because it was a peak-use time, the system was "slow" in responding. After a few moments, I began to fidget, my right foot doing a frenetic tapping that would have elicited the admiration of Gregory Hines. Perhaps twenty seconds elapsed before the screen displayed the desired citations. After I concluded my search and signed off, I realized that the alternative would have occupied considerably more time—locating the appropriate Shepard's unit on the shelves, squinting at the crowded columns of minuscule squiggles, copying the citations, and locating the apposite legal texts on point. "How impatient I've become," I thought. This was by no means the first time I was made aware of the relative ease of conducting an online search, but it always stuns me, like the sun. With computers capable of operational tasks at speeds measured in picoseconds, we find ourselves increasingly restive if our friendly beasts of burden do not provide us with immediate results. We have become like children again, inclined to throw mental tantrums if we do not achieve instant gratification of our information needs.

O brave new society! Computing machines, the Prayer Wheels of the neoteric world, have laid claim to the honorific of ascendant metaphor of this *fin de siècle* century. The current cynosure of the information technologies affecting government reference service today is the proliferating compact disk systems, which have upstaged the now humdrum online services both in expectation and hype. It is becoming difficult to remember that a mere handful of years ago, those selfsame online products were greeted with similarly promiscuous enthusiasm. Whereas formerly the literature of the profession teemed with articles dissecting this or that new electronic file, nowadays one can scarcely avoid reading about the joys of optical technology in the provision of imperishable gigabytes of information.

The consuming public-sector, private-sector argument that characterized the Reagan years continues into the Bush administration. Privatizing government's information functions and delivery systems is an Office of Management and Budget (OMB) crusade, but it is nothing new. Indeed, it was prefigured metaphorically by Charles Wilson, Eisenhower's first Secretary of Defense, who stated in his confirmation hearings before the Senate Armed Services Committee that "What's good for General Motors is good for the country." Although this fatuous aphorism was tempered by Eisenhower's warning of the potential dangers of misplaced power in his famous "military-industrial complex" farewell address to the nation, current policy represents OMB's ardent courtship of business interests; in pursuit of this fatal attraction, the object of OMB's affections can do no wrong. If you substitute the words "information industry" for "General Motors" in Wilson's remarks, executive intent concerning access to government information is expressly predicated.

The amount of literature on this topic would fill a storefront library and spill over into the mean streets,[8] but while the feds temporize and fret over costs, the private sector has been busily producing and marketing a plethora of offline (CD-ROM) as well as online government reference services.[9] So volatile and frenzied has this activity become that there already exists a growing number of CD-ROMs out of print. As usual, the information industry is doing a creditable job of designing value-added features; but that, of course, is not what the privatizing dispute is about.

Nevertheless, the proliferation of the sacred silver frisbees and other hi-tech products is awesome to behold. The metastasization of these vendibles throughout the post-industrial organism is well underway. Whereas the Government Printing Office has reached agreements with a few agencies and the congress (its parent body) to distribute information on compact disk to depository libraries, the private establishment, with its customary zeal and alacrity, offers an array of government reference software to all libraries. Meanwhile, the OMB janissaries spend their time devising cost-effective formulae, as if information was just another fungible commodity, like cabbages and battleships, shoes and sealing wax. Alas, more public policy mischief is concocted in BOGSAT[10] than is dreamed of in our most melancholy reveries.

The following represents a very selective list of electronic gadgetry used to answer law/government reference queries. Once the librarian or user becomes familiar with the search strategies, these systems deliver the requisite textual or bibliographic information much faster and much more conveniently than a comparable effort expended in a manual search for similar or identical information.

Commercial Products and Services

The Winter 1988 edition of the *WESTLAW Database List* consists of 103 single-spaced pages of databases, including gateway services like DIALOG, Information America,[11] PaperChase,[12] PHINet,[13] State Net,[14] and VU/TEXT,[15] all of which contain information generated by or for governments. Mead Data Central's LEXIS library files continue to match WESTLAW in quantity as both giants stride apace to capture every conceivable law/government file online.[16]

SilverPlatter, OCLC Reference Services, Information Access Company, Video Laser Systems, Auto-Graphics, Slater Hall, DIALOG On-Disc, EBSCO Electronic Information, Tri-Star Publishing, Brodart, and many other companies are listed in *CD-ROMS In Print*, a disappointing guide which does not provide information on the subjects or fields covered.[17] The competition to produce the friendliest version of perennially useful sources like the *Monthly Catalog*, ERIC, and NTIS allows libraries to subscribe to two or more disk products on a trial basis.

Disclosure Incorporated markets LaserDisclosure, a CD which provides a staggering amount of information filed with the Securities and Exchange Commission: 10-Ks, 10-Qs, annual reports, proxies, and documentation on the more than 6,000 companies traded on the New York Stock Exchange, American Stock Exchange, and NASDAQ.

WILSONDISC offers access to the *Monthly Catalog*, *Index to U.S. Government Periodicals*, and *Index to Legal Periodicals*. A host of health information agencies are ondisk with SilverPlatter, including MEDLINE, POPLINE, and CANCER-CD. The Microsoft Stat Pack contains a melange of statistical information from various agencies. Another Microsoft product on CD, called Small Business Consultant, brings together information from the Small Business Administration, Patent and Trademark Office, and other federal entities. Slater Hall Information Products issues *SHIP discs* consisting of files from the Census Bureau, the Bureau of

Economic Analysis, and from other federal units that gather and/or disseminate data. Congressional Information Service (CIS) offers *Congressional Masterfile*, wherein pre-1970 hearings, committee prints, reports, documents, and executive messages transmitted to the congress during various periods since 1789 have been programmed for access on a single CD. In addition, CIS has an optical disk package which cumulates all the indexed and abstracted information published in *American Statistics Index*, *Statistical Reference Index*, and the *Index to International Statistics*.

This is but a paltry sampling. It may be only slightly facetious to remark that, by the end of this century, virtually all retrospective and current unclassified government information, at least in bibliographic form, will be available online, ondisk, or in a microformat.

Federal Government Products and Services

The neo-mercantilism of the Reagan-Bush era is a philosophy inimical to the unfettered access to government information.[18] As of early 1989, only five projects, three ondisk and two online, were being considered for distribution to depository libraries. The CD-ROM products comprise Bureau of the Census Test Disk No. 2, Environmental Protection Agency (EPA) *Toxic Chemical Release Inventory* (TRI), and volume 131 of the permanent bound edition of the *Congressional Record* (1985). The two online products consist of the Economic Bulletin Board of the Department of Commerce and *Energy Research Abstracts* through the Department of Energy's computer databank.[19] These are "pilot projects," feasibility studies available to a limited number of depository institutions. Of the five, the Census Bureau's disk has advanced more rapidly than the others, and it is anticipated that all depository libraries will eventually have access to its contents.[20]

Other electronic products available through the government agency itself or through the National Technical Information Service (NTIS) are fee-based. The *Toxic Chemical Release Inventory* file became part of the National Library of Medicine's (NLM) Toxicology Data Network (TOXNET) and went online for public access in the Spring of 1989.[21] Other NLM databases publicly available include AIDSLINE, a bibliographic file which is a subset of records from MEDLINE and is the first step in NLM's overall plan for an AIDS Information Service customized database in response to the AIDS crisis; DOCLINE, an automated interlibrary loan request and referral system; AVLINE, audiovisuals online; CHEMLINE, and online chemical dictionary; PDQ (Physician Data Query), state-of-the-art cancer treatment and referral information; GRATEFUL MED (*sic*.), a microcomputer-based software package which provides an interface to selected databases on the National Library of Medicine's well-known MEDLARS system; and many other numeric and bibliographic databases.

The Bureau of the Census has developed prototypes of the 1990 *TIGER/Line File* for all counties in the nation. TIGER, an initialism for Topologically Integrated Geographic Encoding and Referencing, is the geography for the 1990 decennial census; and *TIGER/Line* prototypes identify the codes and geographic coordinates for census tracts, block numbering areas, and census blocks. Each file is contained on a single reel of tape at a cost of $175 per file. Looking ahead, many products of the 1990 count will become available on CD in addition to summary tape and fiche. Few products will appear in print; those that do will be available to users much later than the electronic products.[22]

Government agencies are exploring the use of CD-ROM technology as an alternative to microfiche. The Defense General Supply Center currently distributes some 16,000 sets of fiche to users worldwide from its Hazardous Materials Information System (HMIS) database. But information managers will augment this system by using CD as a distribution format throughout the Department of Defense and its private sector contractors. The HMIS disk's relatively low cost and easy storage will prove so attractive that the microfiche will be phased out. U.S. Geological Survey (USGS) scientists have been studying the CD-ROM potential since 1985, and they have formed a Special Interest Group on CD-ROM Applications & Technology (SIGCAT) to share ideas and relate experiences about the use of disks in the federal government. The USGS has scanned ocean floors out to the 200-mile limit, where potential oil and mining sites are located. The data gathered in these explorations can be stored on one disk, 900 megabytes, representing the entire Gulf of Mexico. Anyone with a PC and enough money can access these data instead of relying upon a stack of magnetic tapes three feet high.

But the government "does not have anything to compete with the [information] industry standard for full-text retrieval software."[23] Consequently, industry sells or leases disks to agencies like USGS, NASA, the Library of Congress, the U.S. Postal Service, and some Federal Depository Libraries (libraries of executive departments and agencies designated pursuant to 44 U.S.C. 1907) for prices ranging from $35 to $90,000 (for highly proprietary financial data).[24] Will ordinary depository libraries throughout the country participate in this electronic largess so that individuals who support these government-industrial-complex activities with their tax dollars reap some benefit on their investment in the nation? Not today, perhaps tomorrow, maybe never.

Easy Listening: The FR on FM

One of the more exotic flowers that bloom in our electronic garden of delights involves transmitting the *Federal Register* to an FM radio station. A description of this innovation was reported in the February 1989 issue of *Administrative Notes*, the official newsletter of the federal depository library program:

> Jack Isemann, Senior Associate in the Office of Innovation and Development, reported on a pilot project GPO [the Government Printing Office] is conducting using the *Federal Register* and nine test sites in the Washington [D.C.] area, including the National Agricultural Library, University of Maryland, Library of Congress Congressional Research Service, Office of Management and Budget, and GPO itself. The pilot is an outgrowth of an unsolicited proposal to the Public Printer to disseminate information overnight using FM (frequency modulation) sub carriers through GPO at costs comparable to the printed product. The 120 day pilot project is being done at no cost to GPO. Tapes are transmitted from a sending unit at GPO over dialup lines at 9600 baud to a host computer in Sunnyvale, California, where some controlling information is added and it is sent back to a radio station in the Washington, DC, area. This is a PC based system, using proprietary software. Tests so far have demonstrated the technology works with no problems of information loss. Files may be searched with boolean logic using various proprietary software.[25]

Two aspects of this reported item are of interest. One is, of course, the technology—the fact that it is feasible to transmit the full text of the *Register* overnight, store it on a computer, and be able to search it the following day using word processing and text scanning software. One is able to access the FR before the print copy arrives in the mail; moreover, keyword searching of the text is possible. Each day's transmission includes a control file consisting of all the files dispatched for that quotidian issue. In addition, the files include GPO's "element identifiers" used in various text database processes and employed to facilitate composition for printing. The other aspect involves policy—the fact that, even though unsolicited, the GPO entered into a project over and above the five JCP-approved pilot endeavors noted *supra*. At this writing, the utility of this mode of transmission to depository libraries and their clientele is unclear.

The New Mandarins

The teleological assumptions of the clockwork universe have been replaced by the latest *deus ex machina*, a high honor indeed to be conferred by scientists and philosophers upon a human artifact possessed of spectacular speed and storage capacity but evincing only the rudiments of artificial intelligence within the confines of narrowly circumscribed algorithms. The information society is driven by time machines, wingéd chariots powered by the laws of physics; their creators and publicists crown these fleet devices with names or acronyms like Interactive Hypermedia, FAX, and WORM.[26] Consumers are initiated into their mysteries by encryptation manuals (such as Xywrite), user guides written in the burgeoning argot of Computerese, the pidgin English of a regnant technology. "We are entering a new temporal world where time is segmented into nanoseconds, the future is programmed in advance, nature is reconceived as bits of coded information, and paradise is viewed as a fully simulated, artificial environment."[27]

TOMORROW

> *No bounds have been fixed to the improvement of the human faculties . . . the perfectability of Man is absolutely indefinite . . . the progress of this perfectability, henceforth above the control of every power that would impede it, has not other limit than the duration of the globe upon which Nature has placed us.*
>
> Marquis de Condorcet[28]

Computer technology has, ironically, resurrected the notorious proposition espoused by eighteenth-century optimists that this is the best of all possible worlds. Moreover, information theory and cybernetics have invaded the field of cognitive psychology to the extent that "the idea of thinking of the self as a set of computer programs is widespread."[29] Turning the anthropomorphic fallacy on its ear, the next generation will redefine nature and self in philosophical terms consonant with the algorithms of the new Deity. Writing about Alan M. Turing, the great English mathematician, David Bolter suggests that the "programmer-God makes the world not once and for all but many times over again, rearranging its elements to suit each new program of creation. The universe proceeds like a program until it runs down or runs wild, and then the slate is wiped clean, and a new game begins."[30] In this *Weltanschauung* old-fashioned notions like free will are dismissed as simplistic.

So brief is the time-frame from the Lonesome Dove days of print materials to the Max Headroom era of electronic information that the future resonates with unlimited promise. In the near future, however, the paradise that some envision may not yet be manifest. One is well advised to remark the cautionary advice of Carol Tenopir, *Library Journal*'s database doyenne. By 1993 she does *not* foresee the advent of dramatically "improved command languages or a common command language," significant reduction in prices, a noticeable "increase in quality of the large databases," the "abandonment of controlled vocabulary indexing," and "an end to the intermediary searcher."[31] The last two predictions, of course, redound to the benefit of the information professional. However, Tenopir's moderating comments remind us once again that extravagant expectation is often the enemy of prediction.

The OTA Report

The Office of Technology Assessment (OTA) is an analytical arm of the U.S. Congress, and its basic mission is to help legislators anticipate and plan for both positive and untoward consequences of technological changes. Having issued earlier reports on the impact of scientific and technical information (STI) on public policy issues,[32] OTA published in October 1988 *Informing the Nation: Federal Information Dissemination in an Electronic Age* (OTA-CIT-396), a study that carries significant implications for government reference sources and services.[33] A twenty-page summary of the report highlighted the salient problems and opportunities expatiated upon in the basic document. Comments and recommendations appropriate to this essay include the following:

(1) The GPO sales program through the Office of the Superintendent of Documents, now largely a print and microfiche operation, could be strengthened by the addition of "selected electronic formats and products." Agencies that sell government information directly to the public (like the Bureau of the Census) should be encouraged to disseminate their products in electronic formats. Private vendors ought not to be dissuaded from competing in the marketplace "to enhance and resell [these government products in] electronic formats."

(2) The Depository Library Program (DLP) must be expanded to include electronic information. "As agencies make increasing use of electronic formats, limiting the DLP to paper and microfiche products would, over time, reduce the type and amount of Federal information available to the public, and would erode the legislative intent of the DLP." Moreover, if the "basic underlying principle of the depository program is to retain

free access to government information for users, then Congress needs to be aware that there may be additional costs associated with the introduction of certain electronic services, and assist depository libraries and GPO in designing and financing ways to make this information available to the public." For several years the Government Documents Round Table (GODORT) of the American Library Association has been advancing this concept by lobbying efforts, position papers, resolutions, letters to members of congress, etc.; the implacable adversary in this struggle is the Office of Management and Budget.

(3) To fulfill these desired changes *supra*, OTA recommends that Congress "amend the Printing Act, Depository Library Act, and Paperwork Reduction Act to provide statutory direction for specific institutional and technical/management alternatives, as well as to provide general philosophical guidance on electronic information dissemination." OTA outlines this philosophical issue with clarity and brevity:

> At the most basic level, a fundamental cross-cutting issue is public access to Federal information. Debate over the use of electronic formats, privatization, and the like is obscuring the commitment of Congress, as expressed in numerous public laws, to the importance of Federal information and its dissemination in carrying out agency missions, and the principles of democracy and open government. A renewed congressional commitment to public access in an electronic age may be needed.

(4) The Freedom of Information Act (FOIA) "was enacted in an era when paper records were the dominant form of government information. The application of FOIA to electronic formats has created a number of problems. The courts have expressed a need for Congress to clarify gray areas left open by the statute . . . Congress could amend FOIA to bring electronic formats clearly within the statutory purview, define the scope and limits of FOIA searches in an electronic environment, and clarify fees and procedures for FOIA requests for electronic information."

(5) The initiative belongs to Congress, which "has the opportunity to establish a strategic direction for electronic dissemination of legislative branch information. The importance of congressional information to an informed citizenry and the need to ensure equitable channels of access for all interested citizens, including access to electronic formats, are widely accepted in principle. The differences of opinion focus on the means of implementation."[34]

The matter of *equity* is crucial. OTA's three to five year projections indicate that "overall demand for paper formats will decline modestly and the demand for microfiche will drop rather markedly, while the demand for electronic formats will increase dramatically." A General Accounting Office report issued in November 1988 surveyed four nonfederal users groups, selective depository libraries; other public, college, and corporate libraries; scientific and technical associations; and "general associations" such a trade, business, educational, labor, and social welfare organizations. Data from these groups showed a "strong preference for obtaining increasing percentages of Federal information in electronic form and declining percentages in paper and microfiche." Specifically, "the depository library community desires or anticipates decreases in use of paper and microfiche formats and significant increases in online databases and compact optical disks."[35]

Because these technologies are far more timely than receipt of paper or fiche, those without "electronic access are disadvantaged." Librarians and other groups within or outside of governments argue that the federal establishment "has a responsibility to assure equity of access to Federal information in electronic formats as well as in paper. These groups contend that they are or will increasingly be disadvantaged to the extent that Federal information in electronic form is not available through normal channels." In the depository library program, "normal channels" means the right to select electronic products without paying a fee. The information industry and OMB, according to the OTA study, "support" dissemination of federal information in "raw electronic form without software enhancements or searching aids, but oppose government dissemination of enhanced or 'value-added' information." Addressing this position, the OTA study is politely circumspect but clear: OMB and industry policy is in conflict with

> the long-established government role in producing and disseminating value-added information products in paper format and its logical extension to electronic formats. Existing policy does not define "value-added" or specify under what conditions value-added electronic information products are inherently or appropriately governmental versus commercial in nature.[36]

The phrase "information is power" has become a platitude, but the larger truth subsumed therein is not negated. Power today is centralized in the "hands of a small coterie of public bureaucracies and giant corporations." Temporal discrimination is pervasive in post-industrial societies. Laborers remain mired in a "present-oriented temporal ghetto, unable to reach out and claim some measure of control over the future." The old "information rich, information poor" dichotomy is ratcheted up several notches with the advent of systems that can transmit information in speeds approaching that of the googol. Indeed, Rifkin opines that

> whoever controls the data and software of the nanosecond culture will determine how the future will be programmed . . . [The] battle lines are being drawn between those who believe in "enriched informational skills" on the one hand and those who are computer illiterates on the other, conjuring up an image of new class boundaries separating the powerful from the powerless, the privileged from the exploited.[37]

A Nation Informed

While the OTA report represents one of the few positive messages in recent years to bear a congressional entity's imprimatur, it is well to remember that the Office of Technology Assessment has no policy-making authority. By contrast, the Federal Bureau of Investigation, which has considerable clout, has been waging a war of harassment against library users with "foreign" names and pestering directors of libraries to cooperate in identifying certain users of *unclassified* documents readily accessible through *unclassified* print sources like *Government Reports Announcements & Index*, *Scientific and Technical Aerospace Reports*, etc., and their equivalent *unclassified* online databases. To add insult to injury, the FBI had the chutzpah to designate this incursion as a "Library Awareness Program."

According to C. James Schmidt, Chair of ALA's Intellectual Freedom Committee, the Program (pogrom?) "is a broader government effort than originally believed. Currently, it has been determined that 22 federal agencies, under C.I.A. direction, are involved in the program as part of an inter-agency Technology Transfer Intelligence Committee." Moreover, these government units "are empowered by their legitimate statutory charge to investigate domestic intelligence gathering by foreign nationals." Legal counsel advised the Committee that a "permanent injunction against these agencies to cease and desist would not be granted because the courts would construe that the Awareness Program was legal under the statutes, and that [libraries] would be unable to demonstrate sufficient injury."[38]

As Herbert S. White noted, the "diligent search of the unclassified literature for potential nuggets has been an old game, an generally an acknowledged one. . . . The Soviet embassy was, and I suspect remains, one of the best customers of the National Technical Information Service

[NTIS], and the CIA Library did (and perhaps still does) provide interlibrary loan materials to that same embassy."[39] Moreover, the government's tortuous semantic efforts to call these documents "unclassified but sensitive" betoken an oxymoronic paranoia, ironically out of step with continuing arms control negotiations, Détente-PLUS, *glasnost*, and other indicia of international eupepsia.

It is as if we have pledged our fealty to two different national governments, the one which appears to signal, however faintly, a willingness to disseminate freely and equitably certain kinds of information in non-print formats, the other which imagines a gaggle of spies skulking among the stacks and shelves of libraries. The antinomy thus projected suggests a rhetorical question: Are we to become an informed nation or a nation of informers?

CONCLUSION

> *And say, finally, whether peace is best preserved by giving energy to the government, or information to the people. This last is the most certain, and the most legitimate engine of government.*
>
> Thomas Jefferson[40]

The fact that I and many of my colleagues concerned with access to government information resort to lofty quotations from Jefferson, Madison, and other personages in American history demonstrates a failure of constitutional and statutory construction. The public's "right to be informed," in Bernard Fry's felicitous phrase, is an abstract concept.[41] The voluminous literature on this subject employs phrases like "embedded in First Amendment guarantees," "inherent in the Bill of Rights," or "implicit in our constitutional freedoms." But the lamentable truth is that the "Supreme Court has never dealt with this issue directly." Even optimistic scholars qualify their exuberant endorsement of a constitutional right to know. Thomas I. Emerson avers that the " Supreme Court has recognized in a number of cases that the first amendment embodies a constitutional guarantee of the right to know." However, he goes on to note that the High Court "has never clarified the right or pressed it toward its logical borders."[43] It is one thing to assert that there are no theoretical problems in constitutional interpretation; it is quite another thing to cite an explicit Court ruling. Legal scholars have uncovered numerous dicta and dissenting opinions on public access rights but no *ratio decidendi*.[44]

The present Freedom of Information Act (5 U.S.C. 552 *et seq.*), weakened by presidential executive orders, national security directives, and

Attorney General guidelines,[45] is *not* the instrument by which libraries and their users can effectively challenge the government's increasing propensity to withhold information. Its several exemptions, its Catch-22 provisions, its ambiguities, and its time-consuming procedures render it insufficient to the task.

Legislative action, most appropriately in a complete revision of Title 44 of the *United States Code*, is preferable to Berman's call for an FOIA amendment expanding "citizen access to *electronic* public information."[46] Most desirable, in my judgment, would be an extension of the "Penumbra Doctrine" so boldly articulated by Justice Douglas in *Griswold v. Connecticut*.[47] Arising from a justiciable controversy,[48] a First Amendment penumbra *embodying* access to federal government information regardless of format would elevate this implied "right" to that of black letter law.[49] As it stands now, the obligation of executive agencies to disseminate information fully is a political decision. Administrations circumvent this covenant with the people by invoking spurious exigencies like the deficit and national security, or by promulgating philosophical whimsy like the privatizing casuistry.[50] Little can be accomplished until the problem is depoliticized, for a hypothetical question is not justiciable. The suit that Representative Judd Gregg brought against the GPO and the Joint Committee on Printing, for example, was destined to fail. In *Gregg v. Barrett*, 774 F.2d 539 (1985), a federal appeals court upheld a district court's decision that judicial interference in a situation which could be resolved within the Congress would constitute an unwarranted encroachment upon a coequal branch of government.[51]

In the unlikely event that a First Amendment right of access were established as a principle of law under the several penumbra precedents cited and summarized by Justice Douglas in *Griswold*, there would remain many thorny procedural details. Scenarios involving judicial, legislative, or coordinate implementation are capably analyzed by Dockry and others—methods of enforcement, parameters, exemptions, privacy conflicts, cost accountability—but the point of law would be incorporated into constitutional doctrine.[52] After all, every polysci student knows that the Constitution of the United States of America is what the Supreme Court says it is.

One might ask what all these periphrases have to do with government reference sources and services. *Everything*. No longer would GODORT and other organizations with like affinities have to spend valuable time and energy in unequal battle with powerful entities like OMB and the Justice Department. Document reference librarians would be able to devote their full attention and considerable skills toward the provision of government information, employing a combination of the best print and electronic formats, in the service of the only true sovereign in our democracy, the women and men who collectively comprise the body politic. Or, as Wallace Stevens wrote, "Let the lamp affix its beam/The only emperor is the emperor of ice-cream."

Given the composition of the Supreme Court, much less the time and expense consumed in shepherding a justiciable controversy through the gridlocked federal court system, I harbor no illusions about the imminence of this desideratum. But as Shattuck reminds, "the tradition of public access to government dates back to the Constitutional Convention and the Articles of Confederation," and "Out of this early period in our history there emerged a clear American principle of open government . . . "[53] Only of late have we increasingly lost sight of this splendid tradition, this priceless legacy of our forebears.

Perhaps future generations will reclaim yesterday's heritage.

REFERENCES

1. Edward B. Pusey (trans.), *The Confessions of Saint Augustine* (NY: Modern Library, Inc.), p. 253.

2. William Butler Yeats, *Sailing to Byzantium*, IV, 8.

3. The official title of the Plum Book is *United States Government Policy and Supporting Positions* Y4.P84/10:P75/year). A "best seller" when it makes its quadrennial appearance, it is sent to federal depository libraries under Item No. 1022-B (papercopy) or 1022-C (microfiche).

4. Trattner, John H. *The Prune Book* . . . (Lanham, MD: Madison Books, 1988). See *Administrative Notes* 10: 1 (January 1989).

5. *Where to Write for Marriage Records* and *Where to Write for Divorce Records* comprised the other separate pamphlets, now combined into *Where to Write for Vital Records*, issued by the National Center for Health Statistics.

6. *Vietnam Era Medal of Honor Recipients, 1964-1972*, issued in 1973. See Wiley J. Williams, *Subject Guide to Major United States Government Publications, 2nd ed.* (Chicago: American Library Association, 1987), p. 125.

7. *Through the Looking Glass*, ch. I, 2 (1872).

8. At this writing, the proposed revision to OMB Circular A-130 (54 *Fed. Reg.* 214, 1/4/89) has raised disturbing questions for the library community. See also the original Circular A-130, "Management of Federal Information Resources," 50 *Fed. Reg.* 52730, 12/24/85.

9. Existing language in Title 44 of the *United States Code* precludes the distribution of government information in electronic format; moreover, in fiscal year 1990 appropriations hearings, the GPO did not seek additional funds to undertake pilot projects concerning the dissemination of information in electronic

formats to depository institutions. See *Government Publications Review* 16:92 (January/February 1989).

10. BOGSAT: a committee. Stands for Bunch of Guys Sitting Around a Table, a common initialism used in Washington, D.C., dating from the Kennedy administration.

11. Information America includes information in the public domain from several states, such as state Secretary of State Corporate data and Uniform Commercial Code Certificates.

12. PaperChase is a bibliographic record of items indexed in MEDLINE since 1966. About 25,000 citations are added monthly.

13. PHINet contains federal tax materials available through Prentice Hall, Inc., a major commercial distributor of looseleaf topical law reports.

14. State Net contains legislative and administrative information for the federal government and all states; included are bill tracking and regulatory decisions.

15. VU/TEXT includes information from Disclosure, Inc., which provides documents filed pursuant to regulations promulgated by the Securities and Exchange Information.

16. Mead Data Central, in addition to federal and state statutory and case law files, provides the NEXIS library files including important secondary sources like *Congressional Quarterly Weekly Report* and *The National Law Journal*.

17. Nancy Nelson (comp.), *CD-ROMS In Print* (Westport, CT: Meckler, 1987). The publication is issued annually.

18. See Virgil Blake and Thomas Surprenant, "An Information Policy for the Information Age," *Wilson Library Bulletin* 62: 44-46, 112 (May 1988); Arno Penzias, *Ideas & Information: Managing in a High-Tech World* (NY: W.W. Norton, 1989), *passim*.

19. *Government Publications Review* 15:499 (September/October 1988); *Administrative Notes* 10:11 (February 1989); *AALL Newsletter*, October 1988, p. 85.

20. Census Test Disk 2 provides agricultural data for counties from the 1982 Census of Agriculture and retail data by Zip Code from the 1982 Economic Censuses.

21. TRI was mandated by Title III of the SUPERFUND Amendments and Reauthorization Act (SARA) of 1986; the Inventory contains information on the annual estimated releases of toxic chemicals into the environment. The law requires that the data be made publicly available, and I suspect that this is the major if not only reason that the government is responsive to GODORT's demand that this information be made available to depository libraries.

22. *Census and You* 24: 3 (February 1989).

23. Minutes, Federal Publishers Committee Meeting, September 22, 1988, Washington, D.C. (mimeographed), p. 5.

24. *Ibid.*

25. *Administrative Notes* 10: 10 (February 1989).

26. See Ann F. Bevilacqua, "Hypertext: Behind the Hype," *American Libraries* 20: 158-162 (February 1989); William Taylor, "Just the Fax," *PC Magazine*, January 26, 1988, pp. 265-75; S. Blair Kauffman, "Erasable Optical Drives

Announced,'' *American Association of Law Libraries Newsletter* 20: 200 (February 1989).

27. Jeremy Rifkin, *Time Wars: The Primary Conflict in Human History* NY: Henry Holt and Company, 1987), p. 188.

28. Marquis de Condorcet (Marie Jean Antoine Nicolas Caritat), ''Outline of an Historical View of Progress of the Human Mind,'' quoted in John Hallowell, *Main Currents in Modern Political Thought* (NY: Holt, Rinehart and Winston, 1950), p. 132.

29. Sherry Turkle, *The Second Self: Computers and the Human Spirit* (NY: Simon & Schuster, 1984), p. 289.

30. David Bolter, *Turing's Man* (Chapel Hill, NC: The University of North Carolina Press, 1984), pp. 187-88.

31. Carol Tenopir, ''Five Years into the Past . . . Five Years into the Future,'' *Library Journal*, April 1, 1988, p. 63.

32. OTA reports which address the tensions between public access to and national security restrictions on STI include *The Regulatory Environment of Science* (OTA-TM-SET-34), February 1986; *Defending Secrets, Sharing Data: New Locks and Keys for Electronic Information* (OTA-CIT-310), October 1987; and *Science, Technology, and the First Amendment* (OTA-CIT-369), January 1988.

33. *Informing the Nation . . .* , a 333-page report, is available for sale from the Superintendent of Documents for $14 (S/N 052-003-01130-1).

34. U.S. Congress, Office of Technology Assessment, *Informing the Nation: Federal Information Dissemination in an Electronic Age – Summary* (OTA-CIT-397), October 1988, pp. 9, 13-14, 17-18.

35. *Ibid.*, pp. 3-5. See U.S. General Accounting Office, *Federal Information: Users' Current and Future Technology Needs* (GAO-GGD-89-20FS), November 30, 1988.

36. *Ibid.*, pp. 6-7.

37. Note 27, *supra*, pp. 162, 167, 170.

38. *Cognotes*, January 8, 1989, p. 1.

39. Herbert S. White, ''Librarians and the FBI,'' *Library Journal* 113: 54-55 (October 15, 1988).

40. Letter to James Madison, 1787. Quoted in Saul K. Padover (ed.), *Thomas Jefferson on Democracy* (NY: The New American Library, 1946), p. 23.

41. Bernard M. Fry, *Government Publications: Their Role in the National Program for Library and Information Services* (Washington, DC: Government Printing Office, 1978), p. 115.

42. Wallace Parks, ''The Open Government Principle: Applying the Right to Know Under the Constitution,'' *The George Washington Law Review* 26:8 (October 1957).

43. Thomas I. Emerson, ''Colonial Intentions and Current Realities of the First Amendment,'' *University of Pennsylvania Law Review* 125: 755 (1977).

44. The best analysis of this issue is found in David M. O'Brien, *The Public's Right to Know: The Supreme Court and the First Amendment* (NY: Praeger, 1981).

45. See J. Norman Baldwin and Dan Siminoski, "Perceptions of the Freedom of Information Act (F.O.I.A.) and Proposed Amendments by the F.O.I.A. Administrators," *Government Information Quarterly* 2: 132-33 (1985).

46. *Coalition on Government Information Newsletter* 3:5-6 (January 1989).

47. *Griswold v. Connecticut*, 381 U.S. 617, 85 S.Ct. 1678, 1681 (1965). The great jurist stated that "specific guarantees in the Bill of Rights have penumbras, formed by emanations from those guarantees that help give them life and substance."

48. A justiciable controversy is one which is "appropriate for judicial determination, as distinguished from a dispute or difference of a contingent, hypothetical or abstract character." See *Guimarin & Doan v. Georgetown Textile*, 155 S.E.2d 618, 621 (1967).

49. Black letter law, sometimes called horn-book law, is an informal term expressing the basic principles of law generally accepted by the courts or embodied in the plain language of statutes.

50. See John Shattuck, "The Right to Know: Public Access to Federal Information in the 1980s," *Government Information Quarterly* 5: 371 (1988).

51. *Gregg v. Barrett*, 594 F.Supp. 108 (1984), 774 F.2d. 539 (1985). Congressman Gregg wanted the courts to force his colleagues in the House and Senate to stop editing their speeches incorrectly and stop inserting material not delivered on the floor, in order that the *Congressional Record* be a more faithful transcript of proceedings and debates.

52 Kathleen A. Dockry, "The First Amendment Right of Access to Government-Held Information: A Re-Evaluation After *Richmond Newspapers, Inc. v. Virginia*," *Rutgers Law Review* 34: 339-48 (1982).

53. Note 50, *supra*, pp. 369, 370.

Information Policy Issues and Access to U.S. Government Information

Charles R. McClure

SUMMARY. During the end of 1988 and through the Summer of 1989, a flurry of activities occurred as Congress considered legislation regarding management of and access to U.S. government information. This paper identifies and discusses a range of policy issues that evolved from these activities and are likely to affect access to U.S. government information in the immediate years ahead. The paper stresses the importance of addressing these policy issues and offers suggestions for resolving them as a means for increasing access to government information.

As this paper is written in the Summer of 1989, there is a flurry of activity regarding the development of various Federal information policy instruments. A number of factors have contributed to encouraging this activity to take place. One important catalyst was the appearance of *Informing the Nation* (Office of Technology Assessment [OTA], 1988)—a major policy review and assessment of Federal information policies. The issues raised in this report continue to have a significant impact on the library community's access to U.S. government information.

Despite a range of criticisms and concerns over the OTA report, *Informing the Nation* (McClure, 1989), a number of its findings were, in the opinion of this writer, right on target:

Charles R. McClure is Professor, School of Information Studies, Syracuse University, Syracuse, NY 13244.

© 1991 by The Haworth Press, Inc. All rights reserved.

- greater Congressional oversight and direction for Federal information policy is urgently needed (p. 3)
- the Federal government must make a renewed commitment to providing public access to government information (p. 257)
- Federal agencies involved in the dissemination of government information (such as NTIS, GPO, etc.) must better coordinate their activities to improve public access to government information (p. 107)
- private sector information brokers/vendors have an important role to play in the dissemination of government information and providing value added services/products (pp. 312-316)
- Title 44 *USC* pertaining to the production and dissemination of Federal information, the *Freedom of Information Act*, and the *Paperwork Reduction Act* must be revised and updated to accommodate the electronic information age
- the GPO Depository Library Program (DLP) is an essential component in the dissemination of government information, and some restructuring of the program may be necessary to maintain its vitality and effectiveness in an electronic information age (p. 16).

In short, a major accomplishment of the report was its bringing together a broad range of issues related to information policy in a coherent and organized fashion; educating government officials, the various stakeholders, and the public at large as to key issues related to information policy; and drawing increased attention to the importance of information policy to the public at large. The theme of the various findings is clear: government information is the lifeblood of this nation, and every effort must be made to better manage that information and ensure its public accessibility.

But in addition to the appearance of *Informing the Nation*, a number of additional events occurred during the Spring and Summer of 1989, increasing the likelihood that Congress will take action on recommendations and findings from the report:

- the need for Congress to reauthorize the *Paperwork Reduction Act*, and in the process develop clearer guidelines for the Office of Management and Budget (OMB) regarding information policy development—resulting in numerous hearings held by a range of Congressional committees on topics related to government information
- an apparent interest on the part of OMB to reconsider its policy positions regarding access to and dissemination of government information ("Second Advance Notice . . . ," Office of Management and Budget, 1989)
- a decision recently issued by the Government Printing Office (GPO)

General Counsel Grant G. Moy asserting that the GPO has the authority to disseminate federal agency information in electronic format to depository libraries (Government Printing Office, 1989), and GPO's electronic dissemination pilot projects to test the appropriateness of disseminating various types of electronic information through the depository library program
- recognition on the part of many stakeholders, e.g., librarians, information industry spokespersons, Federal officials, researchers, etc., that there are significant problems with the existing Federal information policy system.

While other factors may also be playing a role in encouraging Congress to take action related to federal information policy, there is no doubt that 1989 saw more Congressional interest in this topic than in many previous years.

At this time, it is still too early to determine what the final outcome of all the various Congressional activities will be. But likely as not, there will be a new reauthorization of the *Paperwork Reduction Act*, and it will have some language in it affecting access to government information. But regardless of the results of Congressional activities during 1989, the library community will need to remain vigilant in its concern for and efforts to improve access to U.S. government information.

Thus, this paper provides an overview of selected key issues likely to affect access to government information over the next few years—regardless of Congressional actions to be taken in the immediate months ahead. The issues discussed in this paper are not intended to be a comprehensive list of those that may affect access to government information. Indeed, an effort has been made *not* to review issues such as privacy, copyright/ownership, public-private sector relationships, and others typically discussed in the literature. The issues discussed here, however offer important opportunities for the library community to improve access to government information.

The paper is not a review of the literature related to federal information policies and access to government information. Readers wishing to obtain background information and an overview of topics related to federal information policy and access to government information should review McClure, Hernon, and Relyea (1989), McClure and Hernon (1989), and Office of Technology Assessment (1988). A very useful summary of the recent Congressional activities, stakeholder positions, and the key issues as they have evolved through the Summer of 1989 has been written by McIntosh (1989).

INFORMATION POLICY ISSUES

The issues discussed below are framed in the context of (1) improving access to government information, (2) increasing the awareness of the library community on the importance of these issues in terms of their impact on access to government information, and (3) offering suggestions and strategies to resolve the issues as a means of improving access to government information. Figure 1 provides a summary listing of these issues.

Coordinating Federal Information Policy Development and Information Dissemination Activities

One can hope that legislation resulting from the 1989 "flurry of activities" will help clarify and coordinate federal information policy development information dissemination activities. But regardless of new legislation, there will be a need to continue to work toward better coordination and policy development both between and among the information dissemination agencies and the information policy development agencies.

The information dissemination agencies can be thought of as agencies who have primary mission responsibilities to disseminate government information, e.g., the GPO, National Technical Information Service (NTIS), the Office of Scientific and Technical Information at the Department of Energy (OSTI-DOE), the Defense Technical Information Center (DTIC), and others.

Agencies with primary responsibility for information policy development include the Office of Management and Budget (OMB), Office of Information and Regulatory Affairs (OIRA), the Office of Science and Technology Policy (OSTP), the National Commission on Libraries and Information Science (NCLIS), the Joint Committee on Printing, and of course, a number of other Congressional committees and subcommittees. Further, individual agencies with primary responsibility for government information dissemination such as the GPO and NTIS have significant impact on information policy development on a day-to-day basis.

Better coordination among the policy makers and the information disseminators is needed, and OMB has not been effective in this role (General Accounting Office, 1989, pp. 48-51). With the confirmation of a new director of OSTP during the Summer of 1989 (which included guarantees for a significant increase in the agency's budget), there is a widow of opportunity for this agency to take a much more central role in information policy development. Indeed, a logical point for coordinating government information policy development could be OSTP. Avenues should be

FIGURE 1

SELECTED INFORMATION POLICY ISSUES
AFFECTING PUBLIC ACCESS TO GOVERNMENT INFORMATION

- Coordinating Federal Information Policy Development and Information Dissemination Activities
- Dogmatic Stakeholder Policy Positions
- The "Techno-phoria" View of Information Policy Development
- Storing Large Amounts of Data in Electronic Format Does Not Equate to Accessing and Using that Data
- Responding to User Information Needs
- Importance of Training Users and Intermediaries in Information Technology Uses and Applications
- Evolving Role of Information Resources Management (IRM) in Government Information Management and Dissemination
- Restructuring the Depository Library Program
- Centralized Access to and Directories of Government Information
- Cost-sharing Techniques Among Stakeholders for Improved Public Access to Government Information
- Research on Government Information Policies, and the Access to, and Management and Dissemination of Government Information
- Importance of Value-added Information Services and Products from the Private and Public Sectors

explored for expanding and developing OSTP's role in the development and implementation of government information policy.

Dogmatic Stakeholder Policy Positions

The recent "Second Advance Notice . . . " information policy statement by OMB, Office of Information Regulatory Affairs (1989), is a breath of fresh air in an otherwise predictable, repetitive, and myopic set of policy positions frequently offered by various stakeholders. OMB-OIRA should be congratulated for opening this window of opportunity. The statement is a dramatic departure from a set of tired information policy phrases and principles that served in the past primarily to incite other stakeholders.

Members of the library community, especially representatives of the American Library Association, the Special Library Association, and the Association of Research Libraries (whose spokespersons have been active in recent Congressional hearings on information policies) must look for new approaches, consider compromises, and approach the issues with less emotion and more flexibility. Currently, a number of Congressional staff equate the dogmatism of the library community—regarding information policy—equal to that of the Information Industry spokespersons.

The various stakeholders must move to more moderate positions regarding information policy development. Can the information industry offer policy options that recognize their responsibilities for ensuring public access in addition to maintaining acceptable profit margins? Can the library community recognize that all electronic government information cannot be disseminated to depositories without some cost? Can federal agency officials move more toward developing information systems, services, and products that meet user information needs rather than only agency mission? OMB has made a strong first step in ending stakeholder myopia; other stakeholders can, and must, do the same.

Indeed, a significant stumbling block in the development of federal information policy is the lack of advisory groups composed of different stakeholders from different constituencies. Consistently, policymakers obtain the views of one particular group of stakeholders. Such views are out of context of the concerns and issues of interest to other stakeholder groups. It is important and essential that the stakeholders in information policy development start talking to each other directly to identify (1) possible areas for policy agreement or compromise, and (2) areas where they can agree to disagree.

The "Techno-Phoria" View of Information Policy Development

A number of information policy proposals and perspectives suffer from "techno-phoria," i.e., the wonderfulness of new information technology, especially CD-ROM. The discussion of these new information technology trends appears to be a bit "whiz-bang" and fails to describe the down-side of these technologies, the difficulties in their use, and the fact that many users of and intermediaries for accessing government information have little understanding of how to use and apply these technologies to better access and disseminate government information.

Indeed, some reports, including *Informing the Nation*, read more as a sales promotion for CD-ROM than a balanced view of the problems and issues with the use of the technology. Pearce, in "CD-ROM: Caveat Emptor" (1988) discusses numerous problems and issues with the use of CD-ROM in libraries—most of which are still with us today.

Simply because we will have the capability of mass producing huge databases on CD-ROM disks does not mean that all the various users interested in government information want that information in such a format or could use that information in such a format. Information, regardless of storage device, has no impact until it is retrieved and meets a specific user information need. A broad range of value-added services and products will be needed to make CD-ROM and other information technologies improve access to government information. Techno-phoria phrases such as "limitless arrays of possibilities for electronic dissemination of government information" have to be tempered by considering costs, impacts, and benefits.

Storing Large Amounts of Data in Electronic Format Does Not Equate to Accessing and Using That Data

There appears to be the notion that with these new information technologies for storing government information electronically, someone, somewhere, will in fact be better able to use that information, and use that information to resolve specific needs or decisions. In reality, as one National Oceanic and Atmospheric Agency (NOAA) official stated, they are "drowning in data" and their data centers are really "data cemeteries" ("Early Data . . . , 1989, p. 1250).

A spin-off from the techno-phoria view is confusion about the development and availability of new information technologies and the actual uses/applications of that technology by the user community. While there certainly is the potential for such uses, recent research suggests that a number of the information technologies have vastly outstripped the user's ability to apply that technology successfully in terms of accessing government information (McClure, Bishop, and Doty, 1989a).

The downside of current retrieval technologies is that many are not user friendly, and they tend to increase recall rather than the precision or relevance of those items retrieved. Being able to store the equivalent of 1,500 floppy diskettes of government information on one CD-ROM is of little benefit if librarians cannot *retrieve* that information to resolve the information needs of a particular user. Indeed, recent information policy discussions fail to describe the problems of effective information retrieval with large-scale databases and rather, leave one with the impression that existing and/or prototype retrieval technologies have already eliminated such problems.

Responding to User Information Needs

Designers of many government information services, products, and systems ignore conventional knowledge about how users seek and use information. Indeed, the following statement from *Informing the Nation* (Office of Technology Assessment, 1988, p. 37) is not only inaccurate, it encourages the continued development of ineffective government information services, systems, and products:

> Because Federal agencies collect and/or develop the bulk of Federal information they are generally the most knowledgeable about their own information products and services, and frequently are the best informed about the current and potential users of that information.

Recent research conducted at Syracuse University, School of Information Studies, supports, with some notable exceptions, the direct opposite of this statement—especially the assertion that Federal agencies "are the best informed about the current and potential users of that information." Discussed elsewhere are research findings on information systems design and information gathering and use behaviors which are frequently ignored in the design of government information dissemination activities (McClure, Bishop, and Doty, 1989a, pp. 67-69).

While it is clear that government information systems, services, and products must meet agency missions, they must also be designed such that they accommodate user information needs. In recent stakeholder debates about various information policy alternatives (McIntosh, 1989), the role and importance of the user seems to have been set aside. As stakeholders discuss the design of future government information systems, services, products, and policies, policymakers must make certain that the user perspective and the needs of specific user groups are carefully considered. Librarians can articulate these needs to Federal policymakers and information disseminators.

Importance of Training Users and Intermediaries in Information Technology Uses and Applications

Perhaps the most pervasive issue to be addressed over the next few years regarding access to and use of government information is that many agency officials, intermediaries (including librarians), and individual users are unfamiliar with the use and applications of the new information technologies. In the area of access to federal STI, findings from a recent research project at Syracuse University suggest (McClure, Bishop, and Doty, 1989b):

- there currently is much more information technology available to scientists than they know how to use effectively
- information resources management (IRM) at the federal level, and organizational information management in R&D settings is technology procurement/management driven and fails to consider meeting the needs of individual researchers with that technology
- academia, the private sector, and federal agencies typically have little to no formal programs in place to update and train scientists on how to *use* and apply the various information technologies to *their* particular research areas.

In short, throwing more information technology at users, intermediaries, and researchers is, in and of itself, *not* going to make them more productive or competitive. Indeed, there is an evolving point of view within the scientific community that information technology is a *barrier* to their work, not an aid.

Without doubt, the role and importance of intermediaries who can translate the information technology into practical uses and applications for users will become increasingly important. Some discussions of the new information technology assume that the applications are self-evident and that users and intermediaries will easily understand them, when in fact, the opposite may be true. Librarians must meet this challenge and be knowledgeable operators of the various information technologies that the government will be using (e.g., CD-ROM, online bulletin boards, electronic bibliographic and numeric data files, and high-speed research networks) if information technology is to be harnessed to increase access to government information.

Evolving Role of Information Resources Management (IRM) in Government Information Management and Dissemination

An ongoing issue for Federal information management and dissemination is the role that IRM will play in the future. To date, Federal IRM has been largely concerned with information technology procurement and management and has given inadequate attention to ensuring adequate access to and the effective dissemination of government information (Caudle, 1987). Specific suggestions for improving Federal IRM have appeared in the paper "Federal Information Resources Management (IRM):

A Policy Review and Assessment" (Bishop, Doty, and McClure, 1989) and will not be repeated here.

In 1986, the Federal government spent some $65 billion on research and development (R&D) (National Science Foundation, 1988, p. 3) and only a pittance on the management, organization, and dissemination of the information resulting from that R&D. Littel has changed with this ratio since 1986. In terms of exploiting Federal scientific and technical information (STI), such imbalances severely handicap overall U.S. competitiveness (McClure, 1989b).

Information policy must balance the efforts of Federal acquisition and production of information with management and dissemination of that information. Legislation must specifically direct appropriate agencies to manage, organize, and disseminate the vast storehouse of government information, and Congress must provide adequate resources for IRM personnel to implement strategies for accomplishing such tasks.

Federal IRM personnel are important players in improving public access to government information and ensuring that agencies do not turn into "data cemeteries." However, their potential to play such a role has not been realized. A broad-based educational effort is needed to better utilize Federal IRM personnel in order to ensure public access to government information within the existing Federal information policy system. But currently, many Federal IRM personnel do not understand the basic concepts of IRM, do not know how to implement these concepts in an organizational setting, are unaware of the larger Federal information policy system, and define IRM largely in terms of technology management and procurement.

The library community should recognize the importance of IRM as a means for improving access to government information and should lobby for:

- defining IRM in the context of public service and management-dissemination of information rather than technology procurement and automatic data processing (ADP)
- applying IRM principles and practices not only to internal, administrative data but to STI intended for external dissemination
- requiring Office of Personnel Management to develop IRM job classifications and responsibilities
- clarifying responsibility within the Federal government for developing educational programs to train existing IRM managers in basic skills and educate them to the broader concepts of IRM.

A key opportunity for improving the access to and dissemination of government information is to redefine and clarify the role of Federal IRM managers to understand the design and management of information systems and services that *meet user information needs*. Federal IRM has to move away from managing only the acquisition and storage of government information and pay specific attention to managing the access to and dissemination of that information.

Restructuring the Depository Library Program (DLP)

Informing the Nation. Office of Technology Assessment, 1988, recommended that some restructuring of the DLP might be necessary to meet the challenges of the electronic age. That discussion, however, fails to recognize that the vast majority of the 1400 depository libraries may not have the facilities, the resources, and the staff knowledge to provide access to electronic government information effectively. Once again, it is well to remember that simply because a CD-ROM of population statistics is sent to the depository libraries, such does not mean, in and of itself, that:

- users are aware that such information exists
- there is appropriate equipment at that library to access the necessary information
- the librarian(s) know how to effectively search the CD-ROM database
- the issuing government agency provided adequate indexes and finding aids to the CD-ROM disk.

Further, data reported in a recent user study of academic and public GPO depository libraries (McClure and Hernon, 1989) raises questions about the appropriateness of disseminating certain types of government information, especially electronic STI, through the DLP. Disseminating large amounts of electronic STI through the DLP (as it is currently structured) is unlikely to provide effective access to the STI by the R&D community.

Suggestions for the restructuring of the DLP have been offered by McClure (1982), the Association of Research Libraries (1987), Hernon and McClure (1988, pp. 365-390), and Morton (1989, pp. 15-16). However, a carefully developed assessment of the DLP structure in terms of meeting specific objectives has yet to be done. By and large, the government and the library community assume that if information is deposited into the DLP, responsibilities for providing *access* to that information have been met. This assumption must be questioned, especially as the government moves more into the dissemination of electronic information.

Centralized Access to and Directories of Government Information

While one can agree that dissemination of government information is fundamentally and inherently decentralized, steps need to be taken to promote centralized planning and coordination of government information dissemination activities, provide centralized locator systems to information services and products, and develop directories to assist users in knowing what types of information are available from what agencies. A key problem at this time is that many users and intermediaries do not know what types of government information exist in what types of formats, which agency produced or collected the information, and which agency is responsible for making that information available.

While there may be decentralized dissemination, there can still be centralized coordination, directories, and user assistance to access Federal information. Many government officials speak of "dissemination" when, in fact, they mean distribution. Distribution implies that the government information is simply made available if someone knows enough to request it and knows where to locate it. Dissemination suggests a much more active approach that assists users in finding the information and packages and deliver it to meet the information needs of specific users. This view differs significantly from that proposed in OMB Circular A-130 (Office of Management and Budget, 1985). Typically, the government is involved in distribution of information, not dissemination.

Cost-Sharing Techniques Among Stakeholders for Improved Public Access to Government Information

Simply put, the electronic age requires an expanded resource commitment to maintain and improve public access to government information. While many government officials, librarians, information industry representatives, and others accept the notion that inadequate access to government information, and especially electronic information currently exists, each typically believes that the "other guy" should pick up the expenses for improved access.

Clearly, there are significant pressures on the government for deficit reduction, there are pressures for profit-making in the private sector, and there are pressures on many libraries and other educational institutions in this country to increase their range of services and at the same time reduce costs. All stakeholders benefit from improved public access to government information. No one sector of society can pay for that improved access. Given these factors, cost-sharing strategies among the various stakeholders appears to be the most likely method to improve the resource base for improved management and dissemination of government information.

One implication of this issue is that the library community reconsider its view that "all" government information should be made available to the public, primarily through the depository library program. It is unreasonable to assume that adequate governmental resources are available to accomplish such a task, and further, one can argue that much government information is either inappropriate or unnecessary for distribution to depository libraries. Finally, a number of existing depository libraries, for a broad range of reasons, are unable to successfully disseminate the government information they currently receive.

The library community, government officials, the private sector, and the not-for-profit public sector should explore options for *jointly* supporting the costs associated with increasing access to government information and improving the effectiveness with which that information is disseminated to appropriate audiences. In addition, the library community could take a leadership position by identifying "core" types of government information appropriate for various types of depository libraries.

Research on Government Information Policies, and the Access to, Management and Dissemination of, Government Information

There is a dearth of research related to the management of and access to government information; the costs, benefits, and impacts of competing information policy options; the success of various types of government information services, products, and systems; the results and likely impacts of existing government information policies; and numerous other topics. Indeed, in 1987 Hernon and McClure identified and discussed a number of key research topics (with corresponding research objectives and questions) related to government information (1987, pp. 348-357). Since that time, little progress has been made investigating those topics. A broad range of research and additional investigation is needed as a basis for developing policy to enhance the effectiveness and impact of U.S. government information.

Key Federal agencies such as the OMB, OSTP, NTIS, GPO, and NCLIS (to name a few) can play an important role by supporting themselves, and encouraging other Federal agencies to support research projects broadly related to government information services, policies, products, and systems. Indeed, agency-specific basic and applied research is an appropriate and necessary activity in the design and implementation of information services, products, and systems. Agencies and policymakers must have better knowledge before such systems are designed and before information policies are developed. Without a better base of research, Federal agencies, private sector government information providers, and librarians will continue to design government information systems, products, services, and information policy based on opinion and testimony rather than objective information.

Hernon (1988) recently discussed how a range of government information services, products, and systems are evaluated by testimony rather than by research. There is a body of knowledge regarding methods to evaluate and investigate the success of various government information services, systems, policies and products. Unfortunately, the little research that has been done regarding government information and information policy is oftentimes ignored in the policy development process. Further, little effort is made to investigate key research questions which require attention. The debate over the possible privatization of NTIS in recent years is a good example of this problem. While recognizing that policymaking is an inherently political process, personal testimonials are inadequate replacements for informed and objective policy research.

Generally, Federal funding sources, individual agencies, and other non-government sources consider research related to information policies and the management of government information as low priorities. These funding sources must be made aware of the importance and need for supporting research related to a broad range of information policy issues. Policymakers need a broader base of objective information on existing information policies, their success, and their impact before they rush to design new information systems, products, or services and before policies are revised or created.

Importance of Value-Added Information Services and Products from the Private and Public Sectors

There is a clear need for the Federal government and the library community to encourage new roles for the private sector in the dissemination of government information and becoming involved in the DLP. One possible role has been described by Hanson (1989), who also points out that a private sector infrastructure for the dissemination of government information already exists. The private sector, government agencies, and the depository library community must work together to develop a range of value-added services and products to improve access to government information.

The private sector, may, in fact be better able to respond to new markets and develop new government information products and services. And there is no reason why contractual arrangements cannot be developed that enable private sector vendors to provide, through the depository library program, a range of services and products through various cost-sharing arrangements. However, there has been little constructive discussion among the private sector, the library community, and the Federal agencies to exploit such opportunities.

A number of organizations such as OCLC and the proposed "Reference Point" system (to name but a few) have a very important role to play in the dissemination of government information. These appear to receive little attention by the library community. Especially important is the development of "Reference Point," a public access online national database system currently being developed by Alan Westin (Westin, 1989). This system is likely to include a broad range of government information—much of which is not now available through the depository libraries. Such value-added services and products could have a significant impact on improved access to government information.

IMPORTANCE OF INFORMATION POLICY ISSUES

An important activity is increasing both the library community's and selected user populations' (e.g., the research community) awareness of the importance of developing effective Federal information policies and the need to better manage and disseminate government information resources. Hand-in-hand with increasing awareness is educating stakeholders and the public at large about existing information policy instruments, key information policy issues, and the various policy options available.

Nay-sayers and critics of efforts to develop a more effective Federal information policy system abound. Indeed, it is much easier to tell others that their efforts are ill-advised, inappropriate, etc., than it is to carefully assess the issues, describe specific policy options, conduct policy studies, or develop specific proposals.

Some shortcomings will appear in any constructive effort e.g., the Association of Research Libraries' *Technology & U.S. Government Information Policies: Catalysts for New Partnerships* (1987), OTA's *Informing the Nation*, (1988), OMB's June 9, 1989 information policy initiative, or the various legislative proposals offered during 1989 (to name but a few such efforts). Each of these, however, represents a step forward in the evolution of a coherent and effective set of Federal information policies. These organizations and individuals making such proposals should be congratulated for offering *positive strategies* to resolve Federal information policy issues.

The year 1989 may be remembered as a window of opportunity when significant advances in resolving a range of Federal information policy issues were made. But despite advances that may occur during that year, there will remain a range of information policy issues—such as those discussed above—that will require attention, debate, and analysis, among the various stakeholders. Such debate is both necessary and appropriate in the evolution of U.S. information policies. But the debate must be an informed and knowledgeable one, and it must be one that seeks solutions that increases access to U.S. government information and promotes the overall national competitiveness of this country.

REFERENCES

Association of Research Libraries. *Technology & U.S. Government Information Policies: Catalysts for New Partnerships*. Washington, DC: Association of Research Libraries, 1987.

Bishop, Ann, Philip Doty, and Charles R. McClure. "Federal Information Resources Management: A Policy Review and Assessment." *Proceedings of the 1989 American Society for Information Science and Annual Conference*. Medford, NJ: Learned Information, 1989 (in press).

Caudle, Sharon L. *Federal Information Resources Management: Bridging Vision and Action*. Washington DC: National Academy of Public Administration, 1989.

"Early Data: Losing Our Memory?" *Science* 244 (June 16, 1989): 1250.

General Accounting Office. *Managing the Government: Revised Approach Could Improve OMB's Effectiveness*. Washington, DC: Government Printing Office, May, 1989.

Government Printing Office. "GPO Dissemination of Federal Agency Publications in Electronic Format." Washington, DC: [Memorandum by General Counsel Grant G. Moy], May 22, 1989.

Hanson, Bob. "Can Congress Take the Necessary Steps to Ensure an Informed Nation?" *Government Information Quarterly*, 6 (no. 2, 1989): 153-157.

Hernon, Peter. "Evaluation by Testimonial." *Government Information Quarterly*, 5(1988): 1-3.

——— and Charles R. McClure. *Federal Information Policies in the 1980s: Conflicts and Issues*. Norwood, NJ: Ablex Publishing Corporation, 1987.

———. *Public Access to Government Information: Issues Trends and Strategies*. Norwood, NJ: Ablex Publishing Corporation, 1988.

McClure, Charles R. "Structural Analysis of the Depository Library System: A Preliminary Assessment," in Peter Hernon, ed., *Collection Development and Public Access to Government Documents*. Westport, CT: Microform Review, Inc., 1982, pp. 35-56.

———. "Increasing Access to U.S. Scientific and Technical Information," in Charles R. McClure and Peter Hernon, eds., *U.S. Scientific and Technical*

Information Policies: Views and Perspectives. Norwood, NJ: Ablex Publishing Corporation, 1989b, pp. 319-354.

———, ed. "Symposium on the U.S. Office of Technology Assessment Report: *Informing the Nation*." *Government Information Quarterly*, 6 (no. 2, 1989a): 129-174.

McClure, Charles R. and Peter Hernon. *Users of Academic and Public GPO Depository Libraries*. Washington, DC: Government Printing Office, 1989.

McClure, Charles R. and Peter Hernon, eds. *United States Scientific and Technical Information Policies: Views and Perspectives*. Norwood, NJ: Ablex Publishing Corporation, 1989.

McClure, Charles R., Peter Hernon, and Harold C. Relyea, eds. *United States Government Information Policies: Views and Perspectives*. Norwood, NJ: Ablex Publishing Corporation, 1989.

McClure, Charles R., Ann Bishop, and Philip Doty. "Federal Information Policy Development: The role of the Office of Management and Budget," in Charles R. McClure, Peter Hernon, and Harold Relyea, eds. *United States Government Information Policies: Views and Perspectives*. Norwood, NJ: Ablex Publishing Corporation, 1989a, pp. 51-76.

———. *Impact of High Speed Research Networks on Scientific Communication and Research*. Washington, DC: Office of Technology Assessment, 1989b.

McIntosh, Toby J. "Electronic Age Offers Promises, Problems for Government Information," *Daily Report for Executives* [Bureau of National Affairs], no. 154 (Friday August 11, 1989): C1-C17.

Morton, Bruce. "Perceptions of Power, the People, and the Future Access to U.S. Government Information," *Documents to the People*, 17 (March 1989): 9-17.

National Science Foundation. "Science Resources Studies Highlights" (February 18, 1988): 1-4.

Office of Management and Budget. "The Management of Federal Information Resources" [Circular A-130], *Federal Register*, 50 (December 24, 1985): 52730-52751.

———. "Second Advance Notice of Further Policy Development on Dissemination of Information." *Federal Register*, 54 (June 15, 1989): 25554-25559.

Office of Technology Assessment. *Informing the Nation: Federal Information Dissemination in an Electronic Age*. Washington, DC: GPO, 1988.

Pearce, Karla J. "CD-ROM: Caveat Emptor," *Library Journal*, 113, (February 1, 1988): 37-38.

Westin, Alan. *Reference Point: An Online Public Interest Directory and Information Service for the non-profit Sector and the Active Citizenry*. Teaneck, NJ: Reference Point Foundation, April, 1989.

GPO Regional Depositories

Peter Hernon
David C. Heisser

SUMMARY. This article profiles the 54 regional libraries serving in the depository program administered by the U.S. Government Printing Office. In addition to noting problem areas, the authors encourage the library community and the Federal government to find ways to provide the necessary financial and other support for the depository library program in an electronic and information age.

BACKGROUND

The 1962 Depository Library Act (P.L. 87-579, 76 *Stat*. 352), among its other provisions, formalized pilot programs already in effect in both Wisconsin and New York[1] and created the system of regional libraries. These libraries, limited to two per state, were charged with the maintenance of comprehensive collections held permanently,[2] the provision of interlibrary loan and reference service, and assistance to other depositories in the disposition of unwanted publications. Regionals oversee depository collections and services within the area of their jurisdiction, usually a state. The highest appellate court libraries and Federal libraries are the exceptions. These libraries discard unwanted documents through the Library of Congress and the National Archives and Records Administration.

Based on the recommendations of "the state library authority and a majority of depository libraries within the region," a Senator from the state designates a library as a regional.[3] A library may surrender regional status and revert to a selective depository. If a regional returns to selective status and if there is still an active regional in the state, then the former

Dr. Hernon is Professor, Graduate School of Library and Information Science, Simmons College, 300 The Fenway, Boston, MA 02115.

Dr. Heisser, is Associate Professor and Head, Government Publications and Maps Department, Otto G. Richter Library, University of Miami, P.O. Box 248214, Coral Gables, FL 33124.

© 1991 by The Haworth Press, Inc. All rights reserved.

one may discard (with the permission of the remaining regional) any depository materials held for over five years. In other words, the former regional is treated just like any other selective depository. In some instances, remaining regionals have asked former ones to continue to house their collection until such time as the remaining regional can absorb the former regional's valuable discards.

THESIS

The rationale for regional support of the depository library program remains as valid today as it was in 1962. The role of regional libraries today, however, is constrained by their parent institutions' variable funding and staffing patterns. The problem of finding space to house the regional documents collections continues to be severe, while the prospect of receiving many government publications in electronic format may place added burdens on regional library personnel.

The purpose of this article is to profile the regional libraries (as of fall 1989) and to encourage the library community and the Federal government to seek ways to provide effective and consistent support for the depository program in ensuring public access to U.S. government information.

PROFILE

The 54 regionals are distributed among the following library types:[4]

- Academic (33 or 61.1%)
- State agency (15 or 27.8%)
- Public (5 or 9.3%)
- State historical society (1 or 1.8%).

The 54 libraries comprise 3.9% of the entire depository population (1,396 libraries) and can be found in 44 states.[5] Ten states have the two permitted by the 1962 Act, while the remaining 34 states have one regional. Six states do not have a regional depository. However, in every instance (Alaska, Delaware, New Hampshire, Rhode Island, South Dakota, and Vermont), a regional in another state has assumed interstate responsibilities. The University of Maryland library services Maryland, Delaware, and the District of Columbia. The University of Florida libraries oversees Puerto Rico, and Louisiana State University library handles the Virgin Islands. The University of Hawaii library services the Pacific territories.

According to the *Guidelines for the Depository Library System,* ". . . regional status may be shared by more than one library."[6] In both North Dakota (the first such example) and South Carolina, two university libraries serving as selective depositories share regional status. One library, in effect, is the nominal regional but shares its responsibilities with another library in the state. If, by chance, a third library applied for regional status, the cooperating library might discontinue its role as a supporting regional or itself apply for regional status. The nominal regional might assume the extra responsibilities and displace the cooperating library, or develop a partnership with the library applying for regional status. Clearly, different alternatives might be pursued.

Geographical Location

Using the characterization developed by the U.S. Bureau of the Census, 20 regionals (37%) are located in the South, while 14 (25.9%) are in the West, 14 (25.9%) in the Midwest, and 6 (11.1%) in the Northeast.[7]

Figure 1 depicts the distribution of regional depositories by geographical area. Academic libraries dominate the South, while that geographical region is the only one that does not contain a public library serving as a regional.

Date of Depository Designation

Since libraries designated as regionals must previously have been selective depositories, it might be assumed that on the whole these libraries have held depository status for a number of years. Examination of the year in which the libraries gained their status supports this assumption.

The exact year in which 11 (20.4%) of the libraries gained depository status was not reported in *A Directory of U.S. Government Depository Libraries*.[8] Designation records for these depositories were destroyed in a fire at the Department of the Interior (the original site of the Office of Superintendent of Documents) during the late nineteenth century. All of these libraries obtained their designation before 1870.

The period over which the 43 libraries gained depository status spanned 119 years (1859 to 1978), with the mean being 1903 and the median 1907. Some 17 (39.5%) of the 43 libraries trace their depository status to the nineteenth century, while 14 libraries (32.6%) gained their status in one year – 1907. Land grant college legislation led to the libraries obtaining their status in that year. Using 1907 as the benchmark, 34 libraries (79.1%

Figure 1. Type of Library by Geographical Location

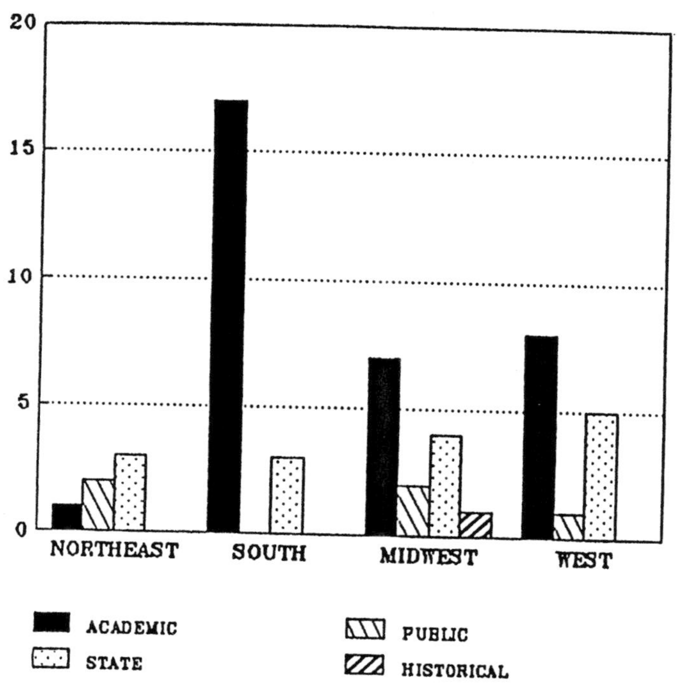

of the 43 libraries) had gained depository status by the end of that year. Between 1909 and 1935, 4 libraries (9.3%) gained their status. The remaining 5 libraries obtained depository status between 1960 and 1978.

Volumes Held

The number of volumes held overall by the library ranged from 106,386 to 5,188,589, with the mean being 1,499,152 and the median being 1,471,363. Ten libraries (18.5%) do not have volume counts exceeding 500,000, while 11 libraries (20.4%) had between 500,000 and

1,000,000 volumes. The remaining 33 libraries (61.1%) had over 1 million volumes.

Academic Regionals

All academic regional depositories are located in public institutions offering the doctorate as the highest degree. Auburn University at Montgomery offers the doctorate but in combination with the primary location of the university—Auburn, Alabama.

Enrollment at the academic institutions ranges from 5,283 to 44,293 students, with the mean being 19,537 and the median being 20,064. Sixteen institutions (48.5%) have enrollments under 20,000, while 14 (42.4%) have enrollments between 20,000 and 30,000. Three libraries (9.1%) have higher enrollments: 34,667, 38,639, and 44,293.

The number of faculty ranges from 306 to 5,382, with the mean being 1,255 and the median being 1,179. Twelve institutions (36.4%) have less than 1,000 faculty, while 19 (57.6%) have between 1,000 and 2,000 faculty. Two institutions (6%) have more than 2,400 faculty.

Over half of the libraries located at these 33 institutions (19 or 57.6%) have membership in the Association of Research Libraries (ARL). Conversely, 14 (42.4%) do not have ARL membership (see Figure 2).

The academic libraries obtained depository status between 1860 and 1971, with 1904 as the mean and 1907 as both the median and mode. The 14 libraries that became depositories in 1907 were all part of academic institutions. Auburn University at Montgomery, which opened in 1967, is the most recent of the 53 institutions to have a library gain depository status.

The libraries hold between 106,386 and 3,807,777 volumes. The mean is 1,812,414 and the median is 1,780,055.

Summary

The "typical" regional library is part of a public, academic institution that offers graduate programs culminating in the doctoral degree. There are more than 1,000 faculty members at the institution and student enrollment is approximately 20,000. There is more than a 50% chance that the library has ARL membership. The library is probably located in the South, and there is probably not another regional in the state. The "typical" regional has held depository status since 1907, or before, and maintains a collection of more than 1 million volumes.

Figure 2. Academic Regionals by Geographical Location

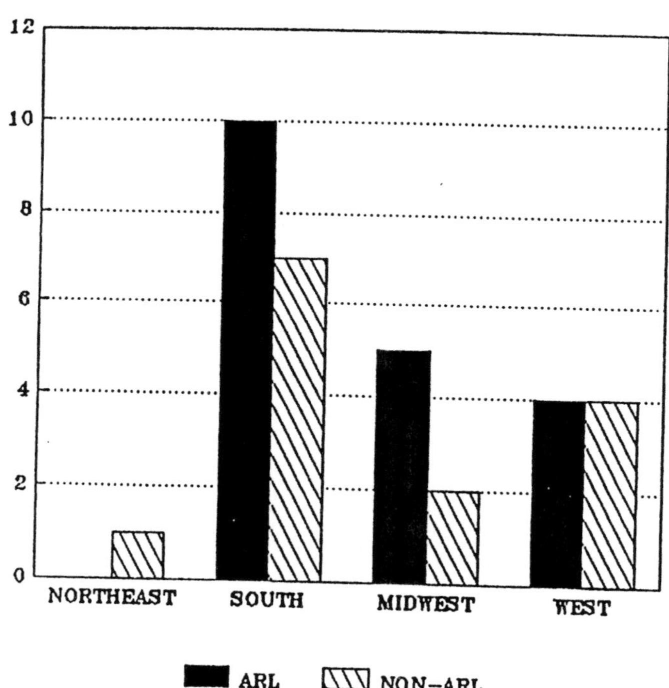

ISSUES

As Faull, a former regional librarian, observed in 1985, for a number of years now, regional depository librarians have expressed their concern "about the ability of their libraries to receive, process, store, and service all the titles and series available on deposit."[9] This section expands on her concern and indicates how the GPO and the library community are trying to cope with the role of regionals as the central linchpin in a depository library network.[10] Indeed, the problems discussed here suggest an attempt to defuse a time bomb that, if it exploded, would severely hamper the effectiveness and efficiency of the depository library program in providing the general public with access to government publications.

In the same article, Faull stated:

> Reworking a slogan from the 1980 presidential campaign, it can be asked if regional libraries are better off now than they were four years ago. Clearly, the answer is "no!" In fact, with more publications entering the depository program . . . regional libraries are probably worse off. If they are to seek relief from problems related to the lack of space to house the massive number of publications actually entering the depository program, the limited number of professional staff assigned to regional collections . . . and inadequate financing for the depository collection and services, the only hope now is that title 44 can be revised.[11]

The library community and the GPO are attempting to confront the issues that Faull raised, but they operate within a gray area concerning the provisions of 44 *U.S.C.* 1912. Unless the statutory law is revised, they have no choice, and that time bomb could explode.

Housing the Publications Sent on Deposit

Between 1978 and 1987, the GPO distributed more than 524,000 titles through the depository program. In addition, depository libraries received microfiche from the Department of Energy, Oak Ridge, and maps from the Geological Survey.[12] Annually, the GPO distributes approximately 40,000 titles: 60% in microfiche and 40% in paper copy. Clearly, regionals receive numerous titles on deposit and must integrate them into the collection. Housing these titles, in either paper copy or microfiche, may present the library with space problems as well as impact its ability to service a rapidly expanding collection.

As a consequence, the GPO permits a regional to serve as a "mini administrative distribution center," whereby the library can funnel some depository items (e.g., maps) to selective depositories serving within its jurisdiction. The regional thereby becomes responsible for depository publications not centrally housed in its collection.

Because regionals need not retain superseded titles (see note 2), the GPO and the library community have discovered a mechanism for bringing some relief to regionals. The Depository Library Council to the Public Printer is developing a list of superseded titles that ultimately might give regionals more latitude with their deselection decisions. (A preliminary list appeared in *Administrative Notes,* 10, 1989, number 9). The assumption behind an expanded list is that regionals should not provide archival collections of superseded materials. Such collections, perhaps, should be left to the Library of Congress and the National Archives and Records Administration.

Format of Depository Publications

At present, regionals must accommodate paper copy and microfiche. In 1989, the Joint Committee on Printing and the GPO conducted a pilot project to explore the feasibility of distributing government information on CD-ROM. The outcome of the study is that CD-ROM will enter the depository program. The Bureau of the Census plans to phase out the production of publications generated on computer-output microform (COM) and replace COM with CD-ROM products. These products will then enter the depository program. In addition, other statistical data, the final version of the *Congressional Record*, and certain reference titles will enter the depository program on CD-ROM.

Regional libraries must receive all formats distributed through the depository program. They either house the publications regardless of format or take advantage of their role as "mini administrative distribution centers." Such a role assumes effective management of resources dispersed among selective depositories.

Additional Constraints

Regionals must follow and maintain the institutions' general library policies, except where these conflict with their legal obligations under Title 44, *United States Code*. The range of services offered by regionals of necessity varies with the amount of institutional support they receive.[13] For example, institutional support for travel in connection with inspections and other duties may be limited. Furthermore, for budgetary reasons, some regionals do not keep records for the documents received.

The range of functions that a regional performs varies as time and institutional support permits. These functions may include:

- Ceremonial duties. The regional librarian, for example, joins in observances for the presentation of GPO certificates to selective depositories
- Inspection duties. The regional librarian is invited to accompany GPO inspectors on their visitations and to give input on the performance of selective depositories
- Communication. The librarian may receive frequent invitations to

speak about documents at conferences and may issue an occasional newsletter

- Adviser. The librarian offers selective depository librarians advice on a host of management questions, ranging from the check-in of problematic microfiche technical reports to the handling of remote storage for documents. Selectives often refer difficult reference questions to the regional, and occasionally a group of selective depository librarians visits the regional for a tour and an opportunity to discuss problems in person
- Intermediary. A selective depository librarian or a library director may request information or advice on a major project, such as the introduction of the GPO cataloging tapes online.

All three of the regional depositories surveyed have embraced the advent of electronic indexes and other commercial products on CD-ROM. However, the arrival of depository documents on CD-ROM gives rise to a mixture of enthusiasm and concern. While the regionals themselves can incorporate the electronic resources smoothly into their operations, they are concerned about being able to offer needed support to less-well-equipped selective depositories. They anticipate an increasingly demanding role for themselves in training and advising staff of selectives. There is strong sentiment for the development of gateway software that will simplify the problem of public access to government information.

BUILDING FOR THE FUTURE

Regional depositories can be likened to the foundation of a building: either they provide the basis by which the entire depository library program grows and meets its statutory responsibilities, or they are unable to assist other depositories and meet challenges effectively. Both the GPO and the library community are trying to prevent the foundation from becoming increasingly shaky and to assist the regionals in accomplishing their intended purpose. The number of regionals may never exceed 54, while a decline in the number would have broad implications for the depository library program, that is, unless a regional in another state assumed interstate responsibilities.

To provide relief to regionals, the GPO has developed strategies such as shared regional status, "mini administrative distribution centers," and an expanded concept of superseded titles subject to deselection. These strategies might be interpreted as comprising a legal gray area. Undoubtedly the size of that gray area will expand unless new legislation is enacted. Since the 1970s, there have been several calls for structural revision of the depository program, in an effort to provide a mechanism for improved public access to government publications and information.

Various librarians and educators have proposed another component in the structural hierarchy of the program. Such proposals have called for the maintenance of a backup collection that would relieve regionals of the requirement of accepting and retaining all items distributed through the depository program. There would be either "a national collection [within the GPO] or a system of super-regionals with federal support."[14] Perhaps regionals might concentrate their holdings on publications pertaining to their state or geographical area. At the same time, some regionals, known as "super regionals" might have more complete collections and provide interlibrary loan service to other regionals and selective depositories.

None of the proposals has lead to a structural change in the depository program. The reason is that 44 *U.S.C.* 1912 does not distinguish among regionals or create levels of regional depositories. Clearly, for there to be a structural change, legislation would have to be introduced into Congress and the one section of the *United States Code* rewritten.

Congress would probably not consider just the one provision or the chapter pertaining to the depository library program – Chapter 19. Rather, it would view the chapter as one component in a review of those Title 44 provisions relating to printing and perhaps reauthorization of the Paperwork Reduction Act (P.L. 96-511). In 1979, legislation introduced into Congress provided for improved administration of public printing services and the distribution of government publications. The bill, however, encountered opposition and ultimately died in the 96th Congress.[15]

In the first session of the 101st Congress, Representative Robert Wise of West Virginia introduced H.R. 2381, which proposes to "reform information dissemination policy functions of the Director of the Office of Management and Budget." The legislation, which has been linked to the re-authorization of the Paperwork Reduction Act, would require agencies to make available to the depository program all public information products, including those in electronic formats; and to participate in the creation of an index of public databases maintained by the government.

At the same time, the Subcommittee on Printing and Procurement of the House Committee on Administration is holding a series of hearings regarding possible revision of Title 44; the first of which was held on May 23, 1989. Such hearings underscore the point that nineteenth century legislation for an "ink on paper" era guides current printing statutes and that this legislation inadequately deals with the electronic collection and dissemination of government information. It is too early to predict what will emerge from the legislative review. Undoubtedly *Informing the Nation*[16] has served as a catalyst for linking the GPO and the depository library program to the review. With this in mind, the library community might want to examine the depository library program and offer a revised structure that addresses the role of the program in an electronic age.

As Franklin Reeder, of the Office of Management and Budget, has written, "with more and more federal databases available primarily if not exclusively on magnetic or optical media, what structure will fulfill the role of the Federal Depository Library System?"[17] The creation of "mini administrative distribution centers" and other gray area remedies are not an adequate answer to his question.

Any review of the depository program should explore those alternative structures that have already been identified in the literature.[18] The Association of Research Libraries (ARL) provides the most recent model for coping with electronic government information. The positive reception that this model has received underscores the importance of engaging in planning and of having a framework ready for policymakers to consider.

ARL formed its Task Force on Government Information in Electronic Format to:

> develop a framework for understanding—philosophically, functionally, and fiscally—the patterns that exist for government information today, and the shifts in those patterns resulting from the introduction of government information in electronic formats.[19]

The Task Force report *Technology & U.S. Government Information Policies: Catalysts for New Partnerships* provides that framework.[20] In its discussion of regional depositories, the report states that:

> As resource sharing becomes more expensive, the ability and willingness of some regionals to serve as resource centers are in question. As the pattern of resource sharing among different kinds of depository libraries changes with the introduction of electronic formats, it is possible that participating libraries will define new scopes for their depository collections and offer a more focused but well defined array of services for the collection.
>
> The particular kind of electronic format chosen to make government information available to depositories will probably largely determine the willingness of depository libraries to add it to their collections.[21]

Clearly, the report focuses on the needs and role of ARL depositories and views them as the *central* component in the depository program. They can serve as the center for an interlocking network in the state. The report, however, does not detail the network structure, indicate how the libraries can compensate for inadequate funding, and link documents departments with computer centers and a decentralized operation. Neither does the report discuss the relationship between ARL regionals and the other academic and non-academic regionals. (As already noted, not even all academic regionals are affiliated with ARL institutions.) The ARL consists of libraries that well serve their academic communities. The question is more "How outstanding are they as depositories?" In other words, are they a good role model, and how effective would they be as the linchpin in a depository network?

It is not the role of the report or the ARL to provide the type of analysis encouraged in this essay. The impetus for change—selection of the *best* model for the depository program—must come from professional library associations; the Depository Library Council to the Public Printer; the Joint Committee on Printing, GPO's oversight committee; and others. At the same time, the private sector, including the Information Industry Association, must have an opportunity for a fair hearing of its viewpoints.

CONCLUSION

The electronic collection and dissemination of government information may serve as the catalyst for change. Building a viable depository library structure for the next century will require careful planning and undoubtedly revision of 44 *U.S.C.*, Chapter 19. Change is all the more important because the depository library program at present is more than a safety net for providing access to government publications and information. It is an important channel by which the public gains access to information sources produced and distributed by the government.[22]

NOTES AND REFERENCES

1. Depository libraries in both Wisconsin and New York could transfer control of publications held at least twenty-five years to the State Library in New York or the State Historical Society of Wisconsin, with the permission of the Superintendent of Documents.

2. Some ephemeral and superseded publications need not be retained.

3. *Guidelines for the Depository Library System* (Washington, D.C.: GPO, 1988), point 12-1e. See also 44 U.S.C. 1912.

4. The profile is based on data gathered from Joint Committee on Printing. *A Directory of U.S. Government Depository Libraries* (Washington, D.C.: GPO,

1987); *American Library Directory* (New York: Bowker, 1988); and *The College Blue Book* (New York: Macmillan, 1987).

5. The GPO supplied the authors with a list of regional depository libraries dated April 1989.

6. See *Guidelines for the Depository Library System*, section 12-1a.

7. The percentages are subject to rounding. For a graphic depiction of the geographical regions and the states comprising each region, see Peter Hernon, Charles R. McClure, and Gary R. Purcell, *GPO's Depository Library Program* (Norwood, NJ: Ablex Publishing Corp., 1985), p. 47.

8. Joint Committee on Printing. *A Directory of U.S. Government Depository Libraries*.

9. Sandra K. Faull, "'State Plans': Their Development and Potential for Regional Depository Libraries Participating in the GPO Depository Program," *Government Information Quarterly*, 2 (1985): 157-167.

10. Ridley Kessler, Jr., the regional librarian for North Carolina, has completed a major survey of regional libraries, their services, functions, staffing, and funding.

11. Faull, "State Plans," p. 165.

12. Peter Hernon and Charles R. McClure, *Public Access to Government Information*, 2nd edition (Norwood, NJ: Ablex Publishing Corp., 1988), p. 95.

13. The information contained in this section resulted from interviews conducted in June 1989 with Gary Cornwell and Janet Swanbeck, University of Florida Libraries, Gainesville; Frank Wihbey, University of Maine at Orono; and Julie Schwartz, Connecticut State Library, Hartford.

14. Depository Library Council, "Summary of Meeting," St. Paul, Minnesota, April 28-30, 1980 (mimeograph), p. 6. Also see Peter Hernon and Charles R. McClure, *Public Access to Government Information*, 2nd edition (Norwood, NJ: Ablex Publishing Corp., 1988), p. 374.

15. Hernon and McClure, *Public Access to Government Information*, pp. 72-74.

16. Congress. Office of Technology Assessment, *Informing the Nation* (Washington, D.C.: GPO, 1988).

17. Franklin S. Reeder, "Directions in Federal Information Resources Management: A View from the Office of Management and Budget," *Information Management Review*, 4 (1989): 29-37.

18. See Hernon and McClure, *Public Access to Government Information*, Chapter 16.

19. Association of Research Libraries, "Technology & U.S. Government Information Policies: Catalysts for New Partnerships," *Government Information Quarterly*, 5 (1988): 267.

20. *Technology & U.S. Government Information Policies: Catalysts for New Partnerships* (Washington, D.C.: Association of Research Libraries, 1987).

21. Association of Research Libraries, "Technology & U.S. Government Information Policies: Catalysts for New Partnerships," pp. 274-275.

22. Charles R. McClure and Peter Hernon, *Users of GPO Academic and Public Depository Libraries* (Washington, D.C.: GPO, 1989).

Documents Search Strategies and General Reference Search Strategies: An Analysis and Comparison

Marilyn K. Moody

SUMMARY. This article describes and analyzes the search strategy step in the document reference process. It uses documents and general reference models to point out the unique aspects of the documents search strategy as well as those which are similar to the general reference search strategy. The documents search process is also analyzed from three different cognitive points of view. Suggestions for improving documents reference service through a better understanding of the documents search strategy are included.

INTRODUCTION

Although it has often been noted that documents reference service requires a different approach than general reference service, there has been little analysis of why this is so, or even what that different approach or process might be. General reference librarians often show both dislike and

Marilyn K. Moody is Head, Access Services, Iowa State University Library, Ames, IA 50011.

© 1991 by The Haworth Press, Inc. All rights reserved.

puzzlement for the seemingly arcane and elaborate process involved in documents reference work. While documents librarians do not seem to have such an aversion to general reference work, they may have difficulties in transferring their documents reference skills to the general reference setting.

There is a need for a better understanding of the factors in the documents reference process which are similar to general reference queries and those which are unique to the documents reference process. The general reference models which have been developed provide a framework for analyzing areas for improvement in answering general reference questions. A similar framework is needed to assist in the description and evaluation of documents reference service. While some aspects of the general reference models may be applied to the documents reference process, there is also the need for analysis of the documents reference process as a unique function.

This article discusses one specific part of the reference process, the search strategy. Although the concept of the search strategy is described in different ways by various models, in general the search strategy is understood as the step in the reference or information process where the reference librarian is actively seeking the answer to the user's query, either by formulating a procedure for conducting the search or consulting individual sources to find the answer to the query. This step is integrally entwined with the reference interview process, and in fact parts of the interview process are often being conducted simultaneously with the search strategy step.

While the search strategy is often shown or charted as a very purposeful step in the reference process, in reality it may be quite intuitive. Studies of the reference process have found that reference librarians often have a very difficult time explaining why they used a particular strategy or consulted an individual source. In fact, one of the frequently cited rules of reference service states, "When you know the answer is in a source, it is."[1] Of course in these cases the reference librarian is using his or her past experiences and knowledge to pinpoint a source, but the cognitive process involved does not necessarily follow any kind of pre-mapped or even outwardly rational process.

This article is concerned mainly with the type of search strategy that occurs at a general reference desk or documents reference desk. The reference process as analyzed is primarily a manual search process, although the searching of databases is often one step in the process.

MODELS OF THE GENERAL AND DOCUMENTS REFERENCE PROCESS

There are several models of the general reference process, but until recently there were no models aimed specifically towards government documents. Two basic search strategy models for government documents are now available which can be analyzed and compared to general reference models. The general reference models used in this article are representative models only, and no attempt has been made to comprehensively analyze the many general reference process models which have been developed.

Sears and Moody's Documents Search Strategies

In their book, *Using Government Publications*, Sears and Moody describe a government documents search strategy which uses the categorization of document reference questions by type as its first step.[2] The five types of questions identified are known item searches, subject searches, agency searches, statistical searches, and special techniques searches. Within each of these individual types, broad categories of sources are listed as sub-steps in the search process. While some of these sources are similar to the ones listed in general reference models, others are quite specific to the documents search strategy. After presenting this basic search strategy model, the remainder of the two volume work in which this strategy is developed is devoted to individual chapters describing the results of applying these search strategies to specific topics. Each chapter describes more specific search steps pertinent to each particular topic, as well as identifying and describing the use of individual document sources.

The known item search is used for questions about a specific bibliographic item. The search strategy is quite similar to the general reference strategies discussed later in this article. The sources listed for consultation in a known item search include online catalogs and databases; local card catalogs and files; the *List of Classes* and Andriot's *Guide to U.S. Government Publications*; and indexes and abstracts. With the exception of the *List of Classes* and *Andriot*, these sources are very similar to those used in the general reference models for locating specific bibliographic or holdings information.

According to Sears and Moody, government document subject searches also follow a basic search strategy similar to the general reference search strategies. Sources to be consulted include online catalogs and databases; card catalogs and local files; bibliographies; and indexes and abstracts. A fifth step is listed as "Integration of Other Search Strategies," which recognizes that other search strategies, such as an agency or statistical search strategy, may be important sub-searches of the documents subject search strategy. While this basic search strategy is much like a general reference subject search, the multitude of bibliographic tools involved in searching government documents make this process more complicated and specialized than one might assume from looking at the listing of possible sources.

The third strategy considered by Sears and Moody is the agency search, which is somewhat unique to documents searches. The most comparable activity in general reference work might be a corporate author search, yet the use of an agency search strategy is far more extensive. Agency searches are used to find information about or by a specific agency, but the types of questions answered by this type of approach are more complex than might first be realized. Sources listed for use in various steps of the agency search include the *List of Classes*; ready reference tools, (particularly *The U.S. Government Manual*); annual reports; regulations; and indexes and abstracts. All of the sources listed for the known item search or subject search might also be used as a related search to an agency search. Sears has also expanded upon the description of the basic agency search by adding identifying grant programs of agencies, analyzing agency budgets, and providing more extensive sources for laws and regulations as additional steps in the agency search.[3]

The fourth type of documents search process is the statistical search. Sources listed under this strategy include ready reference sources (such as *Statistical Abstract*); statistical compilations (such as *Agricultural Statistics*); census materials; indexes and abstracts; and online databases. While statistical sources may be listed in the general reference strategy, they are usually not nearly as heavily emphasized or as important as they are in the documents search strategy.

The last search strategy described in Sears and Moody's model is the special techniques search strategy. Special technique searches are complex, multistep, multifaceted search strategies which are unique to a special topic or type of material. The steps involved in these searches must be described in detail individually, as the steps involved do not follow either the general reference search strategy or the other document search strategies. A characteristic of these searches is that they are almost impossible to carry out without prior knowledge of the steps and nuances involved. Examples include searches for historical information, national archives material, legislative histories searches, budget analyses, treaties, technical reports, patents and trademarks, federal specifications and standards, and Foreign Broadcast Information Service Reports (JPRS/FBIS). These searches are potentially the most frustrating searches for those unfamiliar with documents search strategies, as the application of general reference search strategies provide almost no help in locating answers for questions in these areas.

The Documents Search Strategies of POINTER

The only other specific documents search strategy that has been reported was developed as part of an expert system produced by Karen Smith.[4] Smith's POINTER is a microcomputer system that suggests the use of selected documents sources for users. In doing so, it uses a similar approach as Sears and Moody to categorize questions by type. Both POINTER and *Using Government Publications* were designed to simulate the search strategies an expert documents searcher might use in answering queries, so it is not surprising that they are quite similar in approach.

POINTER is organized into the following main sections: titles; numbers; subjects; names addresses or phone numbers; grants, fellowships, or employment opportunities; executive branch; legislative branch; judicial branch; and general indexes for subject searching. The first two, title and number, are aimed at categorizing the needs of users who are generally seeking a known item. Since POINTER is designed to be used in a particular library, and for use directly by patrons, it provides far greater detail to the known item search than Sears and Moody. The subject search includes additional subdivisions, such as the subdivision "projections," which seek to further categorize the query.

The executive branch section of POINTER corresponds somewhat to the agency search and includes such sub-topics as regulations or treaties. The special techniques found in the legislative branch and judicial branch are treated separately. Each categorization then lists basic sources within the documents collection which can be used to begin the search for answers to questions within these categories. Since POINTER is designed to be used at times when the librarian is not available, it does not attempt to comprehensively describe the possible sources and strategies that might be used by a documents reference librarian. It does, however, attempt to duplicate the categorization of questions that a documents librarian might use to begin the search process.

The recognition that the application of general reference search strategies did not produce the most efficient and effective documents search was the impetus behind the development of both of these models. By basing the creation of strategies on the actions of an experienced documents librarian, these models seek to provide several advantages over traditional search strategies. They have the ability to provide a faster search, reduce the number of searching or retrieval steps, concentrate on the sources and steps most likely to produce results quickly, and identify sources not found by traditional search strategies. Depending on the situation, the use of these search strategies may provide a more comprehensive search or reduce the time spent searching documents indexes or databases.

General Reference Search Strategies

The structure of the documents oriented strategies can be contrasted with those describing the general reference process. One of the most comprehensive general reference process models is that of Jahoda and Braunagel.[5] Their work, *The Librarian and Reference Queries: A Systematic Approach*, is devoted to providing a framework and decision-making model of the general reference process. The overall steps in their process can be summarized as follows:

1. Receive query
2. Message selection or identification of the essential information of the request
3. Negotiate query and revise query statement if necessary
4. Select types of answer-providing tools
5. Select specific titles of tools to search
6. Translate query words into language of answer-providing tool
7. Conduct search, select and submit answer

Steps four and five of this reference process are the ones which involve formulation of a search strategy. As is typical of general reference search strategies, the types of categories listed include biographical sources, card catalogs, union lists, dictionaries, encyclopedias, geographical sources, guides to the literature, handbooks, manuals, indexes, bibliographies, texts, non-biographical directories, primary publications, yearbooks, and almanacs. While some of these sources can be used for documents, many are rarely found as documents sources, or are less useful in conducting most document searches. Several types of materials that were listed in the earlier document search models, such as census materials and annual reports, are not even listed as types of sources.

Although this difference in the types of sources listed is important, there is an even more basic difference between the two strategies. At the outset, the strategy for general reference questions is more delineated by the type of source that will answer the question, rather than the overall strategy that needs to be first considered before differentiating the type of source to be used. The selection of type of source only becomes applicable to documents search strategies after the more basic type of question categorization has taken place. Even then it is only applicable when the sources unique to documents are added to the types of sources used for general reference questions. The general reference model provides minimal help for those areas covered by the documents agency search strategy or the special technique search strategies.

Flowchart Models

Another way of presenting the general reference process is through the use of flowcharts such as those developed by Bunge,[6] Swenson,[7] and Stych.[8] Flowcharts try to track not only the types of sources used, but also the decision points along the way that determine when the use of one type of source or strategy is stopped in order to pursue another approach.[9] Some flowcharts include references to specific titles as well as types of sources. Although government publications are not generally included in these models, they do allow the flexibility to include some specific documents sources or types of documents within the models. Swenson's flowchart model, for example, tracks the use of sources in a technical library (Northern Electric Company). Step four of her flowchart is "Select and consult one or more of the following types of publications and their indexes as necessary." Within this step, fourteen types of sources are included. Besides the standard categories (such as encyclopedia or dictionary, reference book, bibliography, or periodical), documents sources such as technical reports, standards and specifications, and patents are listed. Related indexes used with each type of material are also included within the flowchart. While certainly not addressing the different types of searches covered by government publications, this flowchart model does provide a framework for integrating specific types of document sources or search strategies within a more general reference framework.

Doyle and Grimes Model

Another example of this integration, although achieved through a different format than the flowchart, is found in the work done by Doyle and Grimes.[10] They categorize the information process as being part of a bibliographic chain. Their model of the searching or reference process includes the following steps:

1. Determination that a need for information exists
2. Statement of the question in its initial form
3. Delimitation and redefinition of the question
4. Statement of the redefined question
5. Structuring the search
6. Selecting most suitable information sources
7. Analyzing information sources selected
8. Obtaining additional information if necessary
9. Synthesizing information
10. Analyzing information
11. Decision making
12. Evaluation of the effectiveness of the search

At the search strategy level, Doyle and Grimes visualize the selection of sources as part of a "bibliographic chain." Phase I of their bibliographic chain includes information found in the minds of people. They describe these sources as human resources and institutional resources. Phase II includes materials with intellectual content in print form. This phase includes standard types of sources found in other models, such as:

1. Work-in-progress documents
2. Unpublished studies
3. Periodical articles
4. Reports and monographs
5. Annual reviews and state-of-the art reports
6. Books
7. Encyclopedic summaries

Phase III of their bibliographic chain includes indexing and abstracting services, bibliographic lists and essays, and annual reviews and state-of-the art reports (included in both phase II and III).

From this bibliographic chain, Doyle and Grimes go on to suggest ways of applying this search process to various disciplines such as psychology, education, law, philosophy and religion, and the life sciences. Using each item in phase II and III of the bibliographic chain, they list and describe specific sources that can be used for searches in each area. Within this model, documents sources are often listed. While this model may not provide an entry point for some types of documents searches, it does provide a workable model for the integration of documents sources within more general subject searches. It is interesting to note that the authors describe the sources available in research libraries as being of three types: general circulating materials, specific reference works, and special collections, the latter including documents sources. Even with their integration of documents sources, the authors still view documents as a distinctly unique type of material.

Cognitive Models of the Reference Process

A second approach to analyzing the reference process looks at the cognitive process that occurs when a reference librarian is searching for an item. Studies in these areas often use the audio taping or direct observation of reference interviews as the basis of their study. While many of these studies concentrate on the interaction between patron and librarian, they also provide clues to the processing of information and the formation of search strategies that occur during these interactions.

In particular, the work of Ingwersen provides an insightful example of this approach.[11] In his studies, he has looked at the kind of information librarians try to remember in carrying out their searches, as well as the thought processes, search routines, and procedures they tend to develop and rely on. He prefers to use the term search procedure rather than search strategy as more descriptive of the unplanned process that he observes as part of the information retrieval or reference process. He characterizes the search process as being composed of search routines developed on the basis of training and experience. He finds that search strategies are not developed before the search begins. Most librarians begin to act immediately when consulted with a query by consulting titles on shelves, classification schemes, or subject headings in indexes before they have had a chance to develop a search strategy.

Ingwersen characterizes the search modes used by reference librarians into three types: open, semi-fixed, and fixed search mode. The mode that a librarian uses depends on the motives the librarian has in starting the search and the expectations the librarian has for the sources to be used in the search. In an open search mode the motive is to gain additional information which will further the librarian's search. In the fixed mode search, the librarian is seeking to find "*the* document or tool which includes *the* answer." The semi-fixed search mode follows the fixed mode, but along the way the search itself may cause the librarian to engage in more open search behavior. The librarian also has expectations regarding whether there is a source which will provide an answer and in determining the form an answer may take. The actual need for the answer, the topic, and the librarian's environment also influence the way the search is structured.

Ingwersen found that the two groups of librarians he studied in Danish libraries showed distinct differences in their preference for a particular mode. The reference librarians in the study most often preferred an open search mode. The lending librarians in his study, who were more apt to be searching for a specific monograph to answer a patron's query, used the fixed mode. Both types of librarians used the semi-fixed search mode.

It may be that documents librarians rely more often on the fixed or semi-fixed mode than the open mode. The request for information from documents sources is often for a specific document or specific piece of information that can only be found in a limited number of sources. Fixed searches rely more on the search experience and knowledge of specific documents and tools than that of open searches. The smaller universe of possible sources in a documents collection and the fact that a patron may have already somewhat categorized his or her question as a documents question provides a different environment for the documents librarian than that found at the general reference desk. Given the need to learn very specific search strategies to deal with many of the types of documents questions, such as those listed under the special techniques category by Sears and Moody, the fixed mode may be a more appropriate search process for many documents questions. This would also explain why reference librarians, who might favor a more open search mode, could have difficulty in providing documents reference where a more fixed mode is appropriate. While only a hypothesis, it seems that there very well may be a fundamental difference in the way that documents and reference librarians approach their searches from a cognitive point of view.

Information Search Tactics and Idea Tactics

Viewed from another cognitive model of search strategy activity, the librarian's use of information search tactics and idea tactics significantly effect the success of the search process.[12] As described by Bates, information search tactics are moves which are made to further a search within the reference process. Idea tactics are those tactics used to produce ideas which further a search by approaching it in another manner. Bates describes some twenty-nine diverse information search tactics. Information tactics include monitoring tactics that keep the search on track and efficient, tactics for searching through file structures, search formulation tactics, and term tactics used to select and revise the terms used in a search. An example of a specific tactic is that of STRETCH, which Bates defines "To use a source for other than its intended purposes," or BLOCK, which is "To reject in the search formulation, items containing or indexed by certain term(s), even if it means losing some document sections of relevance." Idea tactics include such tactics as WANDER; "To move among one's resources, being receptive to alternative sources and new search ideas triggered by the materials that come into view," and MEDITATE; "To develop and utilize the skill of quickly achieving a mind state in which rational and intuitive capacities work together in solving search problems."

These tactics would seem to be useful to both general reference and documents librarians, although certain tactics might prove to be more useful than others for documents librarians. McClure and Hernon noted that documents librarians seemed to have the most difficulty with questions that had fewer possible sources as answers and required the librarian to translate the question into a search strategy that matched the indexing for government documents.[13] In particular, they suggest that the use of term tactics could improve documents librarians strategies in dealing with these types of questions. They also suggest the use of information and idea tactics as a way of improving documents reference service in general.[14]

Semantic, Episodic, and Schematic Memory

Another approach looks at the types of memory that librarians use in answering questions. Neil has identified three different types of memory used by reference librarians in the reference process.[15] Semantic memory is used in organizing and classifying items. Episodic memory emphasizes experiences or specific episodes that have occurred in the past. Schematic memory is used in such activities as creating a schema for knowledge relating to the types of tools and types of questions that the librarian uses or encounters. Neil uses transcripts of reference transactions and interviews with reference librarians to provide examples of librarians using different types of memory in the reference process.

Semantic memory is the type of memory most developed by education for librarianship and is further developed by the reference librarian's use of classification schemes, indexes, and other items that organize and classify information. Because of the importance of the Superintendent of Documents classification scheme and the reliance on indexing, the documents librarian may use semantic memory even more than the general reference librarian.

Episodic memory uses the librarian's experience to classify questions, patrons, and the use of bibliographic tools into different types. Our earlier discussion of the documents search strategy leads to the conclusion that this type of memory is quite important in helping to classify documents questions. Previous experience with the questions and recall of questions similar to the one at hand improve the documents librarian's chances of properly categorizing the document by type and selecting the search strategy and tools that are most useful.

Schematic memory develops expectations or schema for different events encountered in the reference process. Schema are developed for example, regarding expectations for the use of particular reference tools, the interactions that occur with patrons, and the physical location of items in the library. Although the process of developing schematic memory is the same for both reference and documents librarians, the schema that are developed for each are quite different. For example, schema may be developed for how a specific reference work is used. The schema a general reference librarian develops for the use of a reference work such as the *U.S. Government Manual* is far different from that developed by a documents librarian. How, when, with what type of patron, and for what type of question the *Manual* is used will differ between the two types of librarians.

CONCLUSION

This discussion of search strategies shows that there are significant differences between general reference and documents search strategies. Models of the general reference and documents reference process help to pinpoint those differences as well as show similarities in the process. A further development of models for documents search strategies and study of the cognitive aspects of the search process is needed to provide insight into ways of improving documents reference service.

REFERENCES

1. Nathan A. Josel, Jr., "Ten Reference Commandments," *RQ* 11 (Winter 1971): 146-47.

2. Jean L. Sears and Marilyn K. Moody, *Using Government Publications, Volume 1: Searching by Subjects and Agencies, Volume 2: Finding Statistics and Using Special Techniques* (Phoenix: Oryx Press, 1985-86)

3. Jean L. Sears, "The Government Agency Search Strategy," *RQ* 25 (Summer 1986): 445-449.

4. Smith, Karen F., "POINTER vs. *Using Government Publications:* Where's the Advantage?" *The Reference Librarian* 23 (1989): 191-204, and Smith, Karen F., "Robot at the Reference Desk?" *College and Research Libraries* 18 (September 1986): 486-490.

5. Gerald Jahoda and Judith Schiek Braunagel, *The Librarian and Reference Queries: A Systematic Approach* (New York: Academic Press, 1980).

6. Charles A. Bunge, "Charting the Reference Query," *RQ* 8 (Summer 1969): 245-50.

7. Sally Swenson, "Flow Chart on Library Searching Techniques," *Special Libraries* 56 (April 1965): 239-42.

8. F.S. Stych, " Teaching Reference Work: The Flow Chart Method," *RQ* 5 (Summer 1966): 14-17.

9. See for example, G. Carlson, *Search Strategy by Reference Librarians. Part 3 of the Final Report on the Organization of Large Files* (Sherman Oaks, CA: Hughes Dynamics, Inc., 1964. Available also as NTIS Report Number PB 166 192).

10. James M. Doyle and George H. Grimes, *Reference Resources: A Systematic Approach* (Metuchen, N.J.: Scarecrow Press, 1976).

11. Peter Ingwersen, "Search Procedures in the Library-Analysed from the Cognitive Point of View," *Journal of Documentation* 38 (September 1982): 165-191. See also Peter Ingwersen and Soren Kaae, *User-Librarian Negotiations and Information Search Procedures in Public Libraries: Analysis of Verbal Protocols. Final-Research Report* (Copenhagen Denmark: Royal School of Librarianship, 1980. Available as ERIC Document Number ED 211 051).

12. Bates, Marcia J., "Information Search Tactics," *Journal of the American Society for Information Science* 30 (July 1979): 205-14, and Bates, Marcia J., "Idea Tactics," *Journal of the American Society for Information Science* 30 (September 1979): 280-89.

13. Charles R. McClure and Peter Hernon. *Improving the Quality of Reference Service for Government Publications*, (Chicago: American Library Association, 1983): 43, 46.

14. Ibid, p. 129.

15. S.D. Neil, "The Reference Process and Certain Types of Memory: Semantic, Episodic, and Schematic," *RQ* 23 (Summer 1984):417-423.

Accessibility and Reference Use of the Depository Collection in College and University Libraries

Marilyn L. Hankel
Frances W. Skiffington

SUMMARY. This paper will first present a short history of the many issues involved in government documents librarianship over the years. It then will present an overview of the most frequently used and requested sources of government information. It will by no means be an exhaustive list because it is aimed at the general information provider in an academic library. This general information provider may not be very familiar with federal documents and may even be afraid of them. In this world of rapidly advancing technology, documents can no longer be pushed aside or overlooked as a source of information because access has improved so much. In this overview, the many formats, including the electronic format in which many documents are now available, will also be noted. This electronic format has caused many problems to arise because of the lack of a federal information policy that is clearly defined.

INTRODUCTION

The federal government produces a wealth of information on a wide variety of subjects. The Office of Technology Assessment's report, *Informing the Nation: Federal Information Dissemination in an Electronic Age*, outlines the many types and uses of federal information. For example, the business and financial communities look to government indicators of economic activity as important inputs to business planning and invest-

Marilyn L. Hankel is Business Reference Librarian at the Earl K. Long Library, University of New Orleans and Frances W. Skiffington is Government Documents Reference Librarian at the Earl K. Long Library, University of New Orleans, Lakefront, New Orleans, LA 70148.

© 1991 by The Haworth Press, Inc. All rights reserved.

ment decisions. The agricultural sector depends on government crop and weather bulletins and forecasts to help schedule crop planting. Scientists and engineers benefit from the technical information generated as a result of federally sponsored or conducted research in areas such as supercomputers, solar energy, and superconductors. As a matter of fact, information generated by the federal government spans the whole spectrum of issues and programs relevant to agency missions—from public health crises such as AIDS, to environmental problems such as hazardous waste disposal and water pollution, to demographic and employment trends. At its most basic level, information about governmental processes—such as the *Congressional Record* and the *Federal Register*—is used by citizens and organizations that wish to monitor and participate in a wide range of government activities.[1]

The Depository Library Program serves as a mechanism for the dissemination of this federal information. The Government Printing Office distributes publications free of charge to the approximately 1400 participating libraries. These depository libraries house these documents and provide access to this information free of charge to the public. Academic libraries make up the largest percentage of depository libraries.[2] Historically, this government information has been disseminated mostly in paper to depository libraries, and in the recent past, in microfiche. However, now there is a rapid increase in the use of electronic formats such as floppy disks, magnetic tapes, online, and CD-ROM.[3] There are many commercially produced products that repackage government information and make it more useful for a fee, but now many of the government produced electronic databases are not being distributed free to depository libraries as paper and fiche are distributed. Therefore, the Depository Library Program as it is now structured, may be in jeopardy since more and more government information is being made available only electronically. There is no clearly defined federal information policy at this time.

BACKGROUND

To put the issues of today into perspective, take a brief look back over the issues of the past. What have librarians done over the years to provide access to this government information? As Moody noted, while the Government Documents Roundtable slogan is "Documents to the People," historically, documents librarians have been much more concerned with selecting, obtaining, classifying, and shelving documents than with showing people how to access and use them.[4]

In Moody's survey of 25 years of documents librarianship, she shows how the literature of the early 1960's emphasized acquisition and organization of documents collections. In the mid-1960's documents librarians began to discuss documents reference service, but the emphasis was still on acquisition and organization. In the 1970's, the topic of access to information also began to be recognized as a factor equal in importance to the organization and quality of the documents collection. In the early 1980's, there was an increased awareness of the role of reference service in documents.[5] In Moody's look at 1960-1985, she concluded that librarians generally had not written about documents reference service, had not conducted research on the topic, had not spent much time analyzing it, and had not talked about it at their professional meetings.[6]

The mid-1980's brought an increased awareness of the need for access to government information, and this is reflected in the literature and in discussions at professional meetings. New technologies have drawn documents out of the basement. The general information provider, as well as the documents specialist, must now be aware of what information documents contain. There is also the broader issue of what the future holds for the dissemination of this electronic government information without the existence of a clearly defined federal information policy. Many of these concerns are directed at the documents specialist in publications such as *Documents to the People* and *Government Publications Review*. Now, however, articles about these issues are appearing in journals which have a broader audience such as *RQ* and *Library Journal*.

Some of these issues have been discussed at recent professional meetings. In October 1988 the Louisiana Chapter of ACRL sponsored a program entitled "Documents to the People: Is This Still a Reality?" The speakers included a representative from the Government Printing Office and two very active document librarians. They addressed issues dear to the hearts of documents librarians such as the emergence of the electronic format and its future, the discontinuation of some documents, and privatization. The program was very successful and attracted many librarians outside of those who are specifically documents librarians. GODORT's 1988 Annual Program at the ALA Conference dealt with using government documents to answer some of the toughest reference questions by training the general information provider (not the documents specialist) to use government information.[7] Not only is the government documents librarian interested in access to government information, but the general reference librarian and even the technical service librarian are also all now paying attention, and those that are not, should be.

TECHNOLOGY

Technology has changed the nature of access to government information, as well as its use. Because of this technology, the old issue of how documents collections should be organized and shelved, and where they should be located may no longer be so relevant. Before the technological advances, there were good arguments for locating government documents departments either with or near central reference areas. In libraries where divisional reference exists, government documents are located with subject reference areas such as social sciences, business and/or science and technology reference. Humanities is the only broad subject area not to have many government publications. There may still be political reasons to align with a powerful reference department. As Moody observed, documents departments have traditionally been the last areas of the library to get a computer terminal for online searching, and they are often excluded from plans for automation systems. They have little access to national bibliographic utilities such as OCLC and are typically the last to receive microcomputers.[8]

Even though it is true that documents collections should be visible and not tucked away in some deep, dark dungeon, the issues are different today. As McClure and Hernon noted, the issues relate to the degree to which government documents are bibliographically accessible by the professional reference staff, the degree to which these personnel are knowledgeable about document reference sources, and the degree to which they resolve the information needs of patrons who request government publications.[9]

There is definitely improved bibliographic access to government publications because of new technologies. Examples include the fact that GPO inputs its records into the OCLC system. A library now has the ability to include government documents in its online catalog and there are many online government data bases that can be searched. There is a proliferation of government CD-ROM products.[10] When government documents departments can take advantage of this technology, government information will be accessible in all areas of the library.

Often, in answering a reference question, one of the many government sources is the most appropriate place to refer a patron first. The following sections will present an overview of the vast array of sources and formats available to access government information. It is aimed at the general information provider, not the documents specialist. It, therefore, is not an exhaustive survey, but just the most frequently used and requested sources. Following the overview will be a discussion of what the future holds for government information and federal information policy.

SOURCES

General Sources

The main index for locating a particular government document is the *Monthly Catalog of U.S. Government Publications*. Begun in 1895, the *Monthly Catalog* indexes the publications of all the federal government agencies on all subjects and in all types and formats. Issued monthly by the Government Printing Office and sent to all depository libraries in paper format, the *Monthly Catalog* provides a subject, author, title, and title keyword index, as well as a series and report number index. Beginning with the year 1976, the *Monthly Catalog* is also available in machine readable format. It is available online through Dialog and BRS. Several commercial vendors, such as Marcive, Autographics, and Information Access provide CD-ROM access to the *Monthly Catalog*.

The *Publications Reference File*, better known as the *PRF*, is issued by the Government Printing Office and is an index to the publications currently available for sale by the Superintendent of Documents. It lists forthcoming and recently out of print publications. Access to the *PRF* is by GPO Stock Number, Superintendent of Documents classification number, and an alphabetical sequence which includes subject, title, series, key words and phrases, and personal authors. Issued in microfiche, the *PRF* is excellent for identifying and verifying publications for purchase as it provides availability and price. It is available online through Dialog.

The *Index to Government Periodicals* is the only publication dedicated to indexing the journals published by the U.S. Government. In the front of each volume it lists the titles indexed and the Superintendent of Documents classification number. Issued quarterly and cumulated annually, this index provides subject access to over 184 government journals, and it is available online through BRS and Wilsonline.

The *American Statistics Index (ASI)* is a great source for finding statistical information in federal documents. It contains very detailed abstracts and incredibly detailed indexing by subject, title, report number, geographic breakdown, and more. It indexes depository, as well as non-depository federal documents.

Most people are aware that the U.S. Government collects and publishes a large amount of statistical data. Each year the U.S. Department of Commerce publishes the *Statistical Abstract of the United States*. Not only does it contain summary statistical data on almost every conceivable subject, but at the end of each table it also gives the source of the data if more detail is needed.

Arranged in Superintendent of Documents classification number order, the *List of Classes of U.S. Government Publications Available for Selection by Depository Libraries* is an excellent source for determining which series or titles are issued by the various departments and agencies of the government.

Guide to U.S. Government Publications by John L. Andriot is a current and historical list of series, journals, reports, and publications issued by the government since 1900.[11] Arranged in Superintendent of Documents classification number order, it provides a short history of the creation and authority of each agency and annotations for many of the series. An important feature of this index is that it lists changes in classification numbers and agencies. This makes it much easier to find a publication previously (or later) classed differently from a given number.

The *U.S. Government Manual* is the official handbook of the U.S. Government. It provides comprehensive information on the official and quasi-official agencies of the U.S. Government including boards, committees, and commissions. It gives a summary statement of the agency's purpose and role in the federal government, as well as a brief history of the agency. It lists the heads of the agencies and departments within the agency and also provides addresses and telephone numbers for the agencies.

Business Sources

In the business area, most of the business statistics that patrons request such as the GNP, the consumer price index, the unemployment rate, and the producer price index are all produced by the government. Statistics issued by the U.S. Department of Commerce and the U.S. Department of Labor are those most frequently requested.

There are various ways to approach retrieving which government publication has the particular statistic needed. For those not familiar with business concepts and terminology, it might be useful to consult a reference book such as Michael R. Lavin's *Business Information: How to Find It, How to Use It*.[12] It explains concepts such as GNP and consumer price index, as well as directs one to sources with detailed descriptions of those sources. Another good reference book is Lorna M. Daniells' *Business Information Sources*, which gives detailed abstracts of both government and non-government publications. [13] The *Statistical Abstract of the U.S.*, mentioned above, is often a good place to start to find statistics since each table provides references to the original sources. *ASI*, of course is great if the statistics are hard to find.

The Census Bureau of the U.S. Department of Commerce is one of the biggest producers of statistical information. It conducts the *Census of Population and Housing* every 10 years, and publishes information such as number of inhabitants, race, age, sex, education, income, employment, occupation, number of rooms in a house, number of persons per room, and value of home with many geographic breakdowns. For years not covered by the decennial censuses, the Census Bureau estimates population and housing information by its Current Population Survey and Current Housing Survey. The results of these surveys are reported in several series entitled *Current Population Reports* and *Current Housing Reports*. Of course, they do not contain the kind of detailed information and geographic breakdown that is available in the decennial census reports.

Every 5 years, the Census Bureau publishes the economic censuses, which include the *Census of Retail Trade*, the *Census of Service Industries*, the *Census of Manufactures*, the *Census of Construction Industries*, the *Census of Mineral Industries*, and the *Census of Transportation*. These censuses contain data on number of establishment, receipts or sales, payrolls, and employment by SIC (Standard Industrial Classification) code and geographic breakdowns by states, counties and MSA's. For years not covered by these censuses, information with less detail is reported in several different series such as *Current Business Reports*, *County Business Patterns*, and *Current Industrial Reports*. Other federal censuses include the *Census of Agriculture* and the *Census of Governments* which are also done every 5 years.

Much of this Census information is available in paper or microfiche format. *CENDATA*, produced by the U.S. Bureau of the Census, is an online database that is available through Dialog. It contains selected statistical data on subjects including population, housing, manufacturing, foreign trade and more. As it also includes press releases, information is available more quickly online than in paper copy or microfiche. More and more Census Bureau information is available on floppy disk, magnetic tape, and now CD-ROM. The CD-ROM products from the Census Bureau include *County Business Patterns* and the 1987 *Economic Censuses*. Plans are in progress to make the 1987 *Census of Agriculture* and the 1990 *Census of Population and Housing* available in CD-ROM format. There are those in the data user community who feel that CD-ROM technology has the potential to do for market research what electronic spreadsheets did for financial analysis. [14] The *Census Catalog and Guide* provides information on availability and formats.[15]

The Bureau of Labor Statistics of the U.S. Department of Labor is another agency that produces a great deal of statistical information including employment and unemployment statistics, consumer price indexes, and producer price indexes. Some of the most frequently used reference sources include the *Handbook of Labor Statistics*, *Employment and Earnings*, *Occupational Outlook Handbook*, and the *Monthly Labor Review*. Some of the BLS information is also available on magnetic tape for purchase.

There are many databases in the business area that contain federal documents but are not produced by government agencies. *Disclosure* and *Disclosure/Spectrum Ownership* provide detailed financial information on over 12,000 public companies. This information is derived from reports that must be filed by public corporations with the U.S. Securities and Exchange Commission. *Disclosure* is available through Dialog, Dow Jones News Retrieval, and Mead Data. It is also available on CD-ROM as *Compact Disclosure*. Predicasts' *PTS U.S. Time Series* and *PTS U.S. Forecasts*, available through Dialog, contain government statistics such as GNP, income, and employment. The *Trademarkscan-Federal* database contains records of currently active federal trademark applications and registrations that are filed with the U.S. Patent and Trademark Office. *D&B Donnelly Demographics* provides access to demographic data from the 1980 Census with their own estimates and projections.

Sciences

In the area of science and technology, there are many sources of government information. The government produces many indexes to its enormous collection of scientific and technical reports. *STAR* (*Scientific and Technical Aerospace Reports*) is published by NASA semimonthly and is cumulated annually. It includes all aspects of aeronautics and space research and development. Some of the reports indexed in it are federal government reports and are sent to depositories, but many are not. *Government Reports Announcements and Index* is published semimonthly by the National Technical Information Service of the U.S. Department of Commerce, and it indexes and abstracts U.S. government sponsored research reports. Most of the reports must be ordered from NTIS because NTIS is required to recover its costs. The NTIS database is available online through Dialog and BRS, and is also available on CD-ROM.

Energy Research Abstracts (*ERA*) is semimonthly and provides abstracting and indexing of scientific and technical reports, journals, conference papers, books, patents, theses, and monographs originated by the U.S. Department of Energy, its laboratories, energy centers, and contractors. Many of the reports indexed in *ERA* are available in depository libraries on microfiche. The *DOE Energy* database, the online equivalent of *ERA*, is available through Dialog. *Nuclear Science Abstracts* was published from 1948 until 1976, and provided comprehensive indexing and abstracting of the international nuclear science literature. *ERA* includes U.S. nuclear energy, but the coverage of the world's nuclear literature ceased being published by the government when it stopped publishing *Nuclear Science Abstracts* in 1976. *Nuclear Science Abstracts* is available online through Dialog.

Index Medicus, which is produced monthly by the National Library of Medicine, indexes articles in medical journals by subject and author. *Medline*, the online equivalent of *Index Medicus*, is available through Dialog, BRS, and NLM. It is also available on CD-ROM. Other online government produced databases include *Agricola* of the National Agricultural Library, which is available through Dialog and BRS, and *Cancerlit* of the National Library of Medicine, which is available through Dialog, BRS, and NLM. *Agricola* and *Cancerlit* are also available on CD-ROM now.

One government agency that produces an enormous amount of technical information in geology is the U.S. Department of the Interior. Series such as the *Professional Papers*, *Bulletins*, *Water Supply Papers*, and *Open-File Reports* of the U.S. Geological Survey and the *Minerals Yearbook* of the Bureau of Land Management should be remembered when questions in the field of geology are asked. *GEOREF*, an online database produced by the American Geological Institute, is available through Dialog and includes many government documents.

The *Official Gazette* of the U.S. Patent and Trademark Office is published weekly and contains brief summary descriptions of patents. The Patent and Trademark Office provides free access to *CASSIS*, which is the online database available to the patent depositories in the U.S. Patent information is also available through online databases such as the various *CLAIMS* files which are commercially produced, very expensive, and available through Dialog.

Social Science

It would be most helpful for reference librarians, particularly in the Social Sciences, to have knowledge of the government publications about other countries and foreign relations with other countries. How often are we asked for extensive but concise information on a given country's economic or political system, or its history or cultural heritage? The *Area Handbook Series* issued by the U.S. Department of the Army provides this and additional information on religious beliefs, criminal justice and national security. Some countries represented in the series are Afghanistan, Belgium, China, Finland, Honduras, India, Mexico, Rwanda, and Zimbabwe. Kept in ready reference, this valuable series can be used by all levels of patrons. While the individual countries in this series are not updated frequently, current data can be obtained from the *Background Notes* published by the U.S. Department of State. Additional information on foreign countries can often be obtained by writing to foreign consuls or other members of the diplomatic corps. Names, addresses, phone numbers, staff members, and other information can be found in one of several publications issued by the U.S. Department of State—*Foreign Service List*, *Diplomatic List*, *List of Foreign Consular Officers in the United States*, *Key Officers of Foreign Service Posts*, and *Foreign Consular Offices in the United States*.

Dating back to the Continental Congress in 1775, the U.S. Department of State is the oldest executive department of the U.S. government. While the *Foreign Relations of the United States* is the official record of papers on U.S. foreign policy, the *Department of State Bulletin* provides current information. Published monthly, it contains addresses of the President and the Secretary of State on United States foreign policy.

One commercially produced index which indexes books, periodical articles, and government publications at all levels of government is *PAIS* (*Public Affairs Information Service*). It also covers non-U.S. government publications. Its coverage extends to all issues relating to social, political or economic policy. It is available online through Dialog and BRS and is also available on CD-ROM.

In the field of education, the U.S. Department of Education publishes *Resources in Education* (*RIE*). It indexes the reports and findings, speeches, and books in the field of education. Indexed by subject and author *RIE* provides extensive abstracts on the reports and publications. *ERIC* is the online equivalent of *RIE* and *Current Index to Journals in Education* (*CIJE*) and is available through Dialog and BRS. It is also available from several vendors on CD-ROM.

Congressional Publications

Congressional publications play an important role in a depository library collection. The *Congressional Directory* is the official directory for Congress. It gives a short biographical sketch of all members of Congress as well as their Washington office address, phone number and FAX number, and their address in their home state. The *Directory* lists the committee assignments and office staff of each member of Congress. It also lists members of the press, radio and TV, photographers, and others who are entitled to attend sessions of Congress.

The official record of the debates and proceedings of Congress is the *Congressional Record*. It is published daily when Congress is in session and is cumulated into the bound edition at the end of each session of Congress. The *Journal of the House of Representatives* and *Journal of the Senate* provide a daily list of the proceedings of Congress. Some types of information found in the *Journals* are lists of bills and resolutions introduced, memorial addresses and veto messages of the President. There is also a section on the history of legislation and the action taken.

Most of the work done by Congress takes place in Congressional committees. Once a bill is introduced, it is referred to a particular committee to study the issues, hold hearings, and receive testimony from pertinent witnesses. The verbatim transcript of these proceedings, together with written statements from witnesses, are published as Senate and House *Hearings*. The House and Senate *Reports* series is the mechanism for communicating committee reports and findings and recommendations on the *Hearings* to the whole House or Senate. The House and Senate *Documents* series is the record of Congress containing Presidential messages, annual reports of various executive agencies, and various other documents. At the end of each session of Congress the House and Senate *Reports* and *Documents* are cumulated into the *U.S. Serial Set*.

In order to access the volume of Congressional data, the Congressional Information Service publishes an index, *CIS*. Published monthly since 1970, *CIS* provides comprehensive indexes and extensive abstracts for all the Congressional publications. The abstracts are cumulated annually and the index is cumulated quarterly, annually, and quadrennially. The publications indexed include the House and Senate *Hearings*, *Reports* and *Documents*, *Committee Prints*, *Public Laws,* and other publications. *CIS* is available online through Dialog and is now available on CD-ROM.

Legal Resources

No discussion of sources of government information would be complete without mention of some of the legal resources available. The *Federal Register* is the official publication of regulations, rules and legal notices issued by federal agencies. Issued daily, it includes meeting and hearing notices, public laws, Presidential proclamations, and executive orders. The regulations are cumulated each year and published in the *Code of Federal Regulations* (*CFR*) Online access is available through Dialog.

The *U.S. Statutes-at-Large* provides the text of both public and private laws, as well as the date the law was passed, law number, and citations to the *U.S. Code.* While the *U.S. Statutes-at-Large* covers a single session of Congress, the *U.S. Code* contains all the laws in effect on a stated day. A new edition of the *U.S. Code* is published every six years and is kept up to date by annual supplements. Commercially published, the *U.S. Code Annotated* provides the same basic information as the *U.S. Code*. However, it is easier to use and it annotates sections of the code and provides citations to court cases affecting the laws.

The full text of Supreme court cases can be found in the *U.S. Reports*, which is published by the Government Printing Office and sent to depository libraries. West, a commercial publisher, also publishes the opinions of the Supreme Court in its *Supreme Court Reporter*. The opinions of the lower federal courts and state courts are published in its various court reporter series, such as the *Federal Reporter*, *Federal Reporter, 2nd Series*, *Federal Supplement*, and the many state and regional reporters. The actual court opinions are also available online through *Lexis* and Westlaw.

PILOT PROJECT

The Depository Library Program had a golden opportunity to cooperate with the private sector for free online dissemination of Congressional information through LEGI-SLATE. From July through December 1988, which was then extended to January 31, 1989, the UNO Federal Depository Library, as well as other federal depositories in the New Orleans area, became one of 51 test libraries which became part of a pilot project with LEGI-SLATE. LEGI-SLATE provided access to all of their online data files free for this trial period. Their data bases include information on the status of legislation, voting records, full text of bills, full text of the *Congressional Record* and Committee reports, press briefings, and full text of the *Federal Register*. It also included non-government produced sources such as the *National Journal*, *CQ*, and the *Almanac of American Politics*.

The UNO Library used the service extensively, especially in the Fall 1988. The information searched for most frequently included regulations in the *Federal Register* and the full text of bills that became law during the last two months of the 100th Congress. The full text of the bills, especially those that became law, were available electronically through LEGI-SLATE much more quickly than any printed or microfiche versions.

LEGI-SLATE was eager to continue development of this project for depository distribution of government publications in electronic format. They submitted a proposal to the Government Printing Office whereby GPO would supply the tapes containing the government publications (Congressional material plus the *Federal Register*) to LEGI-SLATE free of charge through December 1989. LEGI-SLATE would then continue to provide the 51 test libraries access to the "official" government publications in its data base at no charge through December 1989. These libraries would have to subscribe to the non-government portions of the data base (*Washington Post*, *National Journal*, etc.).[16] At this time GPO was not willing to participate in the project. According to a letter from Joseph E. Jenifer, Acting Public Printer of the U.S. to LEGI-SLATE, he states "your barter offer is not in our interest nor is it good public policy in that it would make our tapes available to you and others on an uneven basis."[17]

CONCLUSION

As should be painfully obvious by now, in the words of Hernon and McClure, "the universe of government information is large and poorly defined – nobody knows its exact shape or size."[18] Not only must librarians choose from a dizzying array of new technology, but also from a variety of packages and sources, both private and public.[19] However, this electronic technology has increased the ability to access government information and to integrate it into the mainstream of reference. Obviously, the general information provider will not become an expert in the many complexities of documents reference, but at least will be aware of the many sources and value of government information.

At the same time that electronic technology has increased the ability to access government information, it has also taken away from it because there is no clearly defined federal information policy. As a result, electronic government information is not being distributed to depository libraries in the same manner that paper and microfiche are distributed. The Office of Technology Assessment's report, *Informing the Nation: Federal Information Dissemination in an Electronic Age* addresses the federal information policy issue and urges Congress to resolve the problem.[20]

Librarians should also be concerned with government policies and agency budget cuts that have forced the elimination of many government publications. There have also been efforts to privatize some government information. These issues are all complex, but they need to be resolved. Now that the technology exists to access all of the government information more easily, it would not be good for the public if the government discontinues publishing and distributing valuable information to depositories.

REFERENCES

1. Office of Technology Assessment, *Informing the Nation: Federal Information Dissemination in an Electronic Age* (Washington, D.C.: U.S. Government Printing Office, 1988), p.1.

2. Ibid., p. 12.

3. Ibid., p. 1.

4. Marilyn Moody, "Twenty-Five Years of Government Information: Changes in Reference Service Attitudes," *RQ* 25 (Fall 1985): 39.

5. Ibid., pp. 40-44.

6. Ibid., p. 39.

7. "Finding the Answer to Some of Your Toughest Questions: Training the General Information Provider to Use Government Information, GODORT Annual Program: New Orleans, 1988," *DTTP* 17 (March 1989): 19-40.

8. Marilyn Moody, "Critical Issues in Government Information Reference Service," *RQ* 27 (Summer 1988): 480.

9. Charles R. McClure and Peter Hernon, *Improving the Quality of Reference Service for Government Publications* (Chicago: American Library Association, 1983), p. 140.

10. Ibid., p. 141.

11. John L. Andriot, ed. *Guide to U.S. Government Publications* (McLean, VA: Documents Index, 1989).

12. Michael R. Lavin, *Business Information: How to Find It, How to Use It* (Phoenix: Oryx Press, 1987).

13. Lorna M. Daniells, *Business Information Sources* (Berkeley: University of California Press, 1985).

14. Richard Kern, "The 1990 Census: the Good, the Bad, and the Undercount," *Sales and Marketing Management* 141 (July 1989): 51.

15. U.S. Department of Commerce, Bureau of the Census, *Census Catalog and Guide*, (Washington, D.C.: U.S. Government Printing Office, 1989).

16. "LEGI-SLATE Proposes to Extend Pilot Project," *DTTP* 17 (March 1989): 6.

17. Joseph E. Jenifer to Robert D. Hanson, LEGI-SLATE, 13 February 1989, Letter.

18. Peter Hernon and Charles R. McClure, "GPO's Depository Library Program: Building for the Future," *Library Journal* 113 (April 1, 1988): 52.

19. Moody, "Critical Issues in Government Information Reference Service," p. 480.

20. Office of Technology Assessment, p. 1.

Government Sources for Business Reference Inquiries

Priscilla Cheng Geahigan

SUMMARY. This paper attempts to highlight some of the sources published by the Federal government agencies for answering business reference questions. For the convenience of non-government document depository libraries, ordering information is also provided.

INTRODUCTION

Reference librarians are being asked to cope with a variety of business questions in an age when businesses and companies must increasingly rely upon information to remain competitive. Reference requests range from simple questions such as unemployment rates, to complex questions such as targeting of new products to specific markets. One often overlooked source for answering such questions is government documents. The federal government gathers and publishes enormous amounts of technical and statistical data that are in the public domain. The government also publishes many reference books that include business information although they are not advertised as such. Generally, government documents are priced reasonably and are affordable by most libraries. For government document depository libraries, they are even free. Much of this government generated data has also been repackaged by commercial publishers or database producers, usually with valuable additions such as better indexing features or more accessing points. However, informed librarians can retrieve much of the same data from lower cost government documents if they know how and where to find it. The crucial first step in undertaking such a search is to analyse the user's question and decide what data is actually needed.

Priscilla Cheng Geahigan is Head of Reference, Krannert Management and Economics Library, Purdue University, West Lafayette, IN

© 1991 by The Haworth Press, Inc. All rights reserved.

ANALYZING BUSINESS REFERENCE QUESTIONS

Answers to the majority of business reference questions involve some kind of statistical data. Many business questions, such as the question of unemployment rates, are easy to answer and the librarian needs to locate just one statistical source. Others are more complicated and require more expertise. Take the query about the appropriate market for a new product, for example, the question cannot be tackled until the subject is broken down into more precise sub-questions e.g.,

- What kind of product is being promoted?
- What is its SIC (Standard Industrial Classification) code?
- In what kind of establishments or businesses will this product be sold?
- What geographical location (large cities, smaller communities, etc.)?
- What are the characteristics of the target users of the product?
    a. individuals or families?
    b. male or female, or both?
    c. age group—infants, children, teenagers, adults, older groups?
    d. income level—low income, medium income or high income groups?

Once the various components of a complex question have been pinpointed, the librarian is in a better position to decide the best sources to use. In this case, the census publications, and many related current surveys published by the Bureau of the Census can provide the statistical information needed to answer each sub-question. Such socio-economic and demographic data is valuable for market analysis.

REFERENCE GUIDES

Although government documents provide a wealth of information in the business and economic area, many librarians do not use these sources as often as they should. One reason may be that many government document collections are segregated from the regular reference collections. Most libraries do not catalog government documents and, because of this, they tend to be less accessible. To aid librarians who are unfamiliar with business titles and terminology, there are many reference guides published on business and statistical sources.[1] Beginning librarians will find them useful in identifying both government and non-government sources.

The *American Statistics Index* (ASI),[2] available both as printed source and online database, provides in depth indexing of statistical information included in government publications. Not all libraries can afford its subscription fee or have trained staff to search it as an online reference source, however. If the query does not involve statistical information, a subject search to the *Monthly Catalog of United States Government Publications*,[3] the *Index to U.S. Government Periodicals*,[4] and the *CIS/Index*,[5] may yield titles from other pertinent government publications. The Small Business Administration, for example, publishes pamphlets useful to small business management and startups. Many Congressional hearings and reports also present information reflecting the Congress's concerns with individual industries and the general economy. If you do not own any of these reference guides, the Statistical Abstracts of the United States, the all time favorite reference source, and the Census Catalog and Guide, another government document, could provide leads to individual document titles.

This paper will try to highlight some of the sources which are readily available in most of the depository collections. Much of the information included below was obtained from the online GPO (Government Printing Office) Publications Reference File at the time of this writing (September 1989). It will be necessary to verify the ordering information when purchasing. Because the readership of this journal comes from libraries of various sizes, disciplines, and interests, sources below are divided into the "better known" and "lesser known" groups. Each entry includes the following information when available: title, Superintendent of Documents classification number in parenthesis, issuing agency, year or frequency of publication, number of volume or pagination, a 12-digit GPO stock number for ordering purpose, and the purchasing or subscription price. The groupings of the following titles represent the author's own preferences. Business librarians who are familiar with government sources can probably skip the "better known" section.

BETTER KNOWN DOCUMENT TITLES

The following titles are extremely useful in answering basic statistical questions related to business and economics. Most of these titles are familiar to practising librarians. Because of this, detailed annotations are not provided.

Statistical Abstract of the United States, 1989, National Data Book and Guide to Sources (C3.134:989)

Commerce Department. Census Bureau. Data User Services Division.

1989. 984 pages. 003-024-06906-7. $33.00 Casebound/Cloth; 26.00 paperback.

This reference book is the standard summary of statistics on the social, political, and economic organization of the United States. Provides excellent documentation to sources of information.

County and City Data Book, 1988, A Statistical Abstract Supplement. States; Counties; Cities of 25,000 or More; Places of 2,500 or More. (C3.134/2:C82/2/988)

Commerce Department. Census Bureau. Data User Services Division.

1988.958 pages. 003-024-06709-9. $36.00.

Survey of Current Business (C59.11:)

Commerce Department. Bureau of Economic Analysis.

Monthly. 703-036-00000-7. Subscription $18.00.

Contains current business statistics, national income and product statistics, including the Gross National Product, the GNP implicit price deflator, corporate profits, and articles about trends in industry.

National Income and Product Accounts of the United States, 1929-82, Statistical Tables (C59.11/4:In2/929-82)

Commerce Department. Bureau of Economic Analysis.

1986. 438 pages. 003-010-00174-7. $23.00.

A supplement to the Survey of Current Business. It is one of a series of reports that presents the revised National Income and Product Account estimates that resulted from the comprehensive revision released.

Business Statistics: 1986 (C59.11/3:986)

Commerce Department. Bureau of Economic Analysis.

1987. 264 pages. 003-010-00181-0. $16.00.

A biennial supplement to the Survey of Current Business. Presents historical and methodological notes for approximately 2,100 series that appear in the Survey of Current Business. (Note: 1986 edition was published on February, 1988, according to the GPO Reference File. 1988 edition should be available in early 1990).

Economic Indicators (Y4.Ec7:)

Congress. Joint Economic Committee and Executive Office of the President. Council of Economic Advisors.

Monthly. 752-004-00000-5. Subscription $24.00.

Provides national economic conditions statistics such as interest rate, consumer price index, gross national product, disposable personal income, unemployment rate, etc. on a monthly basis. The information is presented in a condensed tabular and chart format. This deceptively plain looking 38-page publication includes a surprisingly large quantity of information within each issue. Since it is published monthly, it is a good source to update statistics obtained from the U.S. Statistical Abstract. If a small library can afford only one updating subscription to statistical sources, this should be the one.

Business Conditions Digest (C59.9:)

Commerce Department. Bureau of Economic Analysis.

Monthly. 703-012-00000-1. Subscription $44.00.

Presents almost 500 economic indicators including the various components of the leading, lagging, and coincidental economic indicators.

Handbook of Cyclical Indicators, 1984 (C59.9/3:In 2/984)

Commerce Department. Bureau of Economic Analysis.

1984. 195 pages. 003-010-00127-5. $5.50 (Out of print as of Feb, 1989).

A supplement to the *Business Conditions Digest.* Provides technical information and historical data on about 300 economic time series in the monthly *Business Conditions Digest*.

CPI Detailed Report. (L2.38/3:)

Labor Department. Bureau of Labor Statistics. Office of Prices and Living Conditions.

Monthly. 729-002-00000-3. Subscription $21.00.

A monthly report on consumer price movements. Includes statistical tables and technical notes on Consumer Price Indexes for all urban consumers and for urban wage earners and clerical workers. Data include groups and items of services and commodities.

Producer Price Indexes (L2.61:)

Labor Department. Labor Statistics Bureau. Office of Prices and Living Conditions.

Monthly. 729-009-00000-8. Subscription $29.00.

Reports on price movements at producers market level, including statistical tables of summary indexes for groups of products and most commodities. Supplement contains changes in relative importance of components of the index and annual averages.

United States Industrial Outlook, 1989: Prospects for Over 350 Industries (C61.34:989)

Commerce Department. International Trade Administration.

Annual [1989]. 552 pages. 003-009-00547-7. $24.00.

Presents information about 350 industries. Special features in this edition include chapters on "Recent Financial Performance of U.S. Manufacturing Corporations," "The U.S. Export Boom and Economic Growth," and "Top 50 Trade Events."

Occupational Outlook Handbook, 1988-89 Edition (L2.3/4:988-89)

Labor Department. Labor Statistics Bureau.

Annual [1988]. 466 pages. 029-001-02943-8. $24.00.

Part of the Bureau of Labor Statistics Bulletin Series (no. 2300). Provides detailed information on about 225 occupations.

Employment and Wages Annual Averages, 1987 (L2.104/2:987)

Labor Department. Labor Statistics Bureau.

1988. 532 pages. 029-001-02983-7. $31.00.

Part of the Bureau of Labor Statistics Bulletin Series (no. 2314). Presents 1987 annual data on employment and wages. The data relate to works covered by unemployment insurance laws and Federal civilian workers covered by the Unemployment Compensation for Federal Employee program.

Employment and Earnings (L2.41/2:)

Labor Department. Labor Statistics Bureau.

Monthly. 729-004-00000-6 Subscription $25.00.

Contains current data on employment, hours, earnings, and labor turnover for the U.S. as a whole, for individual states, and for more than 200 local areas.

Monthly Labor Review (L2.6)

Labor Department. Labor Statistics Bureau.
Monthly. 729-007-00000-5. Subscription $20.00.
Articles are on employment, labor force, wages, prices, productivity, collective bargaining, etc. Regular features include a review of developments in industrial relations, current labor statistical data, etc.

Federal Reserve Bulletin (FR1.3:)

Board of Governors. Federal Reserve System.
Monthly. $25.00 [free to academic and public libraries], order directly from Federal Reserve System, call (202) 452-3244.
Includes a section on financial and business statistics such as money supply, interest rates, flow of funds, international interest and exchange rates, etc. Also presents the "Industrial Production Index" which serves as an economic indicator of the manufacturing industry.

Census Catalog and Guide: 1989 (C3.163/3:989)

Commerce Department. Census Bureau. Data User Services Division.
1989. 416 pages. 003-024-07009-0. $21.00.
Describes the reports, machine-readable files, microcomputer diskettes, microfiche, and maps related to the various censuses, issued from January 1980 through December 1988. Also includes an index and additional information about the censuses.

THE LESSER KNOWN SOURCES

One of the problems in using government publications is their inconsistency which ranges from their quality of publication and indexing, to their frequency and format of publication. Some works, such as the *U.S. Statistical Abstract*, feature excellent indexing and citation of original sources, but the same cannot be said of others. For example, the annual *Agricultural Statistics*, a publication similar to the *Statistical Abstract* in format, only makes reference to agency source but not to specific titles at the end of each table. This discrepancy occurs because documents are produced by different agencies. Another problem with government publications is the common practice of publishing many individual titles under an umbrella series name such as "Bulletin," "Statistical Bulletin," or "Report." As such, much valuable information included in these individual studies is lost to librarians who are infrequent users of these series. Still another problem is that not all publications issued by government agencies are depository items or for sale by the GPO. Many are distributed by issuing agencies or for sale by the National Technical Information Service only. This section will attempt to include recently published titles that may be useful for answering business questions, but are not widely known.

Wage, Income, and Benefits

Earnings of Married-Couple Families: 1987 (C3.186:P60/no.165)

Commerce Department. Census Bureau. Housing and Household Economics Statistics Division. 1989. 55 pages. 803-006-30012-9. $3.00.

Part of the Current Population Reports (Series P-60, Consumer Income, no. 165). This report contains data on the annual earnings of husbands and wives and their combined earnings as married couples for 1987. Presents earnings by three determinants: annual work experience, occupation, and level of educational attainment. Summary statistics for 1981, 1983, 1986 are also provided. Other tables of interest include: "Married-Couple Families with Wives' Earnings Greater than Husbands' Earnings."

Population and 1985 Per Capita Income Estimates for Counties and Incorporated Places (C3.186/27-5:985-86)

Commerce Department. Census Bureau.

1988 in 5 parts. Stock number and price vary.

Part of the Current Population Reports (Series P-26, Local Population Estimates, no. 86-[part]-SC). This is a set of five regional reports containing current population estimates and estimates of per capita income. It is being published biennially within the P-26 Series. Personal Income information is easily found on the national level. Disposable personal income on the state level can be found in the Survey of Current Business. Local personal income data on the county and township level, however, is not easily accessible. Not every user would attempt to find income information in this series since it is entitled Local Population Estimates. The next set which includes 1988 population and 1987 per capita income estimates should be out in 1990.

Social Security Area Population Projections 1989 by Alice Wade (HE3.19:105)

Department of Health and Human Services. Social Security Administration. Office of the Actuary.

1989. 48 pages. Free copy available from agency, call (301) 965-3008.

Part of the *Actuarial Study* (no. 105). This study describes the population projections that underlie the long-range cost estimates for the Old-Age, Survivors, and Disability Insurance Program. Among the various projections through year 2080 are: death rates by sex, age and year, life expectancy by sex, marriage rate, divorce rate, etc. Marketing projections use much of the same kind of information.

Industry Wage Survey (L2.3/3:)

Labor Department. Labor Statistics Bureau.

Stock number and price vary.

A series of surveys published as individual BLS Bulletins. Each report analyses a separate industry on: (1) Occupational averages by major product, by type of area, by size of establishment, and by labor-management contract coverage; (2) Occupational earnings; (3) Establishment practices and employee benefits. Individual surveys are being updated every few years. Industry groupings include department stores, hospitals, hotels and motels, auto dealer repair shops, certificated air carriers, etc.

Area Wage Survey: Metropolitan Area, 1988 (L2.121/)

Labor Department. Labor Statistics Bureau.

Stock number and price vary.

A series of annual surveys published as individual BLS Bulletins (Bulletin no. 3045-[part] for all 1988 surveys). Each survey reports "earnings for all establishments" and "establishment practices and employee benefits" for office and production workers in one metropolitan area.

Local Area Personal Income, 1981-86 (C59.18:981-86/)

Commerce Department. Bureau of Economic analysis. Regional Economic Measurement Division. 1988-. 9 vols. Stock number and price vary.

Includes county and Metropolitan Areas data on Income by Place of Residence, Earnings by Place of Work, etc.

Employers and Child Care: Benefiting Work and Family (L36.102:Em7/7)

Labor Department. Office of the Secretary. Women's Bureau.
1989. 86 pages. 029-002-00076-2. $4.50.

Prepared especially for employers and employees concerned with developing programs and policies to assist in quality and cost efficient child care programs while parents are at work. Describes types of child care arrangements, and provides information that would be helpful in planning and financing child care services supported by employers or labor unions.

Occupational Projections and Training Data: 1988 Edition (L2.3/4-2:988)

Labor Department. Labor Statistics Bureau.
1988. 120 pages. 029-001-02974-8. $5.50.

A Statistical and Research Supplement to the 1988-89 Occupational Outlook Handbook. Presents statistics and technical data underlying information presented in the Handbook.

Projections 2000 (L2.3:2302)

Labor Department. Labor Statistics Bureau.
1988. 145 pages. 029-001-02968-3. $7.50. (Previous editions: Employment Projections for . . .)

Part of the BLS Bulletin (no. 2302). Presents employment projections for the year 2000.

Socio-Economic and Demographic

Social Indicators III: Selected Data on Social Conditions and Trends in the United States (C3.2:So1/2/)

Department of Commerce. Census Bureau.
1980. 645 pages. 003-024-02563-0. $19.00.

Presents a wide variety of data on social conditions and trends in the United States.

Marital Status and Living Arrangements: 1988, March (C3.186/6:988)

Commerce Department. Census Bureau. Population Division.
1989. 91 pages. 803-005-00032-0. $4.50.

Part of the *Current Population Reports* (Series P-20, Population Characteristics, no. 433). Presents detailed characteristics on the marital status and living arrangements of the non-institutionalized population of the U.S. by age, sex, race, Spanish origin, and in some instances, by metropolitan area and region.

Medicare and Medicaid Data Book, 1988 (HE22/19/4:)

Health and Human Services Department. Health Care Financing Administration. Office of Research and Demonstrations.

1988. 143 pages. 017-060-00214-0. $7.50.

Includes Medicare data. Shows trends in enrollees, recipients, use of services, and expenditures. Also provides lists of Medicare carriers and intermediaries, Medicaid agencies and fiscal agents.

State and Local Information

County Business Patterns [1987] (C3.204/3)

Commerce Department. Census Bureau. Economic Surveys Division.

Monthly. Stock number and price vary by state.

A set of 53 annual reports covering state and county employment and payrolls, number and employment size of establishments by industry. The 1987 reports were published in 1989.

State Government Tax Collection in 1988 (C3.191/2)

Commerce Department. Census Bureau. Governments Division.

1989. 54 pages. 003-024-07067-7. $3.00.

Part of the Government Finance series (GF-88-1). Presents data from state taxes including general sales, individual income, corporation net income, motor fuel sales, motor vehicle licenses, tobacco, alcoholic beverage sales, etc.

Energy Consumption

Annual Energy Review, 1988 (E3.1/3:988)

Energy Department. Energy Information Administration. Office of Energy Markets and End Use. 1989. 317 pages. 061-003-00615-9. $16.00.

Presents historical and current data on production, consumption, stocks, imports, exports, and prices of the principal energy commodities in the U.S. Also includes data on international production of crude oil, consumption of petroleum products, petroleum stocks, and production electricity from nuclear-powered facilities.

Monthly Energy Review (E 3.9:)

Energy Department. Energy Information Administration. Office of Energy Markets and End Use.
Monthly. 761-007-00000-9. Subscription $62.00.

Annual Outlook for United States Electric Power, 1988, Projections Through 2000 (E3.50:988)

Energy Department. Energy Information Administration. Office of Coal, Nuclear, Electric and Alternate Fuels.
1988. 91 pages. 061-003-00579-9. $4.50.
Provides electric power projections to the year 2000 for electric supply, fuel consumption, and electricity prices, by region.

Coal Data: A Reference (E3.11/7-7:987)

Energy Department. Energy Information Administration. Office of Coal, Nuclear, Electric, and Alternate Fuels.
1989. 102 pages. 061-003-00614-1. $7.50.
Provides basic information on the mining and use of coal in the U.S.

Petroleum Supply annual, 1988 (Vol. 1) (E3.11/5-5:)

Energy Department. Energy Information administration. Office of oil and Gas.
1989. 170 pages. 061-003-00617-5. $9.00.
Contains information on the supply and disposition of crude oil and petroleum products. This volume includes final data for 1988 on petroleum supply and refinery capacity.

Nonresidential Building Energy Consumption Survey: Commercial Building Consumption and Expenditures, 1986 (E3.43/2:)

Energy Department. Energy Information Administration. Office of Energy Markets and End Use. 1989. 376 pages. 061-003-00613-2. $19.00.

Presents national and regional level estimates of energy consumption and expenditure totals for commercial buildings. Provides data by type of energy and by building characteristics.

State Energy Data Report Supplement, Consumption Estimates 1960-1987 (E3.42:)

Energy Department. Energy Information Administration. Office of Energy Markets and End Use. 1989. 474 pages. 061-003-00610-8. $23.00.

Provides estimates of annual energy consumption at the state level by major economic sector and by principal energy type. Includes residential, commercial, industrial, electric utilities, and transportation sectors.

Space Technology

Commercial Use of Space: A New Economic Strength for America (NAS1.83:113)

National Aeronautics and Space Administration. Office of Commercial Programs. Public Affairs Office. 1989. 24 pages. 033-000-01035-4. $2.25.

Describe space commerce, its benefits for the country. Provides information on four examples of ways in which industry can use space: satellite communications, earth and ocean observations, materials research and processing, and space transportation and industrial services.

Trade and Industry Studies

United States Foreign Trade Highlight, 1988 (C61.28/2:988)

Commerce Department. International Trade Administration. Office of Trade and Investment Analysis. 1989. 492 pages. 003-009-00561-2. $25.00.

Provides tables of data on U.S. foreign trade, in merchandise, manufactures, and agriculture, with the world, all individual countries of the world, and with the major geographic regions, for 1980 through 1988.

Guide to Foreign Trade Statistics (C3.6/2:F76/983)

Commerce Department. Census Bureau.
1983. 159 pages. 003-024-05766-2. $4.75 [Out of Print].

Provides information on the frequency, format, content, and general arrangement of data in the foreign trade statistics published by the Census Bureau. A good first step guide in deciding which foreign trade statistical series to use.

Trade Performance in 1987 and Outlook (C61.28:987)

Commerce Department. International Trade Administration. Office of Trade and Investment Analysis.
1989. 139 pages. 003-009-00537-0. $7.00.
Presents a comprehensive analysis of United States trade and its role in the world economy.

A Basic Guide to Exporting (C61.8:Ex7/3/986)

Commerce Department. International Trade Administration. Foreign Commercial Service.
1986. 158 pages. 003-009-00487-0. $8.50.
A step by step guide to information on exporting. Includes export strategy, market research, contracts, pricing, and other practical information.

Japanese Solid Wood Products Market: Profile and Outlook (C61.2:W85/3)

Commerce Department. International Trade Administration. Office of Forest Products and Domestic Construction. Basic Industries Sector.
1989. 220 pages. 003-009-00553-1. $11.00.
Includes sections on impediments to increased solid wood products exports to Japan, Japanese consumption of forest products; Japan's forest resources, Japan's wood based industries, barriers to trade, and international trade.

National Trade Estimate Report on Foreign Trade Barriers, 1989. (PrEx1.14:989)

Executive Office of the President. Office of the U.S. Trade Representative.
1989. 220 pages. 041-001-00347-9. $11.00.
Documents significant foreign barriers to U.S. trade. Includes an appendix which defines various types of trade barriers.

Guide to Telecommunication Markets in Latin America (C61.8:M34)

Commerce Department. International Trade Administration.
1989. 92 pages. 003-009-00556-6. $4.50.
Summarizes information on the telecommunications authorities, the networks, and the expansion plans of the telecommunications industries of the countries of Latin America and the Caribbean.

Annual prospects for World Coal Trade, 1989. (E3.11/7-9:989)

Energy Department. Energy Information Administration. Office of Coal, Nuclear, Electric, and Alternate Fuels.
1989. 120 pages. 061-003-00616-7. $6.00.
Provides a world coal trade outlook for the countries of the world which export coal.

Survey of Government Assistance for the World's Hard Coal Industries (C61.2:C63/5)

Commerce Department. International Trade Administration. Office of Energy. 1989. 197 pages. 003-009-00558-2. $10.00.
Investigates the existence and use of subsidies and incentives that foreign nations give their coal industries. Includes industry profiles for 22 countries that mine hard coal, defined as anthracite, bituminous, and subituminous coals.

Annual Survey of Manufactures (C3.24/9-9:986)

Commerce Department. Census Bureau. Industry Division.
Annual, in various parts. Stock number and price vary.
An annual update to the Census of Manufactures, published for each of the years between the Censuses. Reports include "Statistics for Industry Groups and Industries," "Geographic Area Statistics," "Value of Product Shipments," etc.

Current Business Reports: Monthly Wholesale Trade, Sales and Inventories (C3.133:)

Commerce Department. Census Bureau. Business Division.
Monthly. 703-018-00000-9. Subscription $9.00.
An updating service for the Census of Wholesale Trade. Contains monthly statistics for sales and inventories of merchant wholesalers for selected kinds of businesses for the United States.

Current Business Reports: Retail Trade (C3.138/5:)

Commerce Department. Census Bureau. Business Division.
Monthly. 703-017-00000-2. Subscription $36.00.
An updating service for the Census of Retail Trade. Consists of three subtitles: "Advance Monthly Retail Sales," "Monthly retail Trade Sales, Inventories," and "Annual Sales, Year-End Inventories, Pur-

chases, Gross Margin, and Accounts Receivable, by Kind of Retail Store."

Agriculture and Farm Sector

Agricultural Prices (A92.16:)

Department of Agriculture. National Agricultural Statistics Service. Agricultural Statistics Board.

Monthly with annual summary issue. 701-005-00000-7. Subscription $28.00.

Provides comparative information on prices received by farmers for various commodities, and prices paid by farmers for commodities and services, interests, taxes and farm wage rates.

Agricultural Chartbook, 1989 (A1.76/2:989)

Department of Agriculture.

1989. 111 pages. 001-019-00611-1. $5.50.

Consists of charts which illustrate the current economic health of American agriculture. The charts move from the national and international arenas, to farm economic health measures, and crop and livestock trends.

Food Consumption, Prices, and Expenditures, 1966-87 (A1.34:773)

Department of Agriculture. Economic Research Service.

1989. 111 pages. $5.00. Order directly from ERS, call (800) 999-6779.

Part of the Statistical Bulletin series (no. 773) Presents historical data on per capita consumption of major food commodities, prices, nutrient availability, food expenditures, and U.S. income and population.

Economic Indicators of the Farm Sector (A 93.45:)

Agriculture Department. Economic Research Service.

Five issues per year. 701-015-00000-2. Subscription $14.00.

Each of the five issues has a unique subtitle: "Production and Efficiency statistics," "National Financial Summary," "Farm Sector Review," "Cost of Production," and "State Financial Summary."

Small Business

State of Small Business: A Report of the President Transmitted to the Congress, 1989. Together With the Annual Report of the United States Small Business Administration. (SBA1.1/2:989)

Small Business Administration.
1989. 216 pages. 045-000-00255-1. $6.00.
Presents statistics and interpretations of small business trends in 1989. Includes supplementary tables and sections on small business financing and on procurement.

Handbook of Small Business Data, 1988 (SBA1.19:D26)

Small Business Administration. Office of Advocacy.
1988. 354 pages. 045 000-00253-5. $10.00.
Presents detailed statistics on the small business economy. Data were gathered from the Bureau of Labor Statistics, the International Revenue Service, and from Dun and Bradstreet.

Directory of Women Business Owners: Megamarketplace East/West, 1987. (C1.37/3:987)

Commerce Department.
1987. 264 pages. 003-000-00651-4. $12.00.
Designed to assist women business owners in locating new marketing opportunities and to aid purchasing officials in finding new suppliers. Based on information from the Megamarketplace East and West Conferences. Includes names, addresses, and telephone numbers of businesses owned by women, federal agencies, and state and local governments.

Franchise Opportunities Handbook, 1988 (C61.31:988)

Commerce Department. International Trade Administration and Minority Business Development Agency.
1988. 303 pages. 003-009-00528-1. $16.00.
An annual directory which contains brief summary of the terms, requirements, and conditions under which each franchise is available.

Franchising in the Economy (C61.31/2:986-88)

Commerce Department. International Trade Administration. Office of Service Industries. Finance and Management Industries Division.

1984. 102 pages. 003-009-00525-6. $4.75.

Contains information received from an annual survey questionnaire sent out to 2,177 franchisors by the Commerce Department.

Handbook for Small Business: A survey of Small Business Programs of the Federal Government. (Y1.1/3:98-33)

Congress. Senate. Select Committee on Small Business.

1984. 248 pages. 052-071-00680-0. $7.00 [Out of print as of 8-29-89].

Part of the Senate Document Series (no. 98-33). Provides a description of selected Federal programs designed to assist small businesses. Indicates how and where further information can be obtained about these programs.

Government Procurement

Five Hundred Contractors Receiving the Largest Dollar Volume of Prime Contract Awards for Research, Development, Test, and Evaluation, Fiscal Year 1988 (D1.57/2:988)

Defense Department. Directorate for Information Operations and Reports.

1989. 41 pages. 008-000-00528-1. $2.50.

Provides information on the 500 contractors that received the largest dollar volume in Department of Defense prime contract awards.

Laws Relating to Federal Procurement (Y4.AR5/2:L44/2/988)

Congress. House. Committee on Armed Services.

1989. 550 pages. 052-070-06558-3. $16.00.

A useful volume including all of the major legislation relating to federal procurement.

CONCLUSION

It is obvious that no comprehensive listing can be provided in the space of one article. This list of sources only samples the U.S. government documents that can be used to answer routine reference questions in the business and economics area. Readers are encouraged to explore further some of the series mentioned, especially the various censuses and their individual component reports series. Again the *Census Catalog and Guide* is a highly recommended first step. More up-to-date information can also be obtained online directly from some government agencies' electronic bulletin boards. Two related to the business and economics area are the "Economic Bulletin Board" from the Department of Commerce,[6] and the "Electronic Bulletin Board" from the Labor Department.[7] Both are readily accessible to the public. The *Cendata* online database,[8] issued by the Bureau of the Census, is available on the Dialog Information Service. With sufficient guidance from librarians, users from academic, public, and special libraries should be able to take full advantage of the valuable information generated by government sources.

REFERENCES AND NOTES

1. Some of these sources are: *Business Information: How to Find It, How to Use It,* by Michael R. Lavin (Phoenix: Oryx, 1987); *Business Information Sources* by Lorna M. Daniells (Berkeley: University of California Press, 1985); *Business Serials of the U.S. Government,* 2nd edition, ed. by Priscilla C. Geahigan and Robert F. Rose (Chicago: American Library Association, 1988);*Encyclopedia of Business Sources,* 7th edition, ed. by James Woy (Detroit: Gale, 1988); *Handbook of Business Information: A Guide for Libraries, Students, and Researchers* (Englewood, CO: Libraries Unlimited, 1988); and *Statistical Sources,* 12th edition, ed. by Jacqueline W. O'Brien and Steven R. Wasserman (Detroit: Gale, 1989)
2. *American Statistics Index* (Washington, D.C.: Congressional Information Service. Monthly with annual cumulation. Also available as an online database on the Dialog Information System (File 102).
3. U.S. Superintendent of Documents. *Monthly Catalog of United States Government Publications.* Washington D.C.: U.S. Government Printing Office. Monthly. Also available as an online database on the Dialog System (File 66).
4. Infordata International Inc. *Index to U.S. Government Periodicals.* Chicago: Infordata International. Quarterly.
5. Congressional Information Service. *CIS/Index.* Washington D.C., CIS. Monthly, with annual cumulation. Also available as an online database on the Dialog System (File 101).
6. For more information, call (202) 377-1986.
7. For more information, call (202) 523-7343.
8. Available on Dialog both as a standard command driven file (File 580) and as an easy to use menu file (Cendata).

Grant Writing Information in Federal Depository Collections

Diana J. Keith

SUMMARY. Federal government documents collections are a rich source of information about grant writing. This article describes the establishment and ultimate demise of the college's grants office and subsequent efforts to serve the grant writing information needs of faculty and reference librarians. The bibliography lists federal documents by broad subjects and, under each, by government agency.

Kearney State College, Kearney, Nebraska has traditionally been viewed as a teaching institution, as opposed to a research institution. With an ever increasing enrollment, currently in excess of 9,000 students and a steady expansion of program offerings, research has now assumed a much more important role in the mission of the college.

In the past, institutional support for faculty researchers trying to obtain grants was a shared responsibility. The Foundation Office coordinated contacts, supplied information and helped obtain grants from private foundations. There was no grants office to coordinate efforts for grant funding from government entities. The Graduate Office, however, had oversight responsibility and assigned a graduate assistant to help faculty with government grants.

During 1987 a new grants office was established and a full time position, Director of Grants and Contracts, was funded. The purpose of the office was two-fold. The first was to consolidate responsibility for federal grant assistance and the second was to enhance direct support to the faculty for grant writing. The director of the grants office reported directly to the Dean of Graduate Studies/Director of Institutional Support. Office space for the new grants office was created in the college library, Calvin T. Ryan Library.

Diana J. Keith is Head of the Government Documents Section, Calvin T. Ryan Library, Kearney State College, Kearney, NE 68849-7000.

© 1991 by The Haworth Press, Inc. All rights reserved.

The grants office was funded for one year. Although no statistics were kept of the dollar amount of grants for which the new office was responsible, there was a noticeable increase in federal grant activity. While the office was open, the number of grant proposals written and the number of grants actually funded showed a marked increase.

In March, 1987, a grants workshop for faculty was sponsored by the grants office and held in the library. Presenters were the Dean of Graduate Studies and the Executive Vice President of the Kearney State Foundation. Half of the presentation discussed ways to obtain federal grants and the other half was devoted to information about private or corporate funding. Since Calvin T. Ryan Library's federal depository collection was a rich source of grant information, a lengthy bibliography was prepared by the head of the government documents section and copies were handed out at the workshop. The bibliography was designed to assist faculty research efforts and increase awareness of resources in the documents collection.

Funding for the grants office was made available for a one year period only. Permanent funding was requested from the state legislature the following year. Unfortunately funds were not appropriated and the grants office was forced to close in July, 1988. Because of the obvious need for the office, it is hoped that funding can be restored during the next legislative biennium.

The federal government is not only a source of grant funding but also publishes extensively in the area of grant information. Federal documents provide up-to-date information and complement information found in standard grant reference sources that are privately published. The federal government documents collection of C. T. Ryan Library is a separate collection of approximately 160,000 paper titles and over 100,000 microfiche. The library selects 48% of the item numbers available to depositories and has been a depository since 1962.

When the grants office closed, the central focus for coordinating federal grant research on campus was lost. However, interest was still high and faculty needed access to current information about grants. One way of serving this need was to update the bibliography of federal document sources that was prepared originally for the grants workshop. Not only would such a list assist faculty, but it would also help reference librarians become more aware of grant information in the collection and enable them to utilize it more fully. The revised bibliography was sent to all department chairpersons and deans, and copies are available in the library. The documents department also publishes a monthly newsletter which lists new government documents. A section is devoted to grant information and serves to update the bibliography on a continuing basis.

The following bibliography is an abridged version of the full grants bibliography and reflects selections of this particular depository. It is intended to be selective rather than comprehensive. Only titles published since 1985 have been included. Titles were selected to cover the broadest possible range of subjects and include actual grant application booklets and forms, manuals about how to prepare a grant application, information about how grants are reviewed, and examples of grants funded in the past. Two of the most important sources of current federal grant information are not included on the bibliography because they are so general in nature as to not fit any specific category. These are the *Catalog of Federal Domestic Assistance* (Office of Management and Budget, Executive Office of the President, annual with semiannual supplement, PrEx 2. 20: (year), item 853-A-1), and the *Federal Register*, (Office of the Federal Register, National Archives and Records Administration, daily, AE 2. 106: (volume/issue), item 573-C).

Titles are arranged by broad subjects and listed under each according to the issuing agency. In some cases, an agency has published only one or two titles and these were consolidated within each subject under the heading "Other Agencies." Broad subjects include arts and humanities; conservation, recreation, and the environment; criminal justice; education (miscellaneous); elementary and secondary education; handicapped, education and services; higher education; library services and librarianship; local and state government; medicine and health; miscellaneous subjects; science; and transportation and aviation. Each entry includes pagination, publication date, and Superintendent of Documents call number. A brief annotation follows titles whose subject coverage is not clear from the title alone.

ARTS AND HUMANITIES

National Endowment for the Arts

Advancement: Arts in Education, Expansion Arts, Inter-Arts, Museum, Music, Theater; application forms and guidelines, fiscal year 1989. 35 p. 1988. NF 2.8/2-19:989

Arts Administration Fellows Program: Application Guidelines. 5 p. 1988. NF 2.8/2-24:989

Arts in Education, Application Guidelines, Fiscal Year 1989.72 p. 1988. NF 2.8/2:989

Challenge Grants: Application Guidelines, Fiscal Years 1987/88. 34 p. 1986. NF 2.8/2-3:987-88

Challenge II Grants: Application Guidelines, Fiscal Year 1989. 54 p. 1987. NF 2.8/2-25:989

Challenge III Grants, Application Guidelines, Fiscal Year 1990. 56 p. 1988. NF 2.8/2-20:990

Dance, Application Guidelines, Fiscal Year 1990. 48 p. 1988. NF 2.8/2-4:990

Design Arts: Application Guidelines. 34 p. 1989. NF 2.8/2-11:990

Expansion Arts, Application Guidelines, Fiscal Year 1990. no paging. 1988. NF 2.8/2-18:990

Film/Radio/Television: Media Arts, Application Guidelines, Fiscal Year 1990. 48 p. 1989. NF 2.8/2-10:990

Folk Arts, 1989-90: Application Guidelines. 24 p. 1988. NF 2.8/2-16:989-90

Guide to the National Endowment for the Arts. 49 p. 1985. NF 2.8: N 21/985

Initiative for Interdisciplinary Artists: Inter-Arts, Application Guidelines, Fiscal Year 1988. no paging. 1988. NF 2.8/2-22:988

Literature: Application Guidelines, Fiscal Year 1989. 40 p. 1987. NF 2.8/2-2:989

Local Programs, Application Guidelines, Fiscal Year 1990. 36 p. 1988. NF 2.8/2-21:990

Museum Programs, Application Guidelines, Fiscal Year 1990. 72 p. 1988. NF 2.8/2-7:990

Music Ensembles, 1989: Application Guidelines. 60 p. 1988. NF 2.8/2-14:989

Music Fellowships: Composers, Jazz, Solo Recitalists, 1990 Application Guidelines, Fiscal Year 1990. 40 p. 1988. NF 2.8/2-8:990

Music, Music Professional Training, Career Development Organizations, Music Recording, Services to Composers, Centers for New Music Resources, Special Projects: Application Guidelines, Fiscal Year 1989. 56 p. 1988. NF 2.8/2-5:989

Music Programs: Presenters and Festivals, Jazz Management, and Jazz Special Projects: Application Guidelines. 52 p. 1989. NF 2.8/2-9:990

Opera-Musical Theater, 1989-90 Performance Season: Application Guidelines. 48 p. 1988. NF 2.8/2-12:989-90

Presenting Organizations, Artist Communities, Services to the Arts: Application Guidelines, Fiscal Year 1990. 60 p. 1989. NF 2.8/2-23:990

State Programs: Application Guidelines, Fiscal Years 1987-88. 15 p. 1986. NF 2.8/2-17:987-88

Theater: Application Guidelines, Fiscal Year 1989, 1989-90 Performance Season. 56 p. 1988. NF 2.8/2-6:989-90

Visual Arts Fellowships, 1989-90: Application Guidelines. 16 p. 1988. NF 2.8/2-13:989-90

Visual Arts, Grants to Organizations, 1989: Application Guidelines. 36 p. 1988. NF 2.8/2-15:989

National Endowment for the Humanities

Challenge Grants: Guidelines, Application Materials, and Administrative Requirements. 22 p. 1987. NF 3.8:C 35/3

Challenge Grants Program: Guidelines and Application Materials. 34 p. 1987. NF 3.8/2-4:987

Division of Education Programs, Guidelines and Application Instructions. 53 p. 1987. NF 3.17:987

Division of Fellowships and Seminars; list of awards, fiscal year 1987. n.p. 1988. NF 3.20:987

Division of Research Programs. 44 p. 1988. NF 3.2:R 31/5/988 (A description)

Faculty Graduate Study Program for Historically Black Colleges and Universities, Guidelines and Application Materials. 18 p. 1988. NF 3.8/2-7:989

Faculty Projects, Summer College Humanities Programs for High School Juniors, Historically Black Colleges and Universities. various paging. 1986. NF 3.8/2-8:986

Humanities. (Periodical; issued six times per year.) National Endowment for the Humanities. 1980- . NF 3.11:(volume/numbers)

Humanities Instruction in Elementary and Secondary Schools. 44 p. 1988. NF 3.2:H 88/988 (Summaries of 1988 projects)

Humanities Projects in Libraries and Archives, Guidelines and Application Instructions. 43 p. 1988. NF 3.8/2-10:988

Humanities Projects in Museums and Historical Organizations. 32 p. 1987. NF 3.8/2-5:987

Initiative on the Foundations of American Society. 12 p. 1987. NF 3.2:F 82

Interpretive Research: Humanities, Science and Technology, Application, Instructions, and Forms. 9 p. + app. 1988.NF 3.2:R 31/7

Interpretive Research Projects, Application Instructions and Forms. 10 p. + app. 1988. NF 3.2:R 31/8

Methods of Payment, Financial Reporting Requirements, Financial Reporting Forms. various paging. 1987. NF 3.2:P 29/987

NEH Fellowships, University Teachers, College Teachers, and Independent Scholars: Guidelines and Application Forms. 16 p. + app. 1988. NF 3.13/4:988

The 1989 Summer Seminars for College Teachers. 36 p. 1988. NF 3.13/2-3:989

1989 Summer Seminars for College Teachers, Guidelines and Application Form for Participants. 23 p. 1988. NF 3.13/2-2:989

1989 Summer Seminars for School Teachers, Guidelines and Application Form for Participants. 40 p. 1988. NF 3.13/3-3:989

1989 Summer Stipends: Guidelines and Application Forms. 12 p. 1988. NF 3.8/2:989 (For college faculty and others working in the humanities)

1989 Younger Scholars, High School Students, College Students: Guidelines and Application Forms. 23 p. 1988. NF 3.8/2-6:989

1990 Summer Seminars for College Teachers, Guidelines and Application Forms for Directors. 16 p. 1988. NF 3.13/2:990

1990 Summer Seminars for School Teachers: Guidelines and Application Form for Directors. 29 p. 1988. NF 3.13/3-2:990

Preservation Programs: Guidelines and Application Instructions. 32 p. 1986. NF 3.8/2-3:986

Public Humanities Projects, Guidelines and Application Instructions. 43 p. 1988. NF 3.8/2-9:988

Reference Materials, Access, Application Forms and Instructions. 12 p. + app. 1988. NF 3.2:R 25/2/988

Reference Materials, Tools: Application Instructions and Forms. 9 p. + app. 1987. NF 3.8:R 25

Regrants: Conferences; application instructions and forms. 7 p. + app. 1987. NF 3.2:R 26

Teacher-Scholar Program for Elementary and Secondary Teachers: Guidelines and Application Instructions. 35 p. 1989. NF 3.18:989

Texts, Publication, Subvention: Application, Instructions, and Forms. 7 p. + app. 1989. NF 3.2:T 31/2/989

Texts, Translations: Application, Instructions, and Forms. 8 p. + app. 1988. NF 3.2:T 31/3

Travel to Collections: Guidelines and Application Instructions. n.p. 1988. NF 3.19:988-89 (Travel to libraries, archives, museums, and other repositories)

Other Agencies

Application Forms, National Gallery of Art, Smithsonian Institution, Center for Advanced Study in the Visual Arts: Curatorial Fellowship. 4 p. 1988. SI 8.2:Ap 5/2

Application for Senior Fellowship. 4 p. 1988. SI 8.2:Ap 5/4

Application for Visiting Senior Fellowship. 4 p. 1988.SI 8.2:Ap 5/3

Application for Associate Appointment. 4 p. 1988. SI 8.2:Ap 5

National Gallery of Art, 1989 Summer Internship Program. 2 p. 1988. Smithsonian Institution. SI 8.2:In 8/2

1989 Conservation Project Supports, Grant Application and Information. Institute of Museum Services. 63 p. 1988. NF 4.10:989

Smithsonian Opportunities for Research and Study in History, Art, Science. 187 p. 1987. Smithsonian Institution. SI 1.44:987-88

CONSERVATION, RECREATION AND THE ENVIRONMENT

U.S. Dept. of the Interior

Land and Water Conservation Fund, Grants-In-Aid Program, Annual Report, Fiscal Year 1984. 58 p. 1985. I 29.107/2:984 (microfiche)

Urban Park and Recreation Recovery Program, Planners' Information Exchange: A Continuing Catalog of Second-Generation UPAPR Planning Grants. National Park Service. 100 p. 1985. I 29.2:Ur 1/2

U.S. Environmental Protection Agency

EPA Ground-Water Research Programs. 41 p. 1986. EP 1.23/9:600/8-86/004 (microfiche)

Solicitation for Research Grant Proposals. Office of Health and Environmental Assessment. 25 p. 1986. EP 1.23/9:600/8-86/028 (microfiche)

CRIMINAL JUSTICE

U.S. Dept. of Justice

NIJ Reports. National Institute of Justice. Bimonthly periodical. J 28.14:(number) (Includes information about the Institute's research and fellowship programs.)

Shaping Criminal Justice Policy: The Research Program of the National Institute of Justice. (Research solicitations, unsolicited research, graduate research fellowships, visiting fellowships). 27 p. 1985. J 28.2: C 86/15

Solicited Research Programs, Fiscal Year 1985, Program Announcement. National Institute of Justice. 28 p. 1985. J 29.9:NCJ-96131

Supplementing the National Crime Survey, Research Solicitation. National Institute of Justice. 8 p. 1986. J 28.2:R 31/6

EDUCATION, MISCELLANEOUS TOPICS

Various Agencies

National Science Foundation Directory of NSF Supported Teacher Enhancement Projects. National Science Foundation. 16 p. 1986. NS 1.44/2:986-87

1987 Guide to Department of Education Programs. U.S. Dept. of Education. 32 p. 1988. ED 1.10/2:987

Opportunities Abroad for Educators: Fulbright Teacher Exchange Program. 13 p. + app. 1988. IA 1.29:988

Reviewing Applications for Discretionary Grants and Cooperative Agreements: A Workbook for Application Reviewers. various paging. 1988. U.S. Dept. of Education. ED 1.2:G 76/9

Vocational Education: Information on the National Research Center's Grant Award Process. 18 p. 1988. General Accounting Office. GA 1.13:HRD-88-56 (microfiche)

ELEMENTARY AND SECONDARY EDUCATION

U.S. Dept. of Education

Application Development Guide, Educational Opportunity Centers Program, Program Year 1988-89. 25 p. 1987. ED 1.8:Ed 8

Application for Grants Under Indian Controlled Schools: Indian Education Program. various paging. 1986. ED 1.2: In 2/11/986

Application for Grants Under Indian Education Programs. various paging. 1987. ED 1.2:In 2/4/987

Application for Grants Under Magnet Schools Assistance Program. various paging. 1986. ED 1.2:M 27/986

Application for Grants Under the Drug-Free Schools and Communities Program, Federal Activities Grants Program. 20 p. 1988. ED 1.2: D 84/5/988

Application for Grants Under the Educational Research Grant Program: Teachers as Researchers Program. 35 p. 1987. ED 1.2:T 22/5 (For elementary and secondary school teachers)

Application for Grants Under the Indian Fellowship Program. various paging. 1987. ED 1.2:In 2/7/988

Application for Grants Under the Law-Related Education Program. various paging. 1987. ED 1.2:G 76/4/987-2

FY 1988 Application for Grants under the Bilingual Education Program. 82 p. 1987. ED 1.2:B 49/3/988

HANDICAPPED: EDUCATION AND SERVICES

U.S. Dept. of Education

(See also: "Higher Education" section)

Application for Grants Under Innovative Programs for Severely Handicapped Children. various paging. 1987. ED 1.2: In 6/987

Application for Grants Under the Rehabilitation Research and Demonstration Program. various paging. 1987. ED 1.2:R 26/4

Application for Grants Under Rehabilitation Research: Fellowships. various paging. 1986. ED 1.2:R 26/3

Application for Grants Under Rehabilitation Research-Field Initiated Research. various paging. 1987. ED 1.2:R 26/987

Application for Grants Under Secondary Education and Transitional Services for Handicapped Youth. 63 p. 1987. ED 1.2:Se 1/987

FY 87 Application for Grants Under Handicapped Children's Early Education Program: Demonstration Projects. various paging. 1987. ED 1.2:H 19/8/987

Handicapped Children's Early Education Program Overview and Directory. 188 p. 1986. ED 1.32/4:985-86 (Descriptions of programs funded by grants)

Instructions and Application for Grants Under the Special Needs Program. 38 p. + apps. 1986. ED 1.2:Sp 3/2

Projects for Initiating Special Recreation Programs for Individuals with Handicaps. various paging. 1987. ED 1.2:R 24/987

HIGHER EDUCATION

U.S. Dept. of Education

Application Development Guide; Special Services for Disadvantaged Students Program, Program Year 1987-88. 25 p. 1987. ED 1.8:St 9/4

Application Development Guide; Talent Search Program, Program Year 1988-89. 23 p. 1987. ED 1.8/3:988-89

Application for Assistance Under the College Facilities Loan Program. 60 p. 1988. ED 1.2:L 78/2/988

Application for Awards Under the Veterans Education Outreach Program. various paging. 1987. ED 1.2:V 64/988

Application for Fulbright-Hays Seminars Abroad Program. various paging. 1987. ED 1.2:F 95/4

Applications for Fulbright-Hays Training Grants: Faculty Research

Abroad Program, Doctoral Dissertation Research Abroad Program. 52 p. 1987. ED 1.2:F 95/987

Application for Grants, Supplemental Funds Program for Cooperative Education. various paging. 1987. ED 1.2: C 78/3/987

Application for Grants Under Adult Indian Education Programs. various paging. 1986. ED 1.2:In 2/9

Application for Grants Under Business and International Education Program. 34 p. 1988. ED 1.2:B 96/2/988 (microfiche)

Application for Grants Under Fulbright-Hays Group Projects Abroad. various paging. 1987. ED 1.2:F 95/3/987

Application for Grants Under Leadership in Educational Administration Development (LEAD) Program. various paging. 1986. ED 1.2:L 46

Application for Grants Under National Graduate Fellowships in the Arts, Humanities, and Social Sciences. various paging. 1986. ED 1.2:N 21/5

Application for Grants Under Rehabilitation Research-Innovation Grants Program. various paging. 1988. ED 1.2:R 26/2/988

Application for Grants Under Special Projects and Demonstrations for Providing Vocational Rehabilitation Services to Severely Disabled Individuals. various paging. 1987. ED 1.2:V 85/4/987

Application for Grants Under Title VI of the Higher Education Act of 1965, as Amended: International Research and Studies Program. various paging. 1986. ED 1.2:G 76/5/986

Application for Grants Under Title VI of the Higher Education Act of 1965, as Amended by the Education Amendments of 1980: Undergraduate International Studies and Foreign Language Program. 30 p. 1988. ED 1.2:G 76/7/988 (microfiche)

Application for Grants Under Title VI of the Higher Education Act of 1965. National Resource Centers and Foreign Language and Area Studies Fellowships. 43 p. 1987. ED 1.2:G 76/8

Application for Grants Under Women's Educational Equity Act Program. various paging. 1987. ED 1.2:W 84

Applications for Grants Under the Academic Facilities Program. 26 p. + apps. 1986. ED 1.2:Ac 1

Application for Grants Under the Cooperative Education Program (Title VIII, Higher Education Act of 1965, as Amended).various paging. 1987. ED 1.2:C 78/2/988

Application for Grants Under the Drug-Free Schools and Communities Program: Training and Demonstration Grants to Institutions of Higher Education. 22 p. 1988. ED 1.2: D 84/4/988

Application for Grants Under the Education for Economic Security Act: Critical Foreign Languages Program. 17 p. 1988. D 1.2:Se 2/4

Application for Grants Under the Educational Research Grant Program: Field-Initiated Studies. 15 p. 1988. ED 1.2: F 45/988

Application for Grants Under the Endowment Challenge Grant Program. 21 p. + app. 1987. ED 1.2:En 2/4

Application for Grants Under the Endowment Grant Program. 31 p. + apps. 1986. ED 1.2:En 2/3

Application for Grants Under the Jacob K. Javits Fellows Program. 15 p. + apps. 1988. ED 1.2:J 32/988 (For doctoral-level study)

Application for Grants Under the Patricia Roberts Harris Fellowships Program, Graduate and Professional Study Fellowships. various paging. 1988. ED 1.2:H 24/988

Application for Grants Under the Program for the National Center for Research in Vocational Education. various paging. 1987. ED 1.2: V 85/5

Application for Grants Under the Secretary's Discretionary Program. various paging. 1986. ED 1.2:Se 2/986

Application for Grants Under the Secretary's Discretionary Program for Mathematics, Science, Computer Learning, and Critical Foreign Languages. 18 p. 1987. ED 1.2:M 42/2/987

Application for Grants Under the Student Support Services Program. 37 p. 1988. ED 1.2:St 9/4

Application for Seminars Abroad Program. various paging. 1986. ED 1.2:Se 5/986

Comprehensive Program: Information and Application Procedures Fiscal Year 1989, Fund for the Improvement of Postsecondary Education. 29 p. 1988. ED 1.23/2:989

Continuation Application for Grants Under Talent Search Program. 27 p. 1986. ED 1.2:T 14/986

Continuation Application for Grants Under the Student Support Services Program. 27 p. 1987. ED 1.2:St 9/3

FY 1988 Application for Grants Under Training Personnel for the Education of the Handicapped. 46 p. 1987. ED 1.2:T 68/5/988

FY 1988 Continuation Application for Grants Under Training Personnel for the Education of the Handicapped. various paging. 1987. ED 1.2: T 68/988

FY 1989 Application for New Grants Under Bilingual Education Program. 70 p. 1986. ED 1.2:B 49/5 (microfiche)

FY 1989 Continuation Application for Grants Under Bilingual Education Program. 54 p. 1986. ED 1.2:B 49/4 (microfiche)

FY 1989 New Application for Grants Under Research in Education of the Handicapped. various paging. 1988. ED 1.2: H 19/7/1989

The Fund for the Improvement of Postsecondary Education: Drug Prevention Programs in Higher Education, Information and Application Procedures. 21 p. 1989. ED 1.23/5:989

The Fund for the Improvement of Postsecondary Education Drug Prevention Program for Students Enrolled in Higher Education, Information and Application Procedures. no paging. 1987. ED 1.2:D 84/3

The Fund for the Improvement of Postsecondary Education: Lectures Program Information and Application Materials. 4 p. 1988. ED 1.23/4:989

Innovative Projects for Student Community Service: Guidelines for Applicants. 14 p. 1988. Fund for the Improvement of Postsecondary Education. ED 1.23/3:988-2

Instructions and Application for Designation as an Eligible Institution for a Grant Under the Strengthening Institutions Program or the Endowment Challenge Grant Program. various paging. 1988. ED 1.2: St 8/4/988

Instructions and Application for Grants Under the Strengthening Institutions Program. 53 p. 1987. ED 1.2:St 8/2/987

New Application for Grants Under Rehabilitation Services Administration Training Program, Long Term Training Projects. 49 p. 1988. ED 1.2:R 26/5/988 (Rehabilitation medicine, vocational evaluation and work adjustment, occupational therapy, speech-language pathology and audiology, and rehabilitation facility administration)

Other Agencies

Educational and Nonprofit Institutions Receiving Prime Contract Awards for RDT & E. U.S. Dept. of Defense. 16 p. 1987. 1.57/8:987 (microfiche)

LIBRARY SERVICES AND LIBRARIANSHIP

Application for Basic Grants Under Library Services for Indian Tribes and Hawaiian Natives Program. U.S. Dept. of Education. various paging. 1987. ED 1.2:In 2/5/987

Application for Grants Under Library Career Training Program. U.S. Dept. of Education. various paging. 1988. ED 1.2: L 61/2/988

Application for Grants Under Library Literacy Program. U.S. Dept. of Education. various paging. 1987. ED 1.2:L 61/3/987

Application for Grants Under the Strengthening Research Library Resources Program. various paging. 1987. ED 1.2:St 8/987

Application for Special Projects Grants Under Library Services for Indian

Tribes and Hawaiian Native Program. U.S. Dept. of Education. various paging. 1987. ED 1.2:In 2/6/987

Library Programs, HEA Title II-C Strengthening Research Library Resources Program: Abstracts of Funded Projects, 1986. U.S. Dept. of Education. 77 p. 1989. ED 1.18:988

LOCAL AND STATE GOVERNMENT

U.S. Environmental Protection Agency

Construction Grants Program for Municipal Wastewater Treatment Works: Handbook of Procedures. various paging. 1984 edition, updated through 1986. EP 2.8:C 76/2

U.S. Dept. of Housing and Urban Development

Activity Management and Reporting System, User Manual. various paging. 1988. HH 1.6/3:Ac 8 (Microcomputer software for producing grantee performance reports by CDBG entitlement grantees)

Environmental Review Guide for Community Development Block Grant Programs. 149 p. 1986. HH 1.6/3:En 8/3/986

Guidelines for Unsolicited Proposals Submitted to the Office of Policy Development and Research. 14 p. 1987. HH 1.6/3: P 94/6/987

News Release Series. (Information about UDAG awards, loans, other grants awarded.) Bimonthly. HH 1.99/5:(year/month)

Other Agencies

Application for Grants Under the Project with Industry. various paging. 1987. ED 1.2:In 2/12 U.S. Dept. of Education. (Businesses and government agencies)

Community Facility Loans, Farmers Home Administration. U.S. Dept. of Agriculture. pamphlet. 1985. A 1.68:1100/2

Handbook 2650.2, Grants Management Handbook for Grantees. ACTION, The Agency for Volunteer Service. 120 p. 1987.AA 1.8/2:2650.2 (Community development)

Uniform Requirements for Grants to State and Local Governments: Compliance Supplement for Single Audits. Office of Management and Budget. various paging. 1985. PrEx 2.2: Au 2/985

MEDICINE AND HEALTH

JOHN E. FOGARTY INTERNATIONAL CENTER FOR ADVANCED STUDY IN THE HEALTH SCIENCES, U.S. DEPT. OF HEALTH AND HUMAN SERVICES

Alexander von Humboldt Foundation Research Fellowships. pamphlet. 1987. HE 20.3702:H 88

International Neurosciences Fellowship Program. pamphlet. 1988. HE 20.3702:In 8/5

International Research Fellowship Program. pamphlet. 1988. HE 20.3702:In 8/3/988

Israeli Ministry of Health Postdoctoral Research Fellowships. pamphlet. 1987. HE 20.3702:Is 7

Japan Society for the Promotion of Science Postdoctoral Research Fellowships. pamphlet. 1988. HE 20.3702:J 27

NIH Visiting Program. (Visiting Fellows, Visiting Associates, and Visiting Scientists.) 10 p. 1987. HE 20.3702:V 82/987

Senior International Fellowship Program. pamphlet. 1988. HE 20.3702:Se 5/988

U.S.-Bulgaria Biomedical Research Exchange Program. pamphlet. 1987. HE 20.3702:B 52/3

U.S. Public Health Service Health Scientist Exchanges: Hungary, Poland, Romania, Soviet Union, Yugoslavia. pamphlet. 1987. HE 20.3702:Sci 2/2

Health Resources and Services Administration, U.S. Dept. of Health and Human Services

Application for Training Grants. various paging. 1987. HE 20.9002: T 68/987

The Maternal and Child Health Research Grants Program, Inventory of Projects. 71 p. 1986. HE 20.9102:M 41/2 (microfiche)

Nurse Practitioner and Nurse Midwifery Program Grants, Program Guide. 16 p. 1986. HE 20.9008:N 93/2

National Center for Health Services Research, U.S. Dept. of Health and Human Services

Grants for Health Services Dissertation Research, 1989. 4 p. 1988. HE 20.6512/6:H 34

HIV-Related Illnesses: Topics for Health Services Research. 11 p. 1988. HE 20.6512/6:H 88

Individual National Research Service Awards. 4 p. 1988. HE 20.6512/6:R 31/2

Institutional National Research Service Awards. 4 p. 1988. HE 20.6512/6:R 31

NCHSR Extramural Research. 7 p. 1988. HE 20.6502:Ex 8/2 (Research areas of interest; application procedures)

NCHSR Offers Grants for Research on Health Care Technology Assessment. 4 p. 1986. HE 20.6512/6:G 76

NCHSR Solicits Proposals for Research in Medical Practice Variations and Patient Outcomes. 4 p. 1986. HE 20.6512/6:M 46

Research Activities. Monthly. 8-10 p. HE 20.6512/5:(numbers) (Reports on health service grants awarded, dissertation grant awards, fellowship awards, and results of research)

The Role of Market Forces in the Delivery of Health Care: Issues for Research. 22 p. 1988. HE 20.6512/6:M 34/988 (Issues; application procedures)

National Institute of Mental Health, U.S. Dept. of Health and Human Services

Announcement: Research on Severely Mentally Ill Persons at Risk of or with HIV Infections. 17 p. 1988. HE 20.8102:Se 8/2/988

Centers for Research on the Organization and Financing of Care for the Severely Mentally Ill. (Grants to establish Centers for Research.) 8 p 1987. HE 20.8102:R 31/6

Introduction – 1987 Program Information, Minority Research Resources Branch. (Small grants research priorities, training programs for minorities, grant application process.) various paging. 1987. HE 20.8102:M 66/8

Mathematical/Computational/Theoretical Neuroscience: Program Announcement. 6 p. 1988. HE 20.8102:M 42

Minority Mental Health Research Centers, Grant Announcement. 10 p. 1987. HE 20.8102:M 66/7

National Institute of Mental Health List of Current Program Announcements. 4 p. 1988. HE 20.8102:P 94/4

Program Announcement: Brain, Immune System, and Behavioral and Neurological Aspects of Human Immunodeficiency Infection. 8 p. 1988. HE 20.8102:H 88/3

Program Announcement: Central Nervous System Effects of Human Im-

munodeficiency Virus Infection, Neurobiological, Neurovirological, and Neurobehavioral Studies. 8 p. 1988. HE 20.8102:H 88/2

Public-Academic Liaison (PAL) for Research on Serious Mental Disorders: Announcement for Applicants. 9 p. 1988. HE 20.8102: An 7/2

Research on Services for the Severely Mentally Ill, Grant Announcement. 7 p. 1987. HE 20.8102:Se 8

Research Support Programs and Activities. 20 p. 1986. HE 20.8102:R 31/3/986

National Institutes of Health, U.S. Dept. of Health and Human Services

Application for International Research Fellowship Awards. 14 p. + app. 1986. HE 20.3002:In 8/4

Biomedical Research Technology Resources: A Research Resources Directory. 141 p. 1987. HE 20.3037/6:987

Digestive Diseases Research at the National Institutes of Health. 34 p. 1988. HE 20.3002:D 56/3

Division of Research Resources, Biomedical Research Technology Program, Program Description, Guidelines for Review of Grant Applications. (Instructions for applicants). 17 p. 1986. HE 20.3008:B 52/3

Grant brochures set. (Includes: staff fellowships, research services awards, predoctoral fellowships, small grants, career development awards, etc.) 15 pamphlet set. 1986. HE 20.3002:St 1

Handbook for Grants Assistants, National Institutes of Health. 276 p. 1988. HE 20.3008:G 76/3

Helpful Hints on Preparing a Fellowship Application to the National Institutes of Health. 12 p. 1987. HE 20.3002:F 33/4

Helpful Hints on Preparing a Research Grant Application to the National Institutes of Health. 12 p. 1987. HE 20.3002:R 31/10/987-2

Information from the National Institutes of Health on Grants and *Contracts*. 10 p. 1986. HE 20.3002:G 76/10

The K Awards, National Institutes of Health. 67 p. 1988. HE 20.3002: C 18/3

Minority Biomedical Research Support Program, Information Brochure, Division of Research Resources. 7 p. 1988. HE 20.3002:M 66/7

Minority Programs, National Institutes of Health. (Apprenticeship, summer, undergraduate, faculty, associates, etc.) 15 p. 1987. HE 20.3002:M 66/5

National Institutes of Health and Academic Research Enhancement Award (AREA): Program Guidelines. 15 p. 1987. HE 20.3008:Ac 1/987

National Institutes of Health Grants and Awards. (An overview.) 29 p. 1986. HE 20.3002:G 76/9/986

National Institutes of Health National Research Service Award, Institutional Grants. 15 p. 1987. HE 20.3002:R 31/13

National Research Service Awards for Individual Postdoctoral Fellows. 11 p. 1986. HE 20.3002:R 31/11

NIH Guide for Grants and Contracts. Weekly periodical. HE 20.3008/2:(volume/number) (Contains grant notices, announcements of dates RFA's and RFP's are available, and ongoing program announcements)

NIH Peer Review of Research Grant Applications. (Explains review process.) 68 p. 1988. HE 20.3002:R 31/15/988-2

Opportunities for Research and Research Training in Biomedical Sciences. 6 p. 1987. HE 20.3002:R 31/14

Preparing a Research Grant Application to the National Institutes of Health: Selected Articles. various paging. 1987. HE 20.3002:R 31/16

Referral Guidelines for Initial Review Groups of NIH. (Guide for referral of grant applications). 206 p. 1986. HE 20.3008:IN 5 (microfiche)

Research Advances and Opportunities in the Biomedical Sciences. 106 p. 1987. HE 20.3002:R 31/987

Public Health Service, U.S. Dept. of Health and Human Services

Application for Public Health Service Individual National Research Service Award. 20 p. + apps. 1986. HE 20.3002:R 31/9

Application for Public Health Service Individual National Research Service Continuation Award. 12 p. + apps. 1986. HE 20.2:In 2

Manual for Financial Evaluations of Public Health Service Awards. (Guide for cost analysis of grant proposals) 127 p. 1986. HE 20.8:F 49/4

PHS Grants Administration Manual. various paging. 1986. HE 20.8/2:986 (updated by *Policy Memoranda*, HE 20.8/3:nos.)

Program Guide, Health Careers Opportunity Program, Public Health Service. 15 p. 1987. HE 20.8:C 18 (microfiche)

Public Health Service Grants Policy Statement. 90 p. 1987. HE 20.2:G 76/987

Referral Guidelines for Funding Components of the Public Health Service. 441 p. 1988. HE 20.8:F 96/2 (Grant funding)

Other Agencies

Announcement: Research on Behavior Change and Prevention Strategies to Reduce Transmission of Human Immunodeficiency Virus. National Institute on Alcohol Abuse and Alcoholism. U.S. Dept. of Health and Human Services. 9 p. 1988. HE 20.8302:H 88

Extramural Research Training and Education Programs. National Cancer Institute. U.S. Dept. of Health and Human Services. Brochures in a folder. 1988. HE 20.3152:Ex 8/folder

Graduate Training Supported by the National Institute of Dental Research. U.S. Dept. of Health and Human Services. 30 p. 1988. HE 20.3402:G 75/988

Grants Administration Information Sources. National Institute of Child Health and Human Development. U.S. Dept. of Health and Human Services. 42 p. 1985. HE 20.3352:G 76/985

National Cancer Institute Grants Process. U.S. Dept. of Health and Human Services. 49 p. 1986. HE 20.3152:G 76/985

Program Project Grant, National Heart, Lung, and Blood Institute, Preparation of the Application. U.S. Dept. of Health and Human Services. 24 p. 1987. HE 20.3202:P 94/6/prep.

MISCELLANEOUS SUBJECTS

NIOSH Grants, Research and Demonstration Projects, Annual Report, Fiscal Year 1985. National Institute for Occupational Safety and Health. 297 p. 1986. HE 20.7126:985 (microfiche)

Office of Museum Programs. Smithsonian Institution. 6 p. 1986. SI 1.2:M 97/7 (Internships, visiting professionals program, minority awards, Native American museums program.)

SAFAH Grants: Aiding Comprehensive Strategies for the Homeless. U.S. Dept. of Housing and Urban Development. 85 p. 1988. HH 1.2:Su 7

Small Business Guide to Federal R & D Funding Opportunities. National Science Foundation. 135 p. 1986. NS 1.20:Sm 1/986

Small Business Innovation Research Program, Listing of SBIR Awardees for Fiscal Year 1985. 142 p. 1986. SBA 1.42:985 (microfiche)

Synopses of Community Demonstration Grant Projects for Alcohol and Drug Abuse Treatment of Homeless Individuals. Alcohol, Drug Abuse, and Mental Health Administration. U.S. Dept. of Health and Human Services. 11 p. 1988. HE 20.8302:C 73

SCIENCE

National Science Foundation

Division of Computer Research, Summary of Awards, Fiscal Year 1985. 97 p. 1985. NS 1.10/7:985 (microfiche)

Earth Science Research and NSF: Opportunities for Support of Research in the Earth Sciences. 9 p. 1985. NS 1.2:Ea 7/3

Federal Funds for Research and Development: Fiscal Years 1986, 1987, and 1988. 257 p. 1988. NS 1.18:36 (A report from the Survey of Science Resources series)

Federal R & D Funding by Budget Function, 1982-84. 85 p. 1985. NS 1.2:F 31/4/982-84 (microfiche)

Federal Support to Universities, Colleges, and Selected Nonprofit Institutions, Fiscal Year: 1986. 193 p. 1987. NS 1.30/2:986 (Detailed statistical tables)

Guide to Programs, National Science Foundation. Annual. NS 1.47:(year) (1989 is newest edition)

Mathematical Sciences Postdoctoral Research Fellowships, with Research Instructorship Option. 13 p. 1986. NS 1.45:986

National Science Foundation Bulletin. Monthly. NS 1.3:(numbers) (Announces new programs and grants)

Project Summaries, Division of Science Resources Studies. 91 p. 1985. NS 1.39/2:985

Teacher Enhancement and Informal Science Education, Program Announcement and Guide. 28 p. 1985. NS 1.20:T 22

Other Agencies

Application for Grants Under the Education for Economic Security Act: Mathematics and Science Program. U.S. Dept. of Education. 15 p. 1988. ED 1.2:Se 2/5

Basic Research Program. U.S. Dept. of Defense. 87 p. 1985. D 1.2:R 31/9/985 (Research needs, accomplishments; contact list of DOD agencies)

The NASA/ASEE Summer Faculty Fellowship Program. 44 p. 1987. National Aeronautics and Space Administration. NAS 1.2:F 11/2

Oportunidades de Investigacion en el Tropico. Smithsonian Tropical Research Institute. Smithsonian Institution. pamphlet. 1985. SI 1.2:Op 5/spanish

Postdoctoral Research Associateships. National Bureau of Standards. U.S. Dept. of Commerce. 203 p. 1985. C13.65:984

Post Graduate Study at the U.S. Geological Survey, Opportunities for the International Earth Science Community. 12 p. 1989. I 19.2:P 84/2

Program Announcement: Minority Science Improvement Program, Guide for the Preparation of Proposals Fiscal Year 1988. 11 p. 1987. U.S. Dept. of Education. ED 1.8:M 66/2

Research Opportunities in the Tropics. Smithsonian Tropical Research Institute. Smithsonian Institution. pamphlet. 1986. SI 1.2:R 31/2/986

TRANSPORTATION AND AVIATION

U.S. Dept. of Transportation

Airport Aid Program, Federal Aviation Regulations Part 152. 89 p. 1986. TD 4.6:152/2 (Eligibility requirements, application procedures, funding of approved projects, record keeping requirements)

National Experimental Projects Tabulation. 487 p. 1986. TD 2.2:P 94/3/986 (microfiche) (Projects resulting from grants; technology transfer possibilities)

Public Roads, a Journal of Highway Research and Development. Monthly periodical. TD 2.19:(numbers)

Out of the Fire and into the Frying Pan – Hope for Patent Reference Service in a Non-Patent Depository Library

Dena Rae Thomas

SUMMARY. The Patent Depository Library (PDL) system is a valuable program which provides important patent collections and services at many locations across the country. Not all of those interested in patent information can travel to a PDL, and reference staff at other libraries often feel uneasy in dispensing patent information. The article suggests that many types of patent inquiries can be addressed with a small investment in time, materials, and training. Delineates four different levels of service, and discusses the means for deciding which is appropriate to a given library. Describes materials and staff training for each of the levels. Introduces advanced service options and discusses several patron types and their possible needs. Integrating a patent reference service component into an existing reference service provides a number of benefits: information to the community, better public relations for the library, and an opportunity for staff development.

The Patent Depository Library system has grown from twenty-two to the present sixty-five libraries during the past twelve years. Although the goal of providing full service public access to patents and patenting information in all fifty states has not yet been achieved, forty-one states and the District of Columbia are now served by at least one Patent Depository Library, or PDL. The patent depositories provide valuable collections and services, reaching an estimated 240,000 people each year. Because not everyone needing patent information lives within convenient driving distance of a PDL, sooner or later, nearly anyone working a general refer-

---

Dena Rae Thomas is Science/Engineering Librarian and Patent Depository Library Representative at the Centennial Science and Engineering Library, General Library, University of New Mexico, Albuquerque, NM 87131.

© 1991 by The Haworth Press, Inc. All rights reserved.

ence desk will receive a query concerning patents or patenting. Reference professionals often experience intimidation when faced with patent questions. The purpose of this article is to offer hope to those libraries which are not PDLs: Many of these questions and concerns can be adequately or at least preliminarily addressed with basic reference tools and time invested in staff training.

This article discusses preliminary considerations and outlines service options so that any interested library can tailor an active program of patent reference service to meet its individual service goals. It examines reference staff training, advanced patent services, and looks at the various kinds of patrons and their information needs. The benefits of providing patent reference service are three-fold: patent reference service provides valuable information to the community, the service is a wonderful public relations vehicle for the library, and the experience provides a challenging opportunity for development of reference skills in the staff.

PRELIMINARY CONSIDERATIONS

Determine Need

How much patron interest in patents is expressed? How often does the reference staff receive patent-related inquiries—once a day, or once a month? Be careful in basing a final judgment on this answer if the response is low. People ask reference questions they think you will be able to answer. If there is no reason to assume you deal in such information, the number of inquiries may be low, although the level of interest is higher.

Agree to Meet the Need at Some Level

Staff enthusiasm and support is vital to the success of instituting an additional component in the reference service. Is there a consensus among staff that this service would be useful? Is there a shared interest among the staff in enhancing their reference skills? Plans to develop a new service will founder unless there is agreement that this service fulfills a need and that the staff is willing to invest time and energy in acquiring new reference skills.

Identify a Coordinator for the Service

A willing individual with some experience in science, technology, or business reference is essential to the success of integrating a new program. In assembling the information you wish to offer, and in deciding the level of service you want to provide, you will certainly want staff input. But designate one intrepid soul as the coordinator for training, policy development, and collection development. This will not involve a tremendous proportion of the individual's time once the initial set-up is completed. I have heard Patent Depository Library Representatives, the people who coordinate services at PDL's, say that about 10% of their time is all they can devote to that part of their job. Most of them have lots of other responsibilities as well. So do not get trapped into thinking, "This would be a great service to offer, but we really need another line to administer it." You will want to get approval of your administration, and their support, of course. Then take a deep breath and just jump right in.

Determine the Level of Service to Be Offered

Analyze patron need, both expressed and anticipated. The frequency of questions received in the past is only one indication of interest. Do you have circulating books about patents or other types of intellectual property? How often have they been checked out? How often have they been stolen? Remember too, that as the skills of your reference staff develop, they will be suggesting use of the patent literature to patrons who did not arrive with specific "patent" questions. You may wish to start small and leave open the possibility for building the service as you get patron feedback. Perhaps community interest is such that you already feel delinquent, in which case a more ambitious program may be appropriate.

Any new service requires some commitment of time, both for staff training and at the desk when you are fielding the questions. There will also be a commitment to allot time and money for collection development. In all likelihood, these amounts will be modest, and other sections of this article will allow you to be more specific in this regard.

SERVICE LEVELS

Suggested levels of service are described below. Each has specific materials and service knowledge associated. (See Appendix for materials suggestions. Annotations explain information content and utility.) As the service levels become higher, assume that each level encompasses the resources and services associated with the previous level.

Level 1 – Information and Referral

Provide free or low cost information pamphlets. These booklets come from a variety of sources, the Patent and Trademark Office (PTO), the Small Business Administration, and bar and inventor associations.

Level 2 – Descriptive/Background

Provide circulating and/or reference books containing detailed information on patent documents, patent searching and patent application procedures.

Level 3 – Preliminary Search Assistance

Include all basic search tools from the PTO in your reference collection: the *Index to the Classification*, the *Manual of Classification,* and *Classification Definitions.* The list, Attorneys and Agents Registered to Practice before the Patent and Trademark Office is also highly recommended.

Level 4 – Extensive/Specialized

Provide online search capabilities which can assist in answering specialized questions: recent patents on interferons; seat belt patents owned by Nissan; all patents to Bernard Schwartz from years 1980-1989. Most libraries will undertake this level of service only after a considerable clientele is established, and often will offer the search capability on a fee basis.

TRAINING

Although each individual on the reference staff will have his own reactions to the training experience, consistency of approach both in learning the information and in transmitting it to the patron is recommended. Some staff will have more of an aptitude and will feel more comfortable in dealing with a great variety of patent questions, but a core of knowledge shared by all is highly desirable. Any library, whether public, academic, or special, receiving patent queries on a regular basis, should provide staff training at a level to ensure correct referrals.

In serving the information needs of patrons with patent questions, any reference staff should be aware of community resources for assistance or information. It is helpful to have a list of commonly requested phone numbers to save staff time and anxiety. When you construct the list, look for the following. What other information collections exist in your area?

Are there law, technical, or business libraries with public access that have collections of gazettes, marketing or technical information? What is the nearest PDL? Be sure to cultivate a good relationship with the PDL Representative and the reference staff to find out what kinds of cooperation are possible. Are there inventor, entrepreneur or other identifiable associations or clubs? Inventors often find that consulting with people who have gone through the patenting process is helpful. What sort of organizations exist to assist individuals in developing and marketing their inventions? Are there any Small Business Institutes, or University Innovation Centers? What sort of state assistance is available through programs administered by Commerce and Industry Departments or the Secretary of State? Are there patent attorneys or agents practicing locally? Inform patrons they can often be located through the yellow pages. Refer patrons inquiring about invention promotion firms to the Better Business Bureau or to the Chamber of Commerce. These organizations may be able to provide an assessment of the firm's reputation.

For level 1 service, the staff should have basic familiarity with the brochures and other information offered, know how to find answers to basic questions about addresses, fees, and forms, and know when to refer a complicated question to a more appropriate source, whether that source is a written one or another information center. Staff should refer all search questions to the nearest PDL.

Libraries offering level 2 service should be familiar with brochures and general information pamphlets, and should additionally know the contents or indexes of the more comprehensive books and feel comfortable in steering a patron to those sources when appropriate.

If your Library has agreed to pursue level 3 service, there are excellent articles describing how to do a patent search (Bibliography: Brown, Ollerenshaw.) There is a video which also explains the search process. (See Appendix, Gilbertson.) Acquire or borrow as many of these resources as possible and schedule organized instructional sessions for your staff. Group training is invaluable because not only does it provide everyone with a consistent and equal exposure to the material, it gives the opportunity for questions to occur and for the answers to benefit all. When training a new staff in patents reference at our PDL, we used our weekly reference meetings as a forum.

PDLs make a policy of confirming that the patron understands the library staff will not do a search for him. Staff are there to give assistance in the search process, but for most of us, nothing in our backgrounds prepares us for the highly specialized inspection of technical literature that a patent search requires. Usually a reminder to the patron, "You are the subject expert in this area," serves to convince him of the prudence behind this policy

Staff at level 4 libraries should know basic differences between patent and trademark law. Ensure the staff is adequately trained in any online databases used. (See Appendix for relevant databases and vendors.) Realistically, most libraries, even if they can offer this level of service, will not have all the reference staff trained in online patents searching. Specialization is a fact of life in the library, and staff trained at this level should have enthusiasm and aptitude. Attending a formal vendor training program featuring patent databases is highly desirable and recommended. Databases vary according to time coverage and types of patents covered: electrical, mechanical and general, chemical, and design. Important note: Avoid implying that a comprehensive patentability search is possible in the online databases. It would be an extremely rare occurrence that the depth of the database would ensure proper time coverage, and that all possible subject words would be anticipated by the searcher and patron. Several articles on patent databases are listed in the Bibliography. See Kulp, Raduazo, and Simmons.

ADVANCED PATENT SERVICE

Patents are technological disclosure documents as well as legal documents. The patent literature is useful in addressing many kinds of questions, of which patentability is only the most obvious. The following are some of the questions most often encountered in patent reference service.

Patentability/Novelty

Many patrons know that novelty is a criteria of patentability, and they want to know "Has my invention already been patented?" This can be ascertained by determining the class/subclass that the patent would belong in if already registered. Once a patron determines the correct class/subclass(es) reference staff may request a CASSIS printout from a cooperating PDL. The printout will list all patents which have ever been registered that class/subclass. If there is a local collection of patent gazettes or full patents, the patron can proceed to screen the list. If there is no collection of gazettes or patents available to the public, staff may wish to suggest that the patron travel to the nearest PDL or to the Public Search Room at the Patent Office for the screening step.

Patrons should be warned that this type of search is preliminary and that many first applications are disallowed because of the existence of prior art. They should also be advised that even a preliminary search can be a very lengthy process. Whether they decide to go ahead with their own search or hire a professional it will be beneficial for them to know something about the patent classification system. A patron may find that his invention has already received a patent, but may discover another area which is opportune for research and development.

Historical Search

This is often very similar to a novelty search. If the invention can be determined to reside in a small number of classes, the researcher may want to inspect all those patents for a historical survey of the invention.

Inventor Search

Sometimes a patron has an inventor name but no patent number, and would like to find the patent number in order to access the information. The PTO publishes an annual Index of Patentees/Assignees, but most non-PDLs will not have the resources to buy yearly volumes. One possibility is to do an inventor search in an appropriate database. It is usually a very straightforward search. Just make sure that the individual was active during the time span covered by the database. You may instead wish to seek assistance from a PDL. They often have long runs of patentee indices.

Patents Applied for But Not Yet Granted

This is a type of inventor search. The patron has read or otherwise heard of a recent invention by Jean Smith in the area of superconductivity. The patron would like to see the patent to determine if there is any information relevant to her own research. If an inventor search online turns up empty, there are a couple of possible reasons. In the U.S., the information contained in an application is usually confidential until the patent is granted. So the application may still be in process. If the patent was disallowed, the information would not become public unless the inventor wrote about it, or re-applied and succeeded in securing a patent. One possibility for uncovering the information would be to check if there is a patent registered in a foreign country which publishes the disclosure upon receipt of the application. Most other patent-granting entities are fast-publishing. Again, this works down to a database question, and it will depend upon your staff expertise and your patron's willingness (probably) to pay for a search.

Document Delivery

Sometimes all a patron wants is a copy of a patent document. He has the number, the country, and the date. Patents can often be obtained through interlibrary loan if your library is a member of a consortium. Otherwise, most patent depositories have photocopying services and the charges can be passed on to the patron. Check by telephone when making a request to ensure that the charges and the method of payment are clearly understood. Copies of U.S. patents may be obtained for $1.50 from the Commissioner of Patents and Trademarks, Washington, D.C. 20231. There are also many commercial document delivery services that will secure patent copies for a fee.

PATRONS

Unless you work in a special or corporate library, your patent clientele will be widely varied. Most of the patent questions we receive at our PDL are from people not affiliated with the University. They are independent inventors, many with full-time jobs, and their patent research is squeezed into evenings and weekends. Although most are interested in a novelty search, often they will need to know the distinctions between different types of intellectual property. Basic information booklets may be helpful in this regard. Many patrons are unfamiliar with library conventions, and anything you can do to make their investigation easier and more productive is heartily appreciated. Patent information has a special value to many people, and you will find that patrons are particularly grateful for your time and attention to their questions. This may result in a definite enhancement of library public relations.

Attorneys and Law Clerks

These patrons are often quite sophisticated in their use and knowledge of libraries. They often have very specific questions and may require online services, access to legal databases, or referral to the nearest PDL.

Industry, R & D People, Faculty, Scientists and Engineers, Business People

These patrons often have nearly the same requirements as above. They may need very current or very specific information which will be most easily available online or through a PDL.

Students – Grammar School Through College

Students often need general information about what to expect from the patent literature. They may have school projects which require them to use the patent literature to solve a problem, or they may be looking at patents/gazette entries as examples of technical writing or for marketing possibilities.

CONCLUSION

Patent reference service can be an exciting and challenging part of the reference service provided at many types of libraries. This article describes preliminary considerations for deciding whether to add this area to your reference capabilities. If you decide to take on this additional responsibility, four levels of service and suggested materials are outlined. The level chosen depends on the needs of your patrons and upon staff time and interest. It is hoped that this information will assist you in building a service which will be useful to your patrons, provide an opportunity to challenge and develop the skills of the reference staff, and enhance the library's image within the community.

BIBLIOGRAPHY

Brown, Eulalie W. "Patent Basics: History, Background, and Searching Fundamentals." *Government Information Quarterly 3* (1986) : 381-405.

Kulp, Carol S. "Patent Databases: a Survey of What Is Available from DIALOG, Questel, SDC, Pergamon, and INPADOC." *Database* 7 (August 1984) : 56-72.

Ollerenshaw, Kay. "How to Perform a Patent Search: A Step by Step Guide for the Inventor." *Law Library Journal* 73 (Winter 1980) : 1-16.

Raduazo, Dorothy. "Online Patent Databases: a Review Article." *Government Publications Review* 13 (March/April 1986) : 277-286.

Simmons, Edlyn S. "How Good an Online Searcher Are You? 20 Questions about Patent Databases." *Online* 12 part one, (September 1988) : 53-56; part two, (November 1988) : 61-64.

Walker, Richard D. "The Dual Utility of Patents; Strength or Weakness?" *Government Publications Review* 12 (July/August 1985) : 305-314

APPENDIX

These are a few favorite sources to assist staff and patrons in understanding patents. It is by no means a comprehensive list, nor a recommendation of these sources to the exclusion of others. As you undertake reference service in this area, you will find favorite sources of your own, which may complement or replace these. This list was compiled in Sept., 1989. Consult *Books In Print* or the *G.P.O Publications Reference File* to confirm currency when ordering materials.

Level 1 Materials

Basic Facts about Patents. U.S. Department of Commerce. Patent and Trademark Office. Washington: U.S. G.P.O, (1988). Available from Superintendent of Documents, Government Printing Office, Washington, D.C. 20402. (202) 783-3238. $2.00, SN 003-004-00641-2.

A general interest booklet useful for answering basic questions. Short sections discuss patent applications and the Disclosure Document Program. A list of PDLs includes phone numbers. Also lists some relevant publications available from the GPO.

General Information Concerning Patents. U.S. Department of Commerce. Patent and Trademark Office. Washington: U.S. G.P.O, 1988. Available from Superintendent of Documents, address as above. $2.00, SN 003-004-00634-0.

Best general information booklet. Comprehensive, though brief, coverage of the basic information: patent laws; conditions for obtaining a patent; patent searches; a list of PDLs (phone numbers are not supplied); Disclosure Document Program; application procedures and forms; patent rights; patent marking; a list of filing, issuance, post-issuance and other fees; and many more areas of interest. The final section, "Answers to questions frequently asked" is especially helpful.

A Guide to Intellectual Property Protection. A collaborative effort of the Minnesota Small Business Assistance Office and Merchant, Gould, Smith, Edell, Welter & Schmidt, P.A. n.p.: Minnesota Department of Energy and Economic Development, 1986. . . . "Available without charge from either the Minnesota Small Business Assistance Office, 900 American Center, 150 East Kellogg Boulevard, St. Paul, MN 55101, (612) 296-3871 or 1-800-652-9747, Minnesota toll free, or from Merchant, Gould, Smith, Edell, Welter, and Schmidt, P.A., 1000 Norwest Center, St. Paul, MN 55101, (612) 298-1055."

Overview of the four types of intellectual property protection: patent, trademark, copyright, and trade secret. Concise, well-written, and easily understood. Excellent booklet for training your staff to recognize the different types of intellectual property. Concludes with a helpful list of answers to "Commonly asked questions concerning intellectual property protection."

Tavela, John, ed. *Can You Make Money with Your Idea or Invention?* Management Publications, U.S. Small Business Administration. Management Aids, Number 2.013. U.S. Small Business Administration. Management Assistance Support Services. Washington, D.C.: U.S. G.P.O., reprinted 1984. $.50. Available from SBA, P.O. Box 15434, Fort Worth, TX 76119.

Presents some of the critical questions the inventor will want to consider before seeking outside assistance in development of and marketing an invention. Although written in a slick, almost glib style, the discussions of invention promotion firms, invention brokers, Small Business Administration programs, and inventor's associations may be helpful.

A Trademark Is Not a Patent or a Copyright. William M. Borchard. United States Trademark Association. Executive Newsletter No. 39. New York: U.S.T.A., 1986. $.75 each, $.50 each in quantities of 100 or more. Available from: USTA Executive Newsletter Committee, United States Trademark Association, 6 East 45 Street, New York, New York 10017, (212) 986-5880.

More detailed legal treatment of trademarks, patents, and copyrights than above listed sources. Includes definition of each type of intellectual property, registration procedures, term of rights, ownership, remedies for infringement and international protection. Concludes with a table comparing functional (utility) patents, design patents, copyrights, and trademarks, in the following areas: what is protected, criteria for protection, how to obtain protection, term, and tests of infringement.

What is a Patent? American Bar Association, Section of Patent, Trademark and Copyright Law. Chicago: American Bar Association, 1982. $1.00. Available from American Bar Association, Section of Patent, Trademark and Copyright Law, 750 North Lake Shore Drive, Chicago, IL 60611.

Topics discussed include: the patent grant, the value of patents, invention evaluation, who may obtain a patent, preparing and filing the application, and exploitation of patents, among others. Well-written, but lack of a table of contents means looking through the sections carefully in order to find specifics

Level 2 Materials

Burge, David A. *Patent and Trademark Tactics and Practice.* (2nd ed.) New York: Wiley, 1984. $33.75. Available from John Wiley & Sons, Inc., Western Distribution Ctr., 1530 S. Redwood Rd., Salt Lake City, UT 84101, (801)972-5828.

McKnelly, Michele and Johanna Johnson. *Patents and Trademarks: A Bibliography of Materials Available for Selection.* n.p.: Patent Depository Library Association, 1989. Available from Patent Depository Library Bibliography Committee, P.O. Box 15068, Dallas, TX 75201. Also available from NTIS.

Levy, Richard C. *Inventing and Patenting Sourcebook.* Detroit, MI: Gale Research Inc., 1989. $75.00. From: Gale Research Inc., Department 77748, Detroit, MI 48277-0748. 1-800-877-4153.

Pressman, David. Stephen Elias, ed. *Patent It Yourself.* (2nd ed.) Berkeley, CA: Nolo Press, 1988. $29.95. Available from Nolo Press, 950 Parker Street, Berkeley, CA 94710.

Level 3 Materials

Aderholt, Alice B., ed. *Index to the United States Patent Classification.* Department of Commerce, Patent and Trademark Office, Office of Documentation. Washington: U.S. G.P.O., 1988. $12.00, SN 903-006-00013-7

Attorneys and Agents Registered to Practice Before the United States Patent and Trademark Office, 1988, as of Mar. 1988. Department of Commerce, Patent and Trademark Office. Washington: U.S. G.P.O, 1988. "Contains the names and addresses of a majority of the individuals authorized to represent inventors before the Patent and Trademark Office. Includes an alphabetical list by surname and a geographical list by state and foreign country." $17.00, SN 003-004-00635-8.

Classification Definitions. Commerce Department, Patent and Trademark Office, Office of Examining and Documentation Control. Washington: U.S. G.P.O, 1987. (full set complete as of Sept. 1985.) 427 microfiche. $85.00, SN 903-004-00000-2.

Manual of Classification of Patents. Department of Commerce, Patent and Trademark Office, Office of Documentation Planning and Support. Washington: U.S.G.P.O., revised Dec. 1988. "Subscription service consists of the two volume basic manual, the current Index to United States Patent Classification, and supplementary material for an indeterminate period. The Index is also sold separately. The manual lists the numbers and descriptive titles of the Patent Office classes and subclasses, as well as the Design classes." $66.00, SN 903-006-00000-5.

Patents, the Search Begins. Madison, Wis.: Audio Visual Resources, College of Engineering, University of Wisconsin-Madison, 1985. Videocassete, sd., col., 1/2 in., VHS format. Jean M. Gilbertson and Steven Sylvester. Excellent introduction to the patent search process. Highly recommended for both staff training and for introducing patrons to the process

Level 4 Materials – Patent Databases

The following is a sampling of the most versatile and most comprehensive of the many patent databases available.

CA Search. Chemical Abstracts Service, Columbus, OH. Corresponding to the print index Chemical Abstracts, CA Search provides international coverage of the chemical literature,including patents, from 1967 to the present. Over 8 million records include bibliographic information and informative abstracts. Available through BRS, DIALOG, ORBIT, and STN.

Claims/U.S. Patent Abstracts. IFI/Plenum Data Corporation, Alexandria, VA. Records contain usual bibliographic information; many also have abstracts. Coverage depends on patent type: chemical patents from 1950 to the present; electrical, general, and mechanical patents from 1963 to the present; design patents from 1980 to the present. Over 2 million records in all. IFI/PLENUM also produces a number of other, more specialized, databases. Available through DIALOG and ORBIT.

Inpadoc. Inpadoc, Vienna, Austria. The database covers patents in all subject areas from 55 patent-issuing authorities. Coverage extends from 1968 to the present, and includes bibliographic and priority information on more than 8 million patent families, representing more than 17 million patents. No indexing or abstracts. Best use is for patent family or equivalent searching. Available through DIALOG and ORBIT.

World Patents Index. Derwent Publications, Ltd., London, England. Coverage, from 1963 to the present, differs according to patent subject matter. The database contains information on more than 6 million patent documents from 30 patent-issuing authorities world-wide. WPI includes extensive indexing and enhanced titles which assist in subject searching of foreign patents. Records include bibliographic information and, for patents 1981 to the present, abstracts. Available through DIALOG and ORBIT

Disinformation, the Exxon Valdez, and the Search for Truth: Government Documents as Reference Sources for Issues of Current National Concern

Robert M. Ballard

SUMMARY. Prior investigations have indicated that government documents are a relatively underutilized resource by most librarians. Almost invariably, these studies have been of academic libraries and librarians. It is highly probable that scholars use documents unobtrusively and may be overlooked in many surveys, but it must be assumed that they are assisted in their use by knowledgeable documents librarians. A survey of documents use by public reference librarians serving 25 geographically dispersed population centers revealed that there was substantial awareness and use of U.S. government documents. Respondents indicated that they believed accredited programs in library education should provide reference librarians with the backgrounds necessary to assist with reference questions which concern current, but historical issues. Privatization or the commercialization of federal information sources is discussed as the possible consequence of the lack of knowledge and use of documents which can be used for reference purposes, as opposed to those which provide technical information. A Current Issues Seminar for programs of library education is proposed. Using current issues of the day as examples, the content of a typical seminar is reviewed.

After the end of a class, a graduate student asked the professor for assistance in locating information about Zambia. She was attempting to

Robert M. Ballard is affiliated with the School of Library and Information Sciences, North Carolina Central University, Durham, NC 27707.

© 1991 by The Haworth Press, Inc. All rights reserved.

locate current printed information for her daughter, who was a high school junior. Each student in the daughter's social science class, had been required to make oral and written reports on a developing nation assigned to them by their instructor. They had been unable to find anything in the local public library or school library, other than that which appeared in encyclopedias and handbooks such as the *Statesman's Yearbook*. The students had been forbidden to use these sources however. The graduate student asked if there was anything that could be suggested to her?

She was directed to the university's documents library, where she saw for the first time the *Area Handbook* on Zambia published by the U.S. Department of the Defense, and *Background Notes* and the *Post Reports*, both published by the U.S. Department of State. After noting the relatively low cost, the graduate student, who was one who was herself planning for a career in a secondary school library, wondered why her daughter's high school library did not have a subscription to *Background Notes*?

Cost of a subscription to this serial, which consists of "short factual pamphlets about various countries and territories," was fourteen dollars in 1989. It is highly probable that it was unknown to the librarian or media specialist at the school. Perhaps every documents librarian or teacher has had experiences similar to this one, in which practical necessity results in one being awakened to the wealth of information available in government documents. Nor is the problem that of lack of exposure to documents in formal courses of study in accredited library schools. Their significance and potential use is probably relegated to a place of secondary importance and hence they are frequently overlooked, if not simply forgotten by all except those specifically charged with their care and maintenance.

We should not make the assumption that there are not many reference librarians who are not only aware of these resource materials, but who have always routinely made maximum and effective use of U.S. government documents. What is additionally being proposed however, is that all reference librarians and information professionals should be able to use U.S. government documents for the purpose of providing sources of documentation in interpreting and discussing issues of current national concern.

The unrealized significance of the 1988 presidential elections, was that serious public debate, meaning discussion by the supposedly educated segment of the general population, was so obviously absent. The unmistakable impression was that the capability of doing so was and is simply lacking, that if factual information or the documents which support them were available, they would not be used or referred to. A populace which lacks the will, knowledge, or formal education which is necessary to understand and discuss issues and ideas, would render the subject of freedom of information null and void. Reference librarians should demonstrate a substantial ability to interpret and analyze statistical data and information from any source, when called on to do so. That information is frequently to be found in a document published by a federal agency.

In her 1985 review article, Marilyn Moody quotes Peter Hernon in stating:

> research is also lacking in areas such as analysis of the types of reference questions asked and user perceptions towards the role and duties of documents librarians. Also, if general reference librarians do not engage in referral, is there any reason to expect documents librarians to differ or that they can answer correctly, the majority of factual questions asked?[1]

When one views the totality of the literature in this area, almost invariably the studies are about academic libraries, academic librarians and reference service, and documents librarians employed by academic libraries. Yet is it not logical to assume that if use of documents and documents reference service is poor in academic libraries, it would be equally bad in public libraries? And similarly, if referrals are seldom made to the documents librarian in academia, that the same will be true in public libraries? Bill Katz states the following:

> More stress on enthusiastic intellectualism would do more to improve the deplorable amount of misinformation, or no information given by at least some reference librarians to innocent readers.[2]

Let us make a clear distinction between reference use of documents and the use of documents for scholarly purposes. Brill and others have certainly substantiated the fact that scholars do indeed use government documents.[3] Perhaps however, the knowledgeable user of government documents, very much like the knowledgeable user of the literature in any subject or discipline area, does so unobtrusively and may be overlooked in many surveys of documents use. Brill's study was unique when compared with others, in that it made use of the techniques of citation analysis in statistically validating the fact that U.S. government documents were heavily cited in leading journals in the area of international relations. One must also assume that these scholars were assisted in their investigations by skilled and knowledgeable documents librarians.

THE SURVEY

The question remains however. If as reflected by the literature, documents use for general and reference purposes in academic libraries is less than substantial, would not a similar situation be expected to be true in public libraries? The author attempted to answer this question by making a survey of reference librarians employed by public libraries in 25 population centers geographically dispersed throughout the lower 48 states. The population centers were selected entirely as based on geographical location and the size of the community served. As listed in the most recent edition of the American Library Directory, with one exception, all served populations of more then 100,000 and less than 500,000. One library serving a population of less than 100,000 was included because it was the state capital and largest metropolitan area in a unique and clearly defined geographical area. The survey was specifically targeted at what might be termed a representative sample of "middle America."

Although it was not a factor which lead to their selection, 15 of 25 of the libraries maintained documents departments. The survey questionnaire asked for specific responses by categories, including not applicable when appropriate. There were only six questions and they were as follows:

1. Are you called on often to assist with questions on current national issues? Example: Ethics in the U.S. Congress.
2. Are you called on often to assist with questions on current international issues? Examples: Problems in the NATO alliance or the student rebellion in China.
3. On a monthly basis, how often do you use U.S. government publications to answer reference questions?
4. If your library has a documents librarian, are reference questions routinely directed to that person as they are to librarians with subject or discipline oriented specialties?
5. U.S. government documents provide excellent source materials for retrospective study of U.S. international policy. Example: the development of U.S. involvement in South East Asia. Assuming that the appropriate documents are available, would you feel conversant in doing so?
6. Should formal programs of library education be expected to provide reference librarians with the background necessary for discussing current historical issues?

Twenty one of 25 questionnaires were returned for a response rate of 84 percent. The analysis of the responses immediately revealed two weaknesses in the questionnaire design. By the cover letter, it was believed that the respondents had been clearly directed to the lesser used government documents in the library collection. This proved in some instances to have been unclear however. It would have been preferable to have specifically identified for exclusion, titles such as the *Statistical Abstract of the United States*, or any document usually found in reference collections. Nor is it clear whether or not the use of the word "document" as well as the expression "government publication" caused difficulties. It is conceivable that several may have viewed documents as being only those publications which are archival in nature. The categories allowed for a response to question three, "monthly use of government publications to answer reference questions," proved to be inadequate. These were 1-5, 6-10, 11-15, and 16 or more respectively. One respondent did not answer this question. Two responded to categories 1-5 and 6-10 respectively, and four indicated that they used government publications to answer reference questions 11-15 times monthly. Sixteen or more was the highest category of response allowed and there were 17 who gave that response.

Seventeen of 21 librarians who returned questionnaires indicated that they are frequently called on to assist with questions on current national issues. Fifteen indicated that they also assisted with questions on current international issues. One reference librarian expected to answer many questions about the student rebellion in China, but stated that at the time the questionnaire was returned, "events were a little too recent for the responses that we expect to receive." Nine of the respondents indicated that when appropriate, reference questions were routinely directed to their documents librarian. There were five who indicated that this was not a routine occurrence at their library, and seven indicated that the question was not applicable, as their library evidently did not have a documents librarian. One person identified himself as a documents librarian, and stated that he answered approximately 200 referrals each month from the reference department of his library. Another respondent stated the following: "I routinely use U.S. government publications, but most of my staff probably would not as they are not trained to do so."

Fifteen of 21 who returned questionnaires indicated that they felt conversant in discussing U.S. international policy. Seventeen of 21 indicated that they believed programs of library education should be expected to provide reference librarians with the background necessary for discussing current and historical issues. The librarian who indicated that at the time that the questionnaire was returned, the events in China were too recent to measure the responses that the library expected to receive, also stated the following:

> . . . recurring workshops on the availability and use of government documents would be stimulating as well as informative. I have attended similar one day workshops on BLS (Bureau of Labor Statistics) documents and state documents.

This study was only expository. Yet if the categories allowed for responses to question number three, "the number of questions answered monthly," were too low, one has to ask why? There was admittedly a lower level of expectation. If these public reference and documents librarians are typical, there appears to be a far greater use and awareness of U.S. government documents than may have been supposed. Until investigative studies prove otherwise, there is little reason to assume that they are atypical. Perhaps at least among public reference librarians, the awareness and use of U.S. government documents is not as poor as might have been imagined. Paraphrasing Katz, a librarian is an intellectual who lives in a country in which one is frequently tainted when so labeled.[4] Yet their public and "enthusiastic intellectualism" in doing what many reference librarians may already be doing well, would help alleviate many misconceptions about them.

Seventeen of 21 respondents answered affirmatively to question number six. Formal programs of library education should be expected to provide reference librarians with the background necessary for the discussion of current and historical issues. Perhaps in reality, herein lies a problem which is national in scope and not limited to the library profession. If the sum total of one's educational experience has not provided an awareness of history, political affairs, or cultural and social affairs, can the library schools make up for the deficiency? Perhaps not, but maybe at least for those with an orientation towards reference work, the effort should be made, whether through formal courses or current issues seminars which would include a historical perspective and identification of sources of documentation.

PRIVATIZATION OF FEDERAL INFORMATION SOURCES

The nation's most serious current information problem is the possibility that certain federal documents, public and printed sources of information which support freedom of speech, may not always be available. Diane Smith states the following:

> Today, a now commodity, government information, has entered the market place, and struggle for its ownership has begun.[5]

The word "privatization" may be viewed as a more socially acceptable expression for the sale of public assets to private industry. The sale of the National Technical Information Service (NTIS), the federal government's designated agency for the distribution of technical information, was deleted from legislation passed in 1988.[6] The danger remains however. Marc Levin provides an excellent summary of the basic issue:

> Privatization as government policy might on the surface seem like a good and politically correct notion. Privatization of NTIS represents a major federal policy shift away from the constitutional and legislative tradition that embraces the concept of an open and free exchange of public information to ensure an informed citizenry.[7]

The library professional associations have led the fight against the commercialization of federal information sources. A greater awareness of the problem should be evident at all levels. If technical information from federal sources is commercialized, can general information sources be far behind? The thesis here is that the absence of discussion of critical and current issues leads to the lack of knowledge and use of U.S. government documents. One still finds it common to hear an expression of distrust "for anything which originated from the U.S. government." Healthy skepticism may be a desirable attribute, but statistical and factual information which originated from a federal agency does not become more meaningful when reprinted commercially and at a substantially higher price. Additionally, statistical charts and other data which are used for illustrative purposes in commercial texts are frequently federal in origin. There is a greater certainty that the removal from the public domain of categories of documents which are seldom used, even if known, could be achieved with the greatest of ease.

CURRENT ISSUES SEMINAR

What would be the components of a "current issues seminar?" Using the headlines of the day and questions asked on the survey, the following might be typical. The issues are the Exxon Valdez oil spill, the trial of Oliver North, a drug related crime problem, a review and analysis of the problems of the Vietnam and the Watergate eras, and the student rebellion in the People's Republic of China. The problem is the identification of documents which aid in the understanding and discussion of these issues.

The alternative is that of being satisfied with interpretations of the commercial and popular media, as opposed to making use of all of the resources available. Nor should an informed citizenry accept any source uncritically. Government publications are produced for many purposes, but whatever the intent, there are those which provide current and factual statistical information on issues of national concern. Those issues frequently become questions asked at the reference desk of a library.

With the qualifiers having been established, let us review current areas of public concern and sources of information about them. The recently concluded North trial may serve to remind us that the constitutionally granted powers of the President are in reality relatively limited and are implied by his selection by the people as their chief executive officer, his authority to select and remove from office the heads of the executive departments, the armed forces, and other major units of the federal government, and the corresponding responsibility of those whom he has selected to follow his direction in establishing national policy and administering national programs. Consequently, when the President or an official or administrator acting on his authority seeks an interpretation of a point of law, the information is obtained from the Office of Legal Counsel of the Attorney General of the United States. The *Opinions of the Office of Legal Counsel of the Attorney General of the United States* are matters of public record and contain the official responses or interpretations of a point of law when requested. If one searches diligently through issues by varying titles of over two decades ago, they will find that President Nixon asked and received an opinion on the legality of wiretapping. A perusal of these interpretations of the law from over two decades past, can help in providing a better understanding of domestic concerns of the administration from another yet comparatively recent era.

As many naturalized citizens have noted, they frequently have a better understanding of U.S. government than those who are native born. The students enrolled in the seminar should have a thorough understanding of the operations of the federal government and the separation of powers of the legislative, executive, and judicial branches of the government. As indicated by recent supreme court decisions, interpretations of the law change with time. Preliminary Prints "Advance Sheets" (Official U.S. Reports) contain dissenting opinions as well as the official opinions as handed down from the bench. The students in the Current Issues Seminar would review and discuss the significant Supreme Court opinions as they occur.

The *Weekly Compilation of Presidential Documents* includes the significant speeches and activities of the President during the preceding week. Documents libraries, a substantial number of them also being federal depositories, and general libraries as well, may also have on their shelves, the *Public Papers of the President*. These would include documents as well as speeches which may not have appeared in the *Weekly Compilation*. They would be useful for the discussion of current and retrospective domestic and foreign policy issues, and for foreign affairs would be supplemented with the *Department of State Bulletin*.

A true understanding of Vietnam cannot be obtained by simply reviewing the history of overt United States military involvement in South East Asia. One must begin a serious review in the middle to late 1940's, though the antecedents truthfully precede even that time period. The graduate student in foreign affairs and the public in general may be interested in knowing the opinion of American diplomats and State Department officials in French Indo-China preceding and during the period of hostilities between the Vietming and the French republic, or the history of the development of U.S. foreign policy with the People's Republic and its precursors. *Foreign Relations of the United States and Diplomatic Papers* would be necessary reading. Issued annually and whenever there are documents which have been released for publication, diplomatic correspondence which was classified or secret at the time is published in this series. This publication may seldom be found in any but larger academic libraries or federal depository libraries, but those who wish to study the foreign policy of this country following World War II and since the emergence of the United States as a major power, will find this series to be invaluable. A review of earlier volumes would indicate that at least one career diplomat, whose advice concerning Indo-China was ignored, was very prophetic in predicting the future course of world events.

The environmental issue of 1989 has certainly been the Exxon Valdez and the Alaska oil spill. This was followed almost immediately by increases in the retail cost of automobile fuel. One competitor oil company placed a full page advertisement in a popular news magazine stating that the major reason for the increase was that OPEC had stopped overproducing. Yet public skepticism was certainly generated by implications from the commercial media that the wasted petroleum, if not the cost of the cleanup would have to be paid for by the public. This writer can recall little that preceded the accident, which would have indicated that the OPEC countries were again operating in the uniform and discipline manner of the OPEC of a decade ago. It would certainly not be difficult for a librarian or any knowledgeable person to statistically validate the fact that they are. What can be stated with certainty is that the Exxon Valdez spill amounted to only approximately 0.6 percent of the total domestic petroleum consumption in the United States for one day. The information necessary to derive this statistic is to be found in the *Monthly Energy Review*, a publication of the Energy Information Administration. Perhaps an oddity of government publishing is the fact that the December issue contained information current through March of 1989. From the December issue we learn that OPEC production increased by 10 percent in 1988, that "relatively low oil prices tend to depress domestic production, . . . and petroleum imports are expected to be the equivalent of 41 per cent of the projected petroleum consumption in 1989."[8] One of the more encouraging observations was almost exactly the same in 1977 as it was in 1967. Since 1977, the average fuel consumed has declined in every year through 1987, the latest year reported.[9] In 1987, the fuel efficiency of passenger cars had improved by 50 per cent in a ten year period. Hopefully, the 1988 statistics when published, will not show a reversal of this trend. This information was obtained from the December issue of the *Monthly Energy Review*. The compilation of charts, tables, and interpretative date may not be appealing to the general reader and library, irrespective of the value of the information. Students enrolled in the current issues seminar would be required to learn to use and analyze the data and charts in this and any appropriate document.

Certainly there could be few issues of domestic concern which are ever more depressing than those of crime and domestic violence. The most recent Uniform Crime Report available to the author was for the year 1987 and released on July 10, 1988. Yet if 1989 is typical of the past, one would discover that Washington, D.C. does not lead the nation in homicides as currently implied by the commercial media.[10] Perhaps the release of the next yearly summary may tell us otherwise. Changes are usually incremental as opposed to being in quantum leaps however. Perhaps what we best understand when reviewing this FBI and Department of Justice publication is that it is a voluntary reporting system, subject to the quantifications of local jurisdictions all over the United States. Even the willingness of citizens to report minor crimes in one locality as opposed to their reluctance to do so in another will tend to inflate the statistics reported negatively in the higher reporting area. Yet the willingness to make a report may also be a reflection of greater confidence in the local law enforcement agencies.

With this publication as well as others, one should be aware of the significance and meaning of the statistical data and the ways in which it is tabulated and reported. For an example, the numerical listing of total crimes in a category is far less meaningful than the previously used crime index per 100,000 population. The latter provided for a much more meaningful comparison by community, and especially when considering communities with similar populations.

Seminar participants would be advised to note when a change is made in the methods of reporting and tabulating data, and to question the reason or reasons for the change. Is it an improvement or is it simply easier to compile? Raw statistical data can be meaningless without a sound basis on which to make comparative observations. These and other issues and sources of documentation using U.S. government publications and any current and reliable printed materials, would comprise the Current Issues Seminar. The subject areas would be determined on a weekly basis as events occurred.

CONCLUSION

A survey of the reference use of U.S. government documents by reference librarians employed by public libraries serving 25 major population centers indicated substantial awareness and use of U.S. government documents. Sixteen of 20 librarians who returned questionnaires indicated that they thought formal programs in library schools should provide reference librarians with the background necessary for the discussion of current historical issues, even though fifteen of 21 indicated that they were capable of doing so themselves. Documents issued by the various federal agencies frequently provide the most current statistical and factual information. If the ability to understand and interpret historical issues is lacking, any people will run the risk of defending a principle or cause, of which censorship and freedom of information are examples, without a knowledge of that which is being omitted, censored, or simply being removed from the public domain. Librarians should view any attempts to privatize any federal information source including the National Technical Information Center entirely in this manner. A "Current Issues Seminar" could provide prospective reference librarians and any student for whom it would be useful, with the opportunity to discuss current national and international problems and possible sources of documentation. The ability to do so could only enhance the status of the library profession.

NOTES

1. Moody, Marilyn, "Government Information," Reference Quarterly, 25(1) Fall 1985, p.43.

2. Brill, Margaret S. "Government Documents as Bibliographic References in the Periodical Literature of International Relations: A Citation Analysis." Unpublished Master's Paper. School of Library and Information Sciences, North Carolina Central University, Durham, NC, April 1987, 48p.

3. Katz, Bill, "The Uncertain Realities of Reference Service," Library Trends, 31(3): Winter 1983, p. 365.

4. Op. cit. pp. 365-366.

5. Smith, Diane, "The Commercialization and Privatization of Government Information," Government Publications Review, 12(1) January-February 1985, p.45.

6. Leacy, Richard, "NTIS Privatization: The Omnibus Trade and Competitiveness Act of 1988," Sci-Tech News, 42(3): August 1988, p. 77.

7. Levin, Marc A., "Government for Sale: The Privatization of Federal Information Services," Special Libraries, 79(3) Summer 1988, p.211.

8. Monthly Energy Review. Washington: U.S. Department of Energy, December 1988, p.9.

9. Ibid. p.23.

10. Uniform Crime Reports for the United States, 1987. Washington: U.S. Department of Justice. Release date July 10, 1988.

Foreign Countries, Young Adults, and Federal Publications: A Reference Solution

Catherine M. Dwyer

SUMMARY. Young Adults doing research on foreign countries can benefit from using federal government documents. A variety of government documents are published on this topic and most are in an easy to use format. One solution to this type of reference question is to start a vertical file of foreign country material.

Reference librarians are often reluctant to use United States government documents. Documents are seen as inaccessible and awkward to use. In many libraries federal documents are classified by Superintendent of Documents or SUDOC number. Librarians who are unfamiliar with the SUDOC system may see it as another barrier to using the documents. With all these strikes against them, documents certainly do not seem like sources that should be recommended to young adult (YA) patrons. (For the purposes of this article patrons from high school through junior college are defined as young adults.) The reality is that federal documents are perfect for young adults doing research or working on papers. YAs can be very comfortable using government documents even when they are not aware that they are using documents.

YAs frequently request information to help them write papers on foreign countries. Encyclopedias, magazine articles, and atlases are all familiar and dependable sources for this type of information. But YAs often have special criteria for their papers. Some are individual criteria based on personal interest or attention span. Others are imposed by the teacher, no more than one encyclopedia may be used, or at least two magazine articles must be used. Teachers may also assign an "other" category for source

Catherine M. Dwyer is affiliated with the University at Albany Library, State University of New York.

© 1991 by The Haworth Press, Inc. All rights reserved.

material, leaving the student and the librarian to fill in the blank. Government documents are the perfect choice to fill that blank. The documents described in this article are brief, providing a maximum amount of information in a few pages. The reading level is aimed at a very general audience so YAs will have little trouble with comprehension. These publications are also fairly current, most are revised annually.

A variety of Federal agencies produce information on foreign countries. One of the most prolific is the Department of State. They publish a series called *Background Notes* (SUDOC S1.123:), one issue for each country of the world. *Background Notes* are usually 8-24 pages long depending on the current significance of the country. Each issue contains both a small map and a full page map of the country, as well as some basic statistics. There are a number of black and white photographs of places and people. The text is divided by topic including education, history, government, economy, and relations with the United States. For larger countries information on treaties, and relations with countries other than the U.S. is included. Of special interest to YAs are the travel notes. These briefly explain the type of clothing needed, some local customs, food availability, and modes of transportation. For a YA who wants more information there is a bibliography of books. *Background Notes* is usually an annual series but the Department of State does fall behind when publishing the information on some countries. The information is generally current enough to be useful.

Also published by the Department of State are *Current Policy* (S1.71/4:) and *Special Reports* (S1.129:). Both of these 2-5 page publications explain the United States' policy toward a certain country or issue. The text is usually a reprint of a speech or statement given by a federal official. YAs may find the language difficult to follow but the topics are very current. The United States' relationship with China, arms control, and the repression of Soviet Jews are covered in some of the recent issues. In addition, *Special Reports* are occasionally published on a major subject and these documents may be 20-30 pages long. The Soviet occupation of Afghanistan and human rights in various countries have both been dealt with in *Special Reports*.

Post Reports (S1.127:) and *Tips for Travelers to*– (S1.2:) are intended for visitors to foreign countries but contain information that YAs find interesting and useful. *Post Reports* are given to employees of the federal government and their families before they go abroad to live. Information about the American embassy, the customs, climate, and food of the host country are all included. There are also chapters on education, health care, transportation, and recreation. There is one *Post Report* for every country with a United States embassy. The series is issued annually, and each publication is 30-40 pages. Similar to the *Post Report* are the *Tips for Travelers to—*. Each pamphlet covers a specific country or area of the world. Visas and passports, penalties for drug use or crimes, shopping, adopting foreign children, and health precautions are all touched on briefly. Both of these publications use easy to understand language and YAs are fascinated by the details of life in other countries.

Regional Brief (S1.71/6:) is a new series being published by the Department of State. Unlike many of the Department's other series this set covers an area of the world rather than an individual country. Southwestern Africa, Eastern Europe, and East Asia have all been subjects of a *Regional Brief*. Every issue contains maps and photographs of the area. Tables, graphs, and chronologies are some of the special features included. Each Regional Brief focuses on a current topic such as economic changes, or the evolution of a new nation. YAs will find these particularly helpful when doing a current events paper.

The Department of State, because of its interest in foreign policy, collects more information than most federal agencies about foreign countries. But other agencies do produce documents with information on foreign countries. As part of the CIA's research on foreign countries, they publish a series of maps. Most CIA maps (PrEx3.10/4:) are published on letter size paper in color. They cover one country or area of the world and may be either topographic or line maps. By cartographic standards these are not wonderful maps. But YAs like them because they are easy to copy and limited in scope. The CIA also publishes maps of drug trade routes, religions of various countries, and population densities.

The World Factbook (PrEx3.15:) is another CIA publication. Unlike the other government documents mentioned here this is actually a book not a pamphlet. Every country of the world is listed in alphabetical order. Most entries take a page or two and consist of a map and some basic information. Categories given are geography, people, defenses, government, economy, and communications. The information provided is very brief, no more than a few lines or statistics. This also is handy for YAs to photocopy. *The World Factbook* is published annually.

Information on business and trade in foreign countries in compiled by the Department of Commerce. This agency produces *Foreign Economic Trends and their Implications for the United States* (C61.11:) or FET. Each FET covers a specific country and runs about 5 pages. For most countries a report is issued annually. The first page consists of statistics such as the GNP, exports, labor force, and money supply. The rest of the report is textual. Current events that are effecting the economy, and a summary of the economy over the past year are included.

Related to business are *Foreign Labor Trends* (L29.16:) which are distributed by the Department of Labor. Like the FET, these reports cover one country and are usually five pages. The first page lists key labor indicators such as productivity, unemployment, and life expectancy. The text examines union activities and the overall economic situation of the country. This series is also issued annually.

The Department of the Interior publishes a multivolume *Minerals Yearbook* (I28.37:) on an annual basis. Before the *Minerals Yearbook* is published the Department distributes a series of preprints from each volume. For every country in the world, there is a preprint, which looks at that country's mineral industry. These preprints are titled, *The Mineral Industry of–* (I28.37/a2:) and are 20-30 pages long. Each preprint is divided into sections on metals, mineral fuels, and industrial minerals. Governmental policies, and import export trade is discussed. Numerous tables supplement the information.

These are just a few of the publications on foreign countries which are distributed by the federal government. Monographs, single page updates, treaties, and defense reports are also available. Most government documents may be purchased through the United States Government Printing Office. For price and ordering information contact the nearest United States Depository library.

The publications listed here cover a variety of topics in a manner that is useful to YAs. They are also similar in format which makes organizing them into a vertical file an easy solution for reference questions. Create a folder for each country of the world and use it to store the government documents recommended here. Other documents, maps, and pamphlets from tourism departments could also be included. Maintaining back issues of the government documents in the file will allow for circulating as well as reference copies. YA users will become familiar enough with the files to begin their research on their own. Creating a vertical file of federal publications on foreign countries will not only make research easier for YAs, it will introduce them to a whole new world of source material.

Providing Technical Report Services in the Academic Library

Thomas W. Conkling

SUMMARY. Technical reports are a valuable information resource for faculty and students in engineering and the sciences. Academic libraries should have service plans designed to handle requests for these materials. This paper reviews some of the options available for providing reference services and document delivery for the technical report literature.

INTRODUCTION

In an age when technology transfer and research are being stressed on university campuses across the country, ready access to technical information resources is becoming increasingly important. Academic librarians are being called upon to support not only the information needs of faculty, students, and staff, but also the needs of industrial users and, in some cases, the staff at local business incubators.

To satisfy these demands, academic librarians and information specialists must be knowledgeable about all forms of technical information and be able to locate needed material for users. Much of this information is

Thomas W. Conkling is Head, Engineering Library, Pennsylvania State University, 325 Hammond Building, University Park, PA 16802.

© 1991 by The Haworth Press, Inc. All rights reserved.

published in books, conference proceedings, and journals, but in addition, a vast amount of scientific and technical data is contained in technical reports. These reports are issued to convey the results of research sponsored by government agencies such as the National Aeronautics and Space Administration (NASA) and the Department of Energy (DOE). Technical reports are rich sources of data since almost half of all research and development in the U.S. is sponsored by the federal government.[1]

This paper examines the issues facing academic librarians in providing reference services and document delivery for the technical report literature and outlines procedures for establishing a basic technical report service program.

TECHNICAL REPORTS IN THE ACADEMIC LIBRARY

The treatment of technical reports in academic libraries follows no specific standards or guidelines. Collections range in size from large depository sets of reports on paper and/or microfiche down to small collections with only a handful of items. The degree of bibliographic control also varies, often inversely with collection size. The reasons for these conditions are many: the varying need for these materials among faculty and students, the interest of the libraries in building report collections, support from the library administration, and budgetary and space constraints. To a certain extent, these factors affect all collections at an academic institution, but the pressure is probably more acute on reports due to the perceived nature of this literature. Technical reports are often viewed as short-lived publications in narrow subject areas that appeal only to very specific users. They also have acquired the reputation of being hard to locate and deliver to the patron.

The quality and dimensions of the reference services for technical reports also varies between institutions. A recent study has pointed out inconsistencies in services that users can expect when asking for assistance with the report literature.[2] In general, academic librarians and staff seem to have a limited knowledge of report verification procedures as well as the very different roles filled by the primary supplier of reports, the National Technical Information Service (NTIS), and the Government Printing Office (GPO). The same study also found that staff members often seemed disinterested when dealing with patron inquiries for technical reports.

For the library user who needs access to technical reports, this material assumes an importance greater than that of any other segment of the collection. This is the central idea to keep in mind when developing services—a request for a technical report must be handled with the same level of concern and expertise shown to other inquiries. With this philosophy, it becomes easier to plan for integrated services to all forms of literature.

ORGANIZING TECHNICAL REPORT SERVICES

The provision of technical report services begins with determining the level of need of the library users and then setting performance standards for the staff. Appropriate levels of service will vary greatly between institutions, but any academic library staff should be able to deliver basic services for the technical report literature. This service should include the proper identification or verification of an item, and, if the report isn't available in the library, the options a user can follow to obtain a copy. A staff that performs at this level is fulfilling the prime objective of public service, i.e., showing the library user the correct path to needed materials.

Preparing librarians and staff to handle such requests requires a certain amount of training, cooperation, and a willingness to spend time learning about resources that may not be requested regularly. A technical reports service program can be implemented in three stages:

1. designating an in-house expert
2. improving staff recognition of the literature
3. establishing document delivery guidelines

Participating staff include those full-time librarians and other personnel who spend appreciable time at public service desks assisting patrons in person or over the phone.

DESIGNATED EXPERT

Designating a librarian or staff member as the resident expert or resource person on technical reports is an essential step in establishing quality services. It makes little difference whether the person is from a general or special section of the library, as long as they are capable and willing to take on the responsibility. Most public service personnel already have some specialization, either subject or collection related, so finding an appropriate person for this position is a natural outgrowth of current staffing practice.

The preparation needed before an individual can operate successfully as the resource person will vary but a good working knowledge can be developed through self-study and contacts with other professionals in the field. The role of the resource person encompasses all matters relating to technical reports. They will be expected to provide the definitive answers on technical report verification and availability, and they should be involved in developing related guides and instructional material. Of course, they need to know the scope of the existing technical report collection at the institution and must clearly understand the workings of NTIS and related information facilities. A thorough familiarity with bibliographic tools and resources is expected. The technical report resource person will also need to be knowledgeable about library policies and guidelines that cover the acquisition and processing of reports, and all public service personnel need to be aware of the resource person and their role. If these conditions are met, a solid foundation will be set for service.

STAFF FAMILIARIZATION

Increasing overall staff recognition and knowledge of the technical report literature can be a difficult task given the complexity of the literature. Government agencies and their contractors have issued hundreds of report series over the years, and it is common for a report to have multiple identifying numbers.

Training an entire staff in the intricacies of the technical reports literature is impractical. A more economical approach to upgrading staff knowledge is through the development of a brief guide or pathfinder that can be referred to when assisting patrons. It should concisely describe the report literature available at the institution, detail the methods to be followed to acquire reports not locally owned, and identify the resource person as the contact for further information. The guide would be required study material for public service staff and would also be available to library users. If carefully prepared, such a guide could go a long way towards eliminating staff and patron confusion over technical report availability and provide a certain level of consistency in the handling of reference questions in this area.

Basic reference tools should be mentioned in the guide. The listing can be brief, but complete enough to include basic directories and indexes. *The Report Series Codes Dictionary*[3] is a recently revised edition of a classic reference work. It is an excellent tool for identifying the originating organization for reports. A similar tool that is regularly updated is the *Directory of Engineering Document Sources*.[4] This comprehensive work contains information on domestic and foreign report series, as well as other documents such as military and industrial standards and specifications. *How to Get It: A Guide to Defense Related Information Resources* [5] is an excellent verification tool for reports and other documents relating the Department of Defense. These tools should be part of all college and university library collections.

Many libraries subscribe to the NTIS publication *Government Reports Announcements and Index* (GRA&I), the single most authoritative work for report verification and availability information. If this source is not available on campus, verification and subject searching can be done online on the NTIS database which is accessible through all of the major search systems. Universities with large science and technology programs will want to provide additional access through abstracts produced by government agencies. NASA's *Scientific and Technical Aerospace Reports* (STAR) and DOE's *Energy Research Abstracts* (ERA) are excellent indexes to the report literature of the respective agencies. The Department of Defense produces an index titled *Technical Reports Awareness Circular* (TRAC) which can be useful for report verification, but it is distributed only to DOD agencies and their contractors and is not intended for public use. The *Monthly Catalog* may be included as a peripheral source, but it is not an important access tool for the technical report literature.

DOCUMENT DELIVERY

A well-rounded technical report service finishes with the patron having the needed document in his hands, or at least the knowledge of how to obtain the document. There are several document delivery options open to academic libraries depending upon the desired level of service. It is important that each institution have a standing policy on technical report acquisitions that is understood by all public service staff. Such a policy will result in more coherent and equitable services for library users.

Interlibrary loan is the usual starting place to request material not locally owned. However, interlibrary loan is not very effective for borrowing technical reports due to the lack of full cataloging of report collections in most institutions. Therefore, if an interlibrary loan is attempted, the process should not end with a search on OCLC or RLIN, but should continue with a phone call to a university or company with a sizable report collection. Most institutions will check their uncataloged holdings for requested reports and respond to such inquiries. The scope of technical report holdings can be roughly determined from tools such as the *Directory of Special Libraries and Information Centers*[6] or the *Union List of Technical Reports, Standards and Patents in Engineering Libraries*.[7]

ON-DEMAND ORDERING

If the library is committed to acquiring technical reports for users, the most cost effective route is to order the report directly from NTIS or a commercial information supply company such as Information on Demand (IOD). Copies of reports on microfiche can be acquired for as little as six or seven dollars each, with a usual delivery time of one to three weeks. Orders can be placed over the phone or via modem with a microcomputer, thus expediting delivery. Considering the staff time that would be consumed in the interlibrary loan process (even if successful), the outright purchase of microfiche copies is almost always more economical. A deposit account maintained with a supplier permits the direct deduction of funds to cover order costs and relieves the library of dealing with multiple invoices and associated institutional red tape. Most suppliers offer various choices for payment of charges.

Occasionally, the situation arises where a report is not available from NTIS or commercial vendors, but only from the information facility of the original sponsor. In most cases, this will be NASA, DOE, or DOD. All of these agencies offer some form of reference and document delivery service to academic institutions, with the eligibility varying according to the institution's status as a contractor. Academic libraries interested in taking advantage of these services should first determine the extent and nature of the government contracts their faculty hold and then contact the facilities directly. The three main information centers are the DOD's DTIC (Cameron Station, Alexandria, VA 22304), the DOE Office of Scientific and Technical Information (P.O. Box 62, Oak Ridge, TN 37831), and the NASA Scientific and Technical Information Facility (P.O. Box 8757, BWI Airport, MD 21240). Libraries that are properly registered are also eligible to request documents with distribution limitations, a category that constitutes a large subset of the technical report literature. Other related services include automatic report distribution programs and access to specialized online information systems.

Libraries that do not wish to acquire technical reports for users should provide the information needed for these individuals to place orders on their own. A supply of order forms can be obtained from NTIS or duplicated from the forms included in each issue of GRA&I. NTIS forms give ordering procedures in great detail. Similar information sheets can be compiled for commercial vendors. If the user is a faculty member with a government research contract, he or she may be able to request reports through their contract monitor, although this is often a lengthy process.

COMPREHENSIVE COLLECTION DEVELOPMENT

The procedures mentioned thus far are used for acquiring materials on a very selective basis. A library that makes a commitment to develop a comprehensive report collection has several options. If the institution is a GPO depository, it should be able to select a broad range of reports on microfiche from DOE and NASA as part of this program. Universities that have aerospace engineering programs are eligible to receive free copies of NASA reports on microfiche as well as paper copies of related tools such as the indexing publication STAR. Libraries registered as government contractors are eligible for document distribution programs from the various agency information centers.

NTIS offers the Selected Research in Microfiche (SRIM) program to any interested institution. Under SRIM, a library completes a subject profile and is then sent regular shipments of new technical reports on microfiche that fall within the selected categories. The cost for the SRIM service is just over one dollar per report received and, if desired, a custom index can be produced for a slightly higher charge. SRIM profiles can be altered by the library as subject needs change. SRIM provides a means for libraries with no GPO or government agency relationships to build a comprehensive technical report collection at a relatively modest cost.

CONCLUSIONS

Government spending on research and development has created an enormous quantity of data that resides in technical reports, so it follows that this literature forms a major source of technical information for engineers and scientists in industry and academia. The challenge facing academic librarians and information professionals in the years ahead is to find effective means of providing access to this resource to increase its impact on productivity and innovation.[8]

For the most part, the options for technical report services discussed here have concentrated on threshold activities, i.e., those steps needed to enable an academic library to deliver adequate services to users requesting technical reports. Services will, of course, vary between libraries depending upon the needs and situation of the particular institution. The ultimate goal for academic libraries is to achieve a degree of consistency and professionalism in the handling of the technical report literature that reflects its importance as an information resource.

REFERENCES

1. Berger, Suzanne et al. "Toward a New Industrial America." *Scientific American* 260: 39-47, 1989.

2. McClure Charles, Peter Hernon, and Gary R. Purcell. *Linking the U.S. National Technical Information Service with Academic and Public Libraries.* Norwood, NJ: Ablex Publishing Company, 1986. pp.82-88.

3. Aronson, Eleanor J., ed. *Report Series Codes Dictionary.* 3rd ed. Detroit, MI: Gale Research Company, 1986.

4. Nathan, Vasantha, ed. *Directory of Engineering Document Sources.* 4th ed. Clayton, MO: Global Engineering Documents, 1989.

5. Schlag, G.A., and C.E. Reed. *How to Get It: A Guide to Defense-Related Information Resources.* Rev. ed. Alexandria, VA: Defense Technical Information Center, 1989. AD-A201600.

6. Darnay, Brigitte T. and Holly M. Leighton, eds. *Directory of Special Libraries and Information Centers.* 12th ed. Detroit, MI: Gale Research Company, 1989.

7. Byers, Dorothy F., ed. *Union List of Technical Reports, Standards, and Patents in Engineering Libraries.* Washington, D.C.: American Society for Engineering Education, 1986.

8. McClure, Charles R. "The Federal Technical Report Literature: Research Needs and Issues." *Government Information Quarterly* 5: 27-44, 1988.

Technical Reports De-Mystified

Ellen Calhoun

SUMMARY. This paper explores some of the reasons why technical reports are so difficult to identify, and gives some hints for accessing technical reports in a government documents collection. The major producers of technical reports are discussed and the many kinds of technical reports are explained. The elements of a typical citation for a technical report are listed, and the differences between report numbers, contract numbers, and accession numbers are articulated. Four of the most useful indexes for verifying technical reports are compared. The emphasis is on U.S. federal technical reports.

Unless your library's government documents collection is fully cataloged, finding a particular government document can be a frustrating experience. Perhaps the most difficult type of document to identify and to help your patrons acquire is the technical report. It pays to know something about technical reports in general when you are trying to help a patron find one in particular. One of the first things you should try to decipher is where the report came from.

PRODUCERS OF TECHNICAL REPORTS

In simple terms, a technical report is an account of work done on a research project which a scientist compiles to convey information to his employer or sponsor or to other scientists. These reports vary greatly in size, scope, significance of content, quality of writing and effectiveness of presentation, but usually represent the first appearance in print of current scientific investigations.

There are three major sources of technical reports – private companies,

Ellen Calhoun is Head, Government Documents Department, Library of Science and Medicine, Rutgers University, Piscataway, NJ 08855-1029.

© 1991 by The Haworth Press, Inc. All rights reserved.

government agencies, and contractors of government agencies. The technical reports which emanate from private companies engaged in industrial research for their own purposes are usually considered proprietary and are not readily distributed outside of the company. They are generally internal reports, and may be described as idea records, correspondence, technical memoranda, project plans, patents, market analysis reports, financial documents, drawings, and plans.[1] United States anti-trust and patent laws foster competition in our free enterprise system, thus encouraging companies to guard information about both techniques and basic scientific discoveries. The internal publication system of many large companies, such as Bell Laboratories, gives scientists within the company the prestige and peer recognition rewards that would otherwise be satisfied by publication in scientific journals.[2] The technical reports produced by private companies are among the most difficult to obtain and in fact may be available only from the company if at all.

A second major source of technical reports is government agencies, including United States federal, state and local governments, foreign country governments, and international agencies. During the 1950s and 1960s the United States was credited with 75 percent of the world's total research and development activities. Today it performs 30 percent of that total.[3] Still, the annual federal funding expenditures for research and development in the major federal executive branch departments and agencies was over $56 billion in 1986.[4] Only one-third of this federal research and technology development is done under direct federal supervision, through field installations run by government employees, government owned and contractor operated facilities, or non-profit contract research centers such as the RAND Corporation.[5] Government laboratories may work exclusively for one agency, or for several; be a joint venture of any agency and one or several universities and be operated as a distinct organizational entity; do fundamental research closely tied to an agency's mission; or even carry on work which is not closely tied to any agency mission.[6] One example is the National Institute of Science and Technology (formerly the National Bureau of Standards) which acts as an agent for other agencies, trade associations, and small-batch manufacturers. Another example is the National Center for Atmospheric Research in Boulder, Colorado, which is funded by the National Science Foundation and operated by a consortium of universities. The 1984 edition of the *Federal Information Sources and Systems* directory from the General Accounting Office lists almost 1700 federal information systems maintained by federal agencies, most of whom produce technical reports.

Two-thirds of federal research is carried out through the third major source of technical reports-contractors of federal agencies, including corporations, universities, organizations, and individuals. Most government agencies require as part of the contract proposal a written report of final research results. Some contracts also stipulate that interim or progress reports be submitted to the sponsoring agency. In 1956, Saul Herner reported that the United States was producing about 150,000 unpublished research reports annually in connection with government-sponsored research.[7] The federal government is still the largest producer of scientific and technical information in the United States today. Most of these reports are submitted to the National Technical Information Service, which serves as a clearinghouse for these federal reports, and for reports prepared by state and local governments and many government research organizations in foreign countries.

These three major sources of technical reports—corporations, government agencies, and their contractors, produce a great variety of material in the conduct of their research. Some types of reports are more readily available than others, so it may help to know what kind of report your patron is looking for.

KINDS OF TECHNICAL REPORTS

The Committee on Scientific and Technical Information (COSATI) identified eight major kinds of technical reports in 1967.[8] Beginning in order with the least formal type, these are:

Preprints: generally a manuscript designed to be circulated among collegues for review, though they may end up being more formally printed or reviewed by an institution or even indexed and distributed by a clearinghouse.

Corporate "proposal type" report: for example, a corporate proposal to an agency when applying for a grant. These are usually proprietary and not available.

Institutional reports: such as the annual or progress reports of government agencies, foundations, corporations, societies, and laboratories. These reports generally give a good overview and include bibliographies.

Contract "progress report": the largest class of technical reports in circulation, produced either monthly or quarterly or as required by the terms of the research contract. The information reported in the progress report may or may not be contained in the final report of the contract.

Contract "final report": probably the most valuable technical report, for they generally give a good overview of the research performed under contract, and have some editorial review before release. There is a great variety in the format, distribution, and indexing of these contract final reports.

"Separate," topical technical report: closest to the journal article in terms of style and type. Many originate with either the sponsor or staff working on a project, and may be released as research memoranda, research notes, or technical memoranda. These reports often appear later in journals in an abbreviated form. At times, the corporation or government laboratory may take the resulting journal article and put the cover of the organization on it, creating a confusing hybrid.

"Book" in report form: survey type materials, such as reviews and state-of-the-art reports. These appear earlier than the commercial book at lower cost.

Committee-type reports: the findings and conclusions of research by scientific advisory groups. Most of these reports include bibliographic annotations, but their style varies greatly. They often have poor distribution and are usually not adequately described in references. Series designations, for example, are often ignored in descriptions of these reports.

The COSATI list is still a valid assessment of the various kinds of technical reports, but in recent years other agencies have identified additional kinds of reports. The Department of Energy includes among its list of 36 types of technical reports, formats such as magnetic tapes, computer codes, video tapes, and floppy disks. Design reports, incident reports, trip reports, and back-up reports are also listed, along with more formal types such as dockets, hearings, and environmental impact statements.[9] With so many types of technical reports produced by so many sources, it's not surprising that technical reports are sometimes difficult to recognize.

ELEMENTS OF A TECHNICAL REPORT

A complete citation for a technical report normally contains the following seven elements: personal author, title, date of report, issuing agency or corporation, report series number, clearinghouse accession number, and contract or grant number. Rarely does a patron approach the reference desk with all of this information. If all is known is the author, title, and date, you will not be able to distinguish the technical report from any other type of publication. If the issuing agency is known, you have a clue that this might be a government document. Technical reports are most frequently cited and requested, however, by a report number.

Report numbers are assigned by the originating agency or agencies, and represent the origin and status of the document. This report number may contain any or all of the following: the initial letters of the name of the issuing agency, such as MIT for Massachusetts Institute of Technology or AERE for Atomic Energy Research Establishment; an indication of the form of the document, such as TN for technical note or PR for progress report; an indication of the status of the document, such as C for classified or S for secret; the date of the report, such as 78/7 for July 1978; the name of the project which is reported; an indication of the subject content of the report, such as H for health or LS for literature search; and a number indicating the series placement of the report. Examples of report codes are:

> NACA-WR-A-6 : 6th Wartime Report issued by the Ames Laboratory of the National Advisory Committee for Aeronautics.
> CONF-8410131 : the 131st conference report sponsored by this agency in October of 1984.
> EPA 600/2-84-036 : the 36th report done in 1984 for the Environmental Protection Agency's environmental protection technology series.

Appended to this article is a list of sources for identifying report series codes. Linking the report series code to the corporate body which produced the work is an important step in identifying the report.

Contract numbers are not as useful for identifying technical reports because they are not unique to one item. Several reports may have been generated from one contract. Also, not every index includes contract numbers. Contract numbers are easy to confuse with report series numbers, for they sometimes include the acronym for the agency awarding the contract. The sequence and format of contract numbers serve as an internal identification code to the contracting agency. Examples of contract numbers are AT(29-2)-2831; DACW 72-74-C-0012; NAS2-9410; AC09-76SROOOOl.

Clearinghouse accession numbers can be extremely useful for verifying technical reports. These numbers are either assigned by the sponsoring agency, in cases where the agency produces its own index, or assigned by the National Technical Information Service to the items it procures for sale. NTIS does not reassign accession numbers to reports it acquires from the federal agencies that have previously assigned their own. The major clearinghouse accession numbers are:

> AD : stands for ASTIA Document. ASTIA (Armed Services Technical Information Agency) is the former name of the Defense Technical Information Center (DTIC). Examples are AD 473920, and for more recent reports, AD-A 694219.
> DE : numbers are assigned by the Department of Energy (DOE).

Examples are DE81016863 or DE84004926 where the first two digits indicate the year of the report.

N : numbers are assigned by the National Aeronautics and Space Administration (NASA). Examples are N64-02345 or N88-238641 where the first two digits indicate the year of the report.

PB : stands for Publications Board. These are assigned by NTIS, and were in one numerical sequence until 1980, when the indexing year was added to the number. Examples are PB239580 and PB80-381264.

These four accession numbers are the ones most frequently encountered, but there are others. At times, these clearinghouses use the report series code as an accession number, instead of assigning a separate accession number.

It helps to know how technical reports are produced and cited when you are trying to decide which of the major indexes and abstracts to use to verify a technical report.

THE MOST USEFUL INDEXES AND ABSTRACTS FOR TECHNICAL REPORTS

Technical reports are generally not listed in regular trade bibliographies or book selection tools, and are irregularly indexed in the major abstracting journals. Although Herner and Herner list 31 abstracting and indexing publications covering technical and research reports,[10] only four of these cover technical reports intensively. These four indexes are produced by the four major clearinghouses mentioned above.

AD accession numbers are used in the biweekly *Technical Abstract Bulletin (TAB)* from DTIC, published since 1953. *TAB* announces the results of research done under defense-related contracts, and is not generally available in most libraries. TAB itself has been classified since 1967, and access to this index is restricted to federal agencies and government contractees. Unclassified DTIC reports are included in *Government Reports Announcements and Index (GRAI)*.

DE accession numbers are used in the semi-monthly *Energy Research Abstracts (ERA)*, published by the Department of Energy since 1976. *Energy Research Abstracts* includes reports from the Department of Energy, its laboratories, energy centers, and contractors. It covers scientific and technical reports, journal articles, conference papers, proceedings, books, patents, theses, and monographs on subjects such as energy and reactor technology, waste processing and storage, fusion technology, and nonnuclear information. If a report listed in *ERA* is designated for the Government Printing Office (GPO) depository library system, the availability element in the report abstract header is indicated as "GPO Dep." This designation, however, has not been consistently included in the abstract, so it is wise to check the depository library's collection to see if the report has actually been received.

N accession numbers are used in the semi-monthly *Scientific and Technical Aerospace Reports* (*STAR*), published by NASA since 1963, and under variant titles by NASA's predecessor NACA since 1915. *STAR* includes scientific and technical reports, translations, patents and patent applications, dissertations and thesis, and research reports issued within 2 years of the index date in the field of aerospace science. All unclassified reports from NASA, its contractors and grantees, other U.S. government agencies, domestic and foreign institutions, universities, and private firms are included. Classified documents are announced in *LSTAR*, which has limited distribution. Many of the reports announced in *STAR* are made available to libraries through the GPO depository system, and these are also listed in the *Monthly Catalog of United States Government Publications*. NASA has a depository program of its own, and libraries participating in the NASA depository program receive all NASA produced and microfiched reports directly from NASA in accession number (N-#) order. However, NASA only lists the GOP regional depository libraries in each issue of *STAR*.

PB accession numbers are used in the biweekly *Government Reports Announcements and Index (GRAI)* from NTIS, published under variant titles since 1946. The NTIS collection now consists of almost 2 million technical reports and over 2500 data and software files. Approximately 70,000 new items are added each year.[11] This fact, plus the significant amount of overlap that exists between these four indexes, indicate that *GRAI* is the first place to look for information on technical reports available in the United States. A 1981 study found that *GRAI* indexed 94.3 percent of the technical reports that appeared in *STAR* and 78.8 percent of those that appeared in *ERA*.[12] Reports from over 450 federal agencies and their contractors are included in GRAI. Emphasis is placed on the physical sciences, but biological sciences, medicine, statistics, agriculture, and the social sciences are covered also. It is important to remember that NTIS does not announce reports older than 5 years in the printed version of *GRAI*. These older reports are only included on their magnetic tape and available through the on-line service.

One other index that is useful for locating technical reports is the

Monthly Catalog of U.S. Government Publications. The *Monthly Catalog* lists all federal scientific and technical reports sent to GPO depository libraries. Contract reports are generally not included. According to a recent study conducted by Margaret Mooney, most titles sent to depository libraries are cataloged by the Government Printing Office and appear in the *Monthly Catalog* within six months of receipt. Scientific reports, however, are not always included so quickly, and 10.3 percent of all titles issued by the Department of Energy examined in the study had not appeared in the *Monthly Catalog* even two years after they had been received by depository libraries.[13] Although the *Monthly Catalog* does include DOE reports of a non-technical nature, the best index to use for DOE technical reports is of course *ERA*. The Government Printing Office does not duplicate the efforts of the Department of Energy, and relies on *ERA* for access to the DOE reports it distributes under the GPO depository program.

USING THE INDEXES

There are some major differences in these indexes that complicate the search for technical reports. First, each uses a different thesaurus, so subject headings are not be consistent from one index to the next. For example, NASA and NTIS use the heading "measuring instruments" while DOE uses "gages and meters."

Second, the sequence of report numbers in the different report number indexes varies according to the weight assigned to the punctuation of the report number. In *STAR*. for example, dashes precede slashes, letters precede numbers, years precede other numbers, and numbers (excluding years) are filed as whole numbers. In *GRAI*, dashes and slashes are of equal weight, letters precede numbers, years precede other numbers, and numbers (excluding years) are filed as whole numbers. This one difference makes a big impact on the ultimate sequence of the numbers in each index.

Report numbers listed as they appear in *STAR*:

ANL-AMD-TM-262
ANL-CT-77-3
ANL-76-XX-73
ANL-77-XX-37
ANL-77-14
ANL-8000-REV-2
ANL/CEN/FE-77-2

Report numbers listed as they appear in *GRAI*:

ANL-AMD-TM-262
ANL/CEN/FE-77-2
ANL-CT-77-3
ANL-76-XX-73
ANL-77-XX-37
ANL-77-14
ANL-8000(REV.2)

GRAI also occasionally uses lower case (i.e., ORNL-tr-1034) and variations in the report numbers themselves, such as adding vol.1 pt.1 when appropriate, and leaving off things like (REV.2). When searching report numbers in an on-line database, it is best to expand your report number. The expand command is more effective than truncation in revealing the placement of the report in the index.

Of the indexes mentioned above, only the *Monthly Catalog* has both a keyword and a title index. A keyword index is available for *GRAI* in microfiche. These keyword indexes are helpful when the complete citation for a technical report is not known. Incomplete citations, however, are best verified using an on-line service, where the ease of combining known elements of the citation can greatly enhance your chances success. The *STAR* and *TAB* databases are available only to federal contractors, but *GRAI, ERA,* and the *Monthly Catalog* are all available through Dialog or BRS. The major cataloging databases from the Online Computer Library Center (OCLC), the Western Library Network (WLN), and the Research Libraries Information Network (RLIN) can also be useful in verifying technical reports.

USING RLIN TO FIND TECHNICAL REPORTS

RLIN can be very helpful in identifying imprecise citations and in determining whether an item actually is a government document. Search features such as truncation, combined searching, subject searching, free-text searching and combined index searching make RLIN a powerful and effective reference tool. The RLIN database includes records from the *Monthly Catalog*, which has been computer produced since 1976, and from the member institutions of the Research Libraries Group (RLG). A recent survey of RLG members indicated that most of the federal depository libraries in the system catalog their current (1982+) document receipts. Colorado State University Libraries has added over 10,000 "fugitive" federal government publications to the database. The items they cataloged during this special project had usually not been supplied to the Superintendent of Documents by the issuing agency, had been sent to NTIS or DTIC, or were available only from the agency itself.[14] More recently, Stanford University has discussed the possibility of adding their technical reports file to the RLIN database. Always look at the full RLIN record, and if possible, at a Library of Congress/Government Printing Office (DCGD) record. Watch for the following MARC fields:

045, or 074 : depository item number
080 : Superintendent of Documents classification number
5xx : notes, sometimes includes a report number
7xx : added entries, sometimes includes a report number

THE ILLUSIVE TECHNICAL REPORT

There will be times when you cannot verify your technical report in any available index, in print or on-line. De-classified technical reports can be especially illusive, but NTIS does add about 10% of the reports that become declassified to its database each year. There also are times when NTIS will indicate that the report is not available from their collection, even though it has a PB accession number. In desperate cases it sometimes pays to go directly to the source of the report. Don't be afraid to use the telephone – it can be one of your best allies. If the report has been done under contract at a university, contact that university's library. The report may be in their uncataloged documents collection, or they may be able to refer you to the proper department where the work was actually done. You may also try contacting the author of the report. If the report has never actually been published, the author may be the only repository for the report. Most are quite willing to discuss their past research with interested parties. If the report has been produced by a government agency, try contacting the agency. Be prepared to be referred on more than once. A lot of legwork and a lot of persistence can bring the reward of positive results.

REFERENCES

1. Lynda W. Moulton, "Building a Special Libraries Database," *Electronic Library*, v.2 n.4 Oct. 1984, p. 264.
2. Peter Hernon, "The Quality of Academic and Public Library Reference Service Provided for NTIS Products and Services," *Government Information Quarterly*, v.3, 1986, p.164.
3. Op. Cit. p.173.

4. Kathleen Eisenbeis, "An NTIS Case Study," *Government Publications Review*, v.15, 1988, p.355-356.
5. Hans Mark, The Management of Research Institutions, 1984. p.6.
6. Op. Cit. p. 194.
7. Saul Herner, "Technical Information," *Scientific Monthly*, v.83 n.2, 1965, p.82.
8. Gary R. Purcell, "Technical Report Literature," in *Public Access to Government Information* by Peter Hernon (Norwood, NJ: Ablex, 1984), p.171-172.
9. Charles R. McClure, "The Federal Technical Report Literature," *Government Information Quarterly*, v.5, 1988, p. 42.
10. Saul Herner, "The Unpublished Government Research Report," *Government Publications Review*, v.13, 1986, p. 101.
11. Kathleen Eisenbeis, "An NTIS Case Study," *Government Publications Review*, v.15, 1988, p. 357.
12. Mary Hardick, *A Guide to Locating Technical Reports in U.S. Government Publications Collections* (Mettrodocs, 1987), p. 14.
13. Margaret T. Mooney, "GPO Cataloging," *Government Publications Review*, v.16, 1989, p. 268.
14. Douglas J. Ernest, "Accessing Federal Government Publications With RLIN," *Government Publications Review*, v.15, 1988, p. 241.

BIBLIOGRAPHY

Adkinson, Burton W. "Primary Scientific Publication and the Federal Government," *Science*. v.140, 1963, p. 613-617.

Burton, R.E. and B.A. Green, Jr. "Technical Reports in Physics Literature," *Physics Today*, v.14. n.10, 1961, p. 35-37.

Eisenbeis, Kathleen. "An NTIS Case Study," *Government Publications Review*, v.15, 1988, p. 355-369.

Ernest, Douglas J. "Accessing Federal Government Publications With RLIN," *Government Publications Review*, v.15, 1988, p. 237-244.

Federal Information Sources and Systems. Washington, DC, U.S. General Accounting Office, 1986. GAO/AFMD-85-3.

Federal Library and Information Center Committee. "The International Flow of Scientific and Technical Information," *Government Information Quarterly*, v.3 n.2, 1986, p. 163-178.

Gray, Dwight E. and Staffan Rosenborg. "Do Technical Reports Become Published Papers?" *Physics Today*, v.9 n.6 June 1957, p. 18-21.

Gray, Dwight E. "Scientists and Government Research Information," *College and Research Libraries*, v.18 Jan. 1957, p. 23-27.

Hardick, Mary. *A Guide to Locating Technical Reports in U.S. Government Publications Collections*. Mettrodocs Monograph One, 1987. ED 287506.

Herner, Saul. "Technical Information—Too Much or Too Little?" *Scientific Monthly*, v.83 n.2 Aug. 1956, p. 82-86.

Herner, Saul and Mary Herner. "The Unpublished Government Research Report: 1959 and 1985," *Government Publications Review*, v.13, 1986, p. 97-104.

Hernon, Peter and Charles R. McClure. *Public Access to Government Information: Issues Trends and Strategies.* Norwood, NJ: Ablex, 1984.

Hernon, Peter and Charles R. McClure. "The Quality of Academic and Public Library Reference Service Provided for NTIS Products and Services: Unobtrusive Test Results," *Government Information Quarterly*, v.3 n.2, 1986, p. 117-132.

Hicks, Margaret S. "Government-Sponsored Research Reports in Three Areas of Physical Chemistry," *Journal of Chemical Documentation,* v. 3, 1963, p. 144-148.

Kline, Eileen. "Strategic Access: Government/Defense Online Databases," *Database*, v.10 n.5, 1987, p. 75-82.

Maizell, R.E. "Locating Unclassified Government-Sponsored Research Reports," *Physics Today*. v.12 n.12 Dec. 1959, p. 42-44.

Mark, Hans and Arnold Levine. *The Management of Research Institutions: A Look at Government Laboratories.* Washington, DC, National Aeronautics and Space Administration, 1984. NASA SP-481.

McClure, Charles R. "The Federal Technical Report Literature: Research Needs and Issues," *Government Information Quarterly*, v.5 n.1, 1988, p. 27-44.

McKee, Jay R. *Bibliography of Finding Aids to Locate Government Technical Reports*. Denver, CO, Martin Marietta Astronautics Group, [1987].

Mooney, Margaret T. "GPO Cataloging Is It A Viable Current Access Tool for U.S. Documents?" *Government Publications Review*, v.16, 1989, p. 259-270.

Moody, Marilyn. "Twenty-Five Years of Government Information: Changes in Reference Service Attitudes," *RQ*, v.25 Fall 1985, p. 39-45.

Morton, Bruce. "U.S. Government Documents As History," *RQ*, v.24 Summer 1985, p. 474-481.

Moulton, Lynda W. "Building a Special Libraries Database," *Electronic Library*, v.2 n.4 Oct. 1984, p. 261-271.

Paul, James H. "Scientific and Technical Information Policy and the Future of NTIS," *Government Information Quarterly*, v.5 n.2, 1988, p. 137-146.

Smith, Ruth S. "NTIS As A Social Science Resource," *Behavioral and Social Sciences Librarian*, v.3 n.2 Winter 1983, p. 37-45.

U.S. Congress. House. Committee on Science and Technology, Subcommittee on Science, Research, and Technology. *Scientific and Technical Information (STI) Activities: Issues and Opportunities.* Washington, DC, Government Printing Office, 1979. Committee Print 95-2 Serial XXX.

Voos, Henry. "The Information Explosion; or, Redundancy Reduces the Charge!" *College and Research Libraries*, v.32 n.1 Jan. 1971, p. 7-14.

Zink, Steven D. "The Impending Crisis in Government Publications Reference Service," *Microform Review*, v.11 n.2 Spring 1982, p. 106-111.

APPENDIX

SOURCES FOR IDENTIFYING TECHNICAL REPORT SERIES CODES

Corporate Author Authority List-1983. Springfield, VA: U.S. National Technical Information Service, 1983.

The most current source, and the first place to look for help in decoding a report number's source. Arranged alphabetically, the beginning section of each letter lists acronyms with referrals to full names. Any government or corporate agency or institution who has ever submitted a technical report to NTIS will be included in this publication. Over 35,000 entries, includes former names of organizations and gives locations (but not addresses).

Dictionary of Report Series Codes, by Lois E. Godfrey and Helen F. Redman. Washington, DC: Special Libraries Association, 1973.

In three sections. Section on Reference Notes explains how technical report numbers are composed by 48 agencies. Section on Report Series Codes (yellow) is arranged by acronym, gives full name and location of agency. Section on Corporate entries (blue) is arranged by agency name, and report code acronym follows. Most useful for Reference Note section, especially Reference 1—Ambiguous Numerical Codes, and Reference 2—Ambiguous Alphabetical Codes.

How to Get It—A Guide to Defense-Related Information Resources, U.S. Defense Technical Information Center. Springfield, VA: NTIS, 1988. (DTIC/TR-89/1; AD-A201 600).

Primarily a guide to sources for procuring technical documents and information resources prepared for, needed by, or of particular interest to the Defense Department. The cross references from report code acronyms to full agency names are particularly useful. Limited to DoD activities, but does include some NTIS, NASA, and DOE report codes.

Government Acronyms and Alphabetic Designations Used in DDC. U.S. Defense Documentation Center. Springfield, VA: NTIS,1972. (AD-743000).

Limited to reports cataloged by the DDC from the Defense Department, federal government, and foreign military organizations. Arranged in 3 parts—by report code acronym, organization name, and DDC numerical code.

Federal Regulations: Overview and Research Guide

Elizabeth A. McBride

SUMMARY. Federal regulatory research often poses a challenge to both the general reference librarian and the documents specialist. This article provides a brief overview of the history of regulation, emphasizing developments since the 1970's and the role of the Office of Management and Budget; reviews the federal rulemaking system from proposed rule to codification to revision; includes an annotated list of the major official and privately produced regulatory publications; and concludes with suggested approaches to five sample research problems. These sample problems range from finding and updating regulations on a specific subject to keeping informed about an agency's regulatory plans.

We pass such fuzzy legislation. Then we pass it on to administrative agencies and say: 'You work it out.' Then members and the President go out and campaign against those 'crazy bureaucrats.'

—Senator Patrick J. Leahy (D-Vt)[1]

Currently each Congress passes some six to seven hundred laws establishing policies and programs which then fall to administrative agencies to implement and enforce. The 99th Congress (1985-86) passed 664 public laws; during the same time period federal agencies published 10,173 final rules to implement existing legislation. The numbers alone testify to the importance of the regulatory process. From the taxes we pay to the quality of the air we breathe, regulations impact our daily lives.

Elizabeth A. McBride is Head, Documents Center, Robert W. Woodruff Library, Emory University, Atlanta, GA 30322.

© 1991 by The Haworth Press, Inc. All rights reserved.

BRIEF HISTORY OF REGULATION

When the republic was young, the functions of government could be handled through the legislative process and a small executive branch. It was not until the second half of the nineteenth century that the growth of the country and the expansion of the role of the federal government resulted in the birth of regulations. Many of the early agencies had some regulatory component but in 1887 a milestone in the history of regulation was reached when, in the wake of troubles in the railroad industry, Congress created the Interstate Commerce Commission, the first agency established for the sole purpose of regulation.

In the twentieth century, government concern with economic and social issues during the depression led to an enormous growth in regulatory activity. It has been estimated that the National Recovery Administration alone issued "some 10,000 pages of 'law'—a greater volume than the total amount of statute law contained in the United States Code."[2] As might be expected the agencies themselves were unable to keep track of regulations that were being issued and, after an embarrassing court case in which the government was defeated because of inaccurate information about the status of a regulation, Congress responded with the Federal Register Act of 1935 (44 U.S.C. Chapter 15).[3] This law directed agencies to file their regulatory documents with the Office of the Federal Register to be published in the new periodical, the *Federal Register*. The first issue of the *Federal Register* is dated March 14, 1936. Presidential executive orders and proclamations were also to be printed in the *Federal Register*.

In 1937 the Federal Register Act was amended to create the *Code of Federal Regulations* (CFR). The purpose of the CFR was to provide a subject arrangement of all the regulations in effect as of a specific date. Like the *United States Code*, the CFR was organized into fifty broad subjects or titles. Many of the titles in the CFR corresponded to those in the *United States Code*.

The Administrative Procedure Act of 1946 (5 U.S.C. 551 et seq.) introduced the concept of public participation into the regulatory process. It required agencies, with some exceptions, to publish their proposed rules in the *Federal Register*. The Act also provided, again with exceptions, for a thirty day period between publication of a regulation in the *Federal Register* and its effective date. Finally the Act allowed other items to be published in the *Register* including agency statements of organization and procedural rules.

INCREASED PRESIDENTIAL CONTROL

The 1960's and 70's saw a tremendous growth of federal regulation and succeeding Presidents sought to influence the regulatory process. President Nixon instituted a "quality of life" review of selected regulations and relied on the Office of Management and Budget to coordinate the regulatory programs of various agencies. President Ford attempted to make agency officials more conscious of the cost consequences of regulations through Executive Order No. 11821. In 1978 President Carter issued Executive Order 12044 requiring agencies to evaluate the need for significant proposed rules and consider their economic impact. Most helpful for the researcher, this executive order also required that regulations be written in "plain English." It further attempted to help the public by generally extending the comment period on proposed rules to sixty days. During his term President Carter created two groups to control the regulatory process. The Regulatory Council was a voluntary group of agency heads who attempted to coordinate regulations. One of the chief responsibilities of the Council was to develop a Calendar of Federal Regulations and publish it semi-annually, the *Federal Register*. The Calendar provided a brief synopsis of the most important regulations under development. President Carter also created the Regulatory Analysis Review Group to review major proposed rules and submit comments on them.

President Reagan had a major impact on the regulatory process through two executive orders. Executive Order 12291 issued in 1981 and Executive Order 12498 issued in 1985 placed major responsibility for coordinating and reviewing proposed executive branch agency regulations (independent regulatory commissions are not covered) in the Office of Management and Budget (OMB). OMB's regulatory review takes place before regulations are ever published in the *Federal Register*. Regulations are screened for adherence to the Administration's priorities and for coordination. All major regulations (defined as those over $100 million in cost) must be accompanied by a regulatory impact analyses (RIA), essentially a cost-benefit study. Executive Order 12498 also requires annual publication of the *Regulatory Program of the United States Government*.[4] This substantial document reviews the overall regulatory plans of each executive branch agency for the regulatory year (April 1 through March 31) and provides descriptions of all significant rule making activities at the prerulemaking and rulemaking stages. A second OMB effort to coordinate possible rulemaking activity is the Uniform Calendar of Federal Regulations published twice a year in the *Federal Register*. Unlike the *Regulatory Program* which previews only the most important of an agency's proposed rulemaking activities, the Uniform Calendar covers almost all federal agencies that issue regulations and all proposed regulatory activity for the year. It provides public notice of an agency's plan "to review, propose and issue regulations."[5] Information given is much briefer than that found in the *Regulatory Program*. The Uniform Calendar is published in the *Federal Register* in April and October each year by OMB's Regulatory Information Service Center. OMB's regulatory review has had a substantial impact on the regulatory process and the number of pages, proposed rules and final rules published in the *Federal Register* has dropped significantly.

Finally there are a number of laws which are not specifically directed to agency rulemaking but impact it nevertheless. One of the most important of these is the Paperwork Reduction Act of 1980 (44 USC 3501). This law created the Office of Information and Regulatory Affairs (OIRA) in the Office of Management and Budget and directed it, among other duties, to review all activities of agencies, including independent regulatory commissions, which require collection of information from ten or more persons. This includes paperwork requirements of proposed rules. OMB's disapproval of proposed paperwork can have an impact on agency rulemaking activity since only the independent regulatory commissions can override OMB's rejection. In implementing the Paperwork Reduction Act each year OMB publishes the *Information Collection Budget of the United States Government* which reports on each agency's efforts to meet OMB targets for reduced paperwork.[6]

Since as Vice President, George Bush chaired the Presidential Task Force on Regulatory Relief whose findings were reaffirmed in President Reagan's Executive Order 12498, it might be expected that the new Bush Administration will continue to pursue a policy of aggressive Presidential oversight of federal regulatory activities through the Office of Management and Budget.

FEDERAL RULEMAKING SYSTEM

As indicated earlier all federal rules and regulations (the terms are synonymous) have as their basis a federal law or executive order which delegates to agencies the authority to engage in rulemaking. Often this authority is quite general, e.g., 'to promote the public health,' other times it may be more specific. In all cases, however, regulation is an extension of the constitutional authority of the President or the Congress and all regulations always refer back to the law or presidential action on which they are based.

Other than notice in the Unified Agenda of Federal Regulations and the *Regulatory Program of the United States Government*, there is little available documentation at the drafting or OMB review stage.[7] Once the proposed rule is fully developed, however, the text is published in the *Federal Register* along background information and an invitation for public comment. There is usually a minimum sixty day comment period.

Final regulations are proposed rules revised to reflect public comments. Although it is estimated that only about 50% of all proposed rules actually receive comments, those that do are often substantially affected by it.[8] Publication of a final rule in the *Federal Register* is official notice of a regulation's existence, establishes its text and effective date, and is evidence acceptable in a court of law.

Regulations are then codified in the annual *Code of Federal Regulations* (CFR) where they are arranged by fifty broad titles or subjects. The CFR contains the text of all regulations in effect in a subject area regardless of date of initial issuance. The regulations are footnoted to refer back to their original publication in the FEDERAL REGISTER as well as their legal basis.

Since regulations are frequently changed, it is possible that new proposed or final regulations on a subject have been issued since the date of the last edition of the *Code of Federal Regulations* and so the whole process of proposed to final to codified regulations should be thought of as a continuous circle(See Figure 1).

MAJOR PUBLICATIONS RELATED TO FEDERAL REGULATIONS

Background Sources

The Federal Register: What it is and how to use it. Washington, D.C.: Office of the Federal Register, 1985 (AE2.108:F31)

This is the latest edition of a handbook used in workshops conducted by the Office of the Federal Register. It reviews the major milestones in the history of regulations and takes the reader through the sources (official only) related to the regulatory process. The text is supplemented by numerous reproductions of sample pages and other graphics.

Federal Regulatory Directory. Washington, D.C.: Congressional Quarterly. 1979/80- .

Now in its fifth edition (1986), the *Directory* is helpful for its extensive

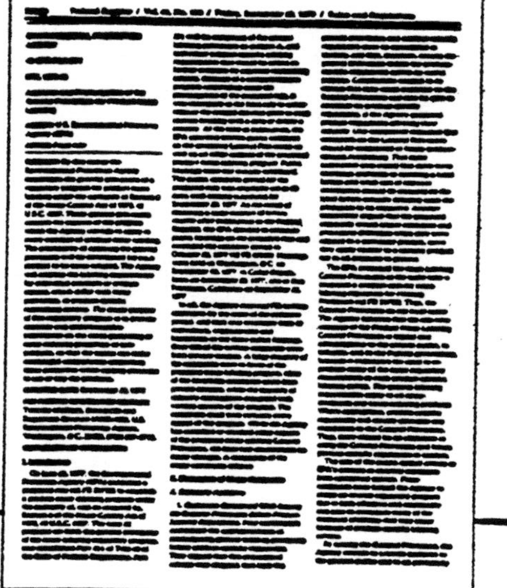

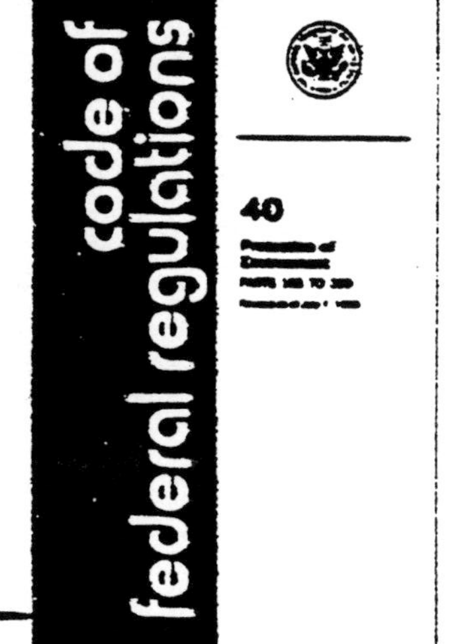

Proposed rule in FEDERAL REGISTER

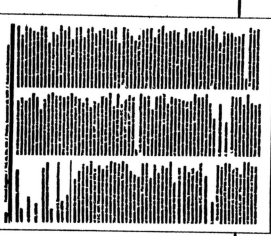

Final rule in FEDERAL REGISTER

Codification in CODE OF FEDERAL REGULATIONS

Figure 1. Federal rulemaking system

overviews of federal regulatory agencies covering their history, functions and personnel. At the end of each agency is a list of information sources including public information contacts, agency libraries/documents rooms, and significant publications. For the most important regulatory agencies, the *Directory* gives major authorizing legislation, names of Congressional oversight committees, and a select bibliography which notes privately published loose-leaf services related to an agency's regulatory area.

Source Documents

Federal Register, 1935- . Daily except on weekends. (AE2.106:)

Each current issue of the *Federal Register* contains a number of important sections beginning with (1) a Table of Contents arranged by agency and (2) a list of CFR parts which are affected in the issue. Both allow regular readers (of which there are many) to quickly scan for item of interest. The bulk of the rest of the issue is devoted to the text or the documents themselves arranged by category:

- Presidential Proclamations and Executive Orders
- Rules and Regulations arranged by agency and CFR section affected
- Proposed Rules also arranged by agency and proposed CFR section affected. Interim rules, rules generated for emergency situations and published without a prior proposed rule, are found in this section as well as general information about an agency's handling of a regulation or important information for the public in dealing with an agency. Agencies also occasionally publish advance notices of rulemaking in this section. These advance notices are intended to allow for extensive public comment.
- Notices, a section containing documents applicable to the public which are not rules and regulations. These include notices of meetings, agency decisions and rulings, hearings or investigations, grant application deadlines, availability of environmental impact statements, Privacy Act issuances, and the like.[9]

The format of the rules and proposed rules sections are similar. The text of the rule is preceded by a summary statement, the effective date, an information contact, and Supplementary Information which can be quite extensive and assist in understanding the purpose of the regulation. It is in the Supplementary Information of final rules that agencies respond to any public comments received. The prefatory information also includes citation to legal authority as well as reference to and earlier appearance in the

Federal Register. The format of notices is generally similar to the rules and proposed rules section.

Beginning in spring 1989 agencies have begun to include Regulation Identifier Numbers (RINs) in the heading information supplied with proposed and final rules. These numbers are also used in the Unified Agenda of Federal Regulations which lists an agency's planned regulatory activity and was discussed earlier. Inclusion of the RINs is intended to help agencies and the public to keep track of regulations at various stages of development.

The final section of the *Register* is Readers Aids which contains Washington phone numbers relevant to regulatory research and a list of CFR Sections Affected showing revisions caused by documents published in the *Federal Register* for the month. The list of CFR Sections Affected cumulates monthly and is a very important tool in discovering the current status of regulations. Arrangement is by CFR part. Readers Aids also lists any public laws which have become available. Each Monday issue of Readers Aids includes a Checklist of the most recent issues of the *Code of Federal Regulations* and their prices.

Proper citation of the *Federal Register* includes volume number and page, e.g., 54 FR 12345.

Code of Federal Regulations, 1938- . Annual. (AE2.106/3:)

The *Code of Federal Regulations* (CFR) contains the full text of all general and permanent regulations published in the *Federal Register*. The regulations listed are those in effect as of the date of the cover. The CFR is organized into fifty broad subjects or titles, e.g., Title 42 is Public Health. Titles are further broken down into chapters (generally corresponding to agencies), parts (covering specific regulatory areas) and sections. Sections contain the actual text of the regulations. The CFR is revised each year in quarterly segments.

Each title of the CFR begins with a brief description of content as well as a reference to and applicable redesignation or distribution tables. Each title, chapter and part of the CFR also begins with a Table of Contents which includes useful cross reference information to other titles and chapters. The authority citation which normally follows gives the legal basis, usually legislative or presidential, under which the regulation is issued. The accompanying source note refers back to the original publication in the *Federal Register*. If a section of the CFR is added or amended later, its source note is appended to that section.

Each volume of the CFR concludes with a List of CFR Sections Affected. Currently this List goes back to 1973. Earlier lists have been separately published as *Code of Federal Regulations List of Sections Affected*, 1949-1963 and *List of Sections Affected*, 1964-1972.[10] Use of these Lists and the various redesignation and distribution tables enables one to track the development of any portion of the CFR over time

Title 3 of the CFR is reserved for an annual compilation of Presidential documents, e.g., proclamations and executive orders, as well as a codification of regulations of the Executive Office of the President. Copies of Title 3 are often permanently retained for reference.[11]

The CFR is typically cited by title, part and section number. More complete citations include the date of the CFR edition as well, e.g., 42 CFR 235.10 (1988).

Differences Between the **Federal Register** *and* **CFR**

While both the *Federal Register* and the *Code of Federal Regulations* contain the text of final regulations there are important differences between the two. Briefly summarized the major differences are:

- The *Federal Register* also contains the text of proposed rules and explanatory information as well as other types of material. The CFR contains the text of final regulations only.
- The *Federal Register* contains the text of regulations as they are published. The CFR contains the text of all regulations in effect *regardless* of the date of publication.
- The CFR is used to find regulations currently in effect on specific topics. The *Federal Register* is used to keep abreast of current and proposed regulations and to update the CFR.

Finding Aids

The following are publications of the Office of the Federal Register unless otherwise indicated:

Federal Register Index. Included with the *Federal Register*, 1936- . Monthly. (AE2.106:)

The official index to the *Federal Register* is the monthly, cumulative *Federal Register Index*. The *Index* provides mainly an agency approach to regulations. Under the name of the agency, entries are arranged by category, e.g., "rules," "proposed rules." Cross references are to other agency names. Since entries contain only limited subject detail, users must frequently resort to multiple "look ups" to locate the specific information they are seeking. The *Federal Register Index* also includes a Guide to Freedom of Information Indexes which is published on a quarterly basis. This Guide lists agency indexes to various information resources that are available for inspection or copying. A typical listing is the National Science Foundation's (NSF) reviewer panelist list which contains the name, state, and institution of individuals who have reviewed NSF proposals.

CIS Federal Register Index, Bethesda, MD: Congressional Information Service, 1984- . Weekly.

The *CIS Federal Register Index* (FRI) is extremely timely, with weekly, monthly, quarterly and semi-annual cumulations. The *Index* is mailed on Friday, one week after the last *Federal Register* issue covered. Access is by a wide variety of subject terms (with liberal cross references), program names, popular names of authorizing legislation, proper names of geographical entities, individuals, companies, and products as well as responsible federal agencies. Specialized indexes allow searching by CFR section numbers and agency docket numbers. There is also a Calendar of Effective Dates and Comment Deadlines for Recent and Pending Regulations in the weekly and monthly issues. A typical entry includes a brief description, issuing agency, date, document type, and *Federal Register* page citation. Only notices of selected agency meetings are excluded from FRI's comprehensive coverage.

Federal Index. Gaithersburg, MD: National Standards Association. vol. 1. 1976/77- . Monthly.

The National Standards *Federal Index* is a monthly index (with annual cumulations) to the *Federal Register*, the *Congressional Record*, and the *Weekly Compilation of Presidential Documents*. While the *Federal Index* does provide subject as well as agency access to the *Register* it is less timely than either of the two indexes cited above and the subject coverage does not approach that offered by the CIS product.

CFR Index and Finding Aids. Annual. (AE2 . 106/3-2:)

The official *CFR Index and Finding Aids* is revised annually as of January 1st. Its major components are a subject/agency index, a list of agency-prepared indexes that appear throughout the CFR, a tables section which refers to laws or presidential documents which are cited in the CFR as legal authority for regulations, a list of laws which require agencies to publish documents in the *Federal Register*, a list of CFR titles and contents, and finally, an alphabetical list of agencies which appear in the CFR with reference to where their regulations may be found.

For most users the important portion of the official *Index* is the subject/agency index which is based on the "Federal Register Thesaurus of Indexing Terms" last published in the *Federal Register* in 1983.[12] Entries in the subject/agency index refer users to CFR titles and parts. Since the *CFR Index* covers regulations in effect as of January 1st each year but the CFR itself is reviewed in quarterly segments it is occasionally possible to find citations to material which does not appear in the latest CFR volumes for that title. In such cases it is necessary to use the *List of CFR Sections Affected* described below to locate the regulations in the *Federal Register*.

The next most useful portions of the *Index* are the authority tables. These tables refer back to the rule making authority for CFR regulations and are based on the authority citations found in the CFR text. Generally reference is to the *United States Code* but where that is unavailable, citations are given to the *Statutes at Large* or individual Public Laws. Presidential documents such as executive orders are also listed when they are cited as the legal basis for rulemaking. It is the responsibility of federal agencies to keep the authorities portion of the CFR current and accurate, so the tables portion should be approached with some caution. The authorities tables are updated in each month's *List of CFR Sections Affected* described below.

Index to the Code of Federal Regulations. Bethesda, MD: Congressional Information Service, 1977/79- . Annual.

While the official *CFR Index* is superior to the official *Federal Register Index* it is still a limited means of access to regulations. In 1980 the situation improved considerably with publication of *Index to the Code of Federal Regulations*, 1977-1979, now produced annually by the Congressional Information Service. The superior access provided by the CIS product is apparent from its size alone: the 1987 Subject/Agency Index of the official *CFR Index* totalled 736 pages; the *CIS Index* provided 3782 pages of Subject Index to the same material. The *CIS Index* uses a controlled vocabulary with numerous cross references to broader, narrower and related terms. Ambiguous vocabulary and indexing practices are clarified through copious scope notes. Public Laws are cited when they are mentioned in the CFR text and are referenced by name versus number.

The basic CIS Subject Index is supplemented by a Geographic Index and a Geographic Proper Names Index. These specialized indexes provide easy access to regulations which deal only with specific political entities or areas, e.g., Florida, Cuba, Yellowstone National Park, etc. Regulations which deal more generally with states, foreign countries or national parks are covered by the general Subject Index. Entries in all indexes refer to CFR title, chapter and part as well as to the headers used in the CIS microfiche version of the CFR.

List of CFR Sections Affected. Monthly. (AE2.106/2:)

Since the *Code of Federal Regulations* is updated only annually and regulations change so frequently, it is necessary for users to search through the *Federal Register* for possible revisions to the CFR sections they are using. The monthly *List of CFR Sections Affected* (LSA) is intended for this purpose. Arrangement is by CFR title, chapter part and section, and reference is given to *Federal Register* pages which contain changes in final rules. Proposed rules are listed at the end of each title and should not be overlooked.

The monthly LSA cumulates throughout the year but since 1973 there has been no single annual issue. Instead the various titles are cumulated annually in scheduled monthly issues, e.g., the December LSA is the annual cumulation for CFR Titles 1-16. Use of the LSA requires a careful check of the Table of Contents page to learn the dates of coverage of the monthly issues for various CFR titles. For example if one is updating 1 CFR (1988) through May 31, 1989, it would be necessary to (1) check the exact date (January 1, 1988) of the Title 1 CFR volume to be updated, (2) check the exact dates (January 3—May 31, 1989) for Title 1 in the May 1989 LSA and, (3) since there is a gap in dates of coverage, consult the December 1988 LSA which contains the 1988 annual cumulations for Title 1 to fill in the missing time period.

Another important function of the LSA is the revisions to Table I, "Parallel Table of Authorities and Rules" that it provides. This section cumulates throughout the year and updates the similar Table found in the annual *CFR Index*.

The *CIS Federal Register Index* has a section, "List by CFR Section Numbers" which is similar in function to the LSA. As with the LSA itself it is important to check the dates of coverage of each issue to make sure all changes to the various titles of the CFR have been discovered.

ELECTRONIC ACCESS

Electronic access to the *Federal Register* is available through several systems. The National Standards Association's Federal Register Abstracts database is updated weekly and covers the *Federal Register* back to 1977. It is available through both Dialog (File 136) and Orbit (FedReg). The

Federal Index is also available on Dialog (File 20). Finally, both LEXIS and WESTLAW provide electronic access to the *Federal Register* from 1980 to the present. Electronic access to the *Code of Federal Regulations* is available through LEXIS from 1981 and through WESTLAW from the 1984 edition. A CD-Rom version of the *Federal Register* and the *Code of Federal Regulations* is available from Video Laser Systems (VLS) in Toledo, Ohio. The CD-Rom product allows key word searching using TMS OPTEXT Research and Retrieval software.

SAMPLE RESEARCH PROBLEMS

Most federal regulatory research falls into one of several areas:

Problem: Finding more about a new proposed or final rule mentioned in the news.
Approach: If it is a very recent regulation, scan the Table of Contents section of the latest *Federal Registers* to locate the text and various explanatory information. If it is somewhat older, use one of the *Federal Register* indexes. Although the official *Federal Register Index* runs one-to-two months behind, the *CIS Federal Register Index* is quite up-to-date, running only a week to ten days behind the *Register*. Electronic indexes may also be used but be careful of dates of coverage. Once a proposed or final rule is located one can contact the official agency person mentioned for further information. It is also possible to contact the Office of Information and Regulatory Affairs (OIRA) of the Office of Management and, Budget, to get copies of agency drafts and OIRA comments.[13]

Problem: Finding regulations in effect on a certain topic.
Approach: Use the official *CFR Index, CIS Index to the Code of Federal Regulations*, or an electronic CFR index to locate appropriate CFR title and part. Update the regulations by using the *List of CFR Sections Affected* and the appropriate Readers Aids sections of recent *Federal Registers*. Remember to check the dates of coverage to make sure that no time periods have been missed. Regulations should be updated through the most current issue of the *Federal Register*.

Problem: Finding regulations issued to implement a specific law.
Approach: Use Table 1, "Parellel Table of Authorities and Rules," in the official *CFR Index* and update with the revisions to Table 1 which are found in the *List of Sections Affected*. Search under U.S.

Code citation as well as public law number. A supplemental check may also be made under the Public Law name in the *CIS Index to the Code of Federal Regulations*; this step does not take the place of using the "Parallel Tables" however.[14] Update further by using the *CIS Federal Register Index* and scanning the Table of Contents of the most recent *Federal Registers*. Unfortunately, neither source has a specific Table of Authorities section and so a check must be made under agency name or subject. Remember to be careful of time periods covered. Remember also that the various tables are not completely reliable and so searching the various CFR indexes under subject may also be necessary.

Problem: Understanding the intent of a regulation found in the *Code of Federal Regulations*.
Approach: Go back to the *Federal Register* using the citation found in the CFR source notes and read some of the accompanying material. If necessary go all the way back to the original proposed rule, normally referenced in the regulation's Supplementary Information section in the *Federal Register*. Contact agency personnel listed or OIRA personnel for further information if necessary.

Problem: Keeping up-to-date on an agency's future regulatory plans.
Approach: Use the *Federal Regulatory Directory* to get background information if needed. Check the latest edition of the annual *Regulatory Program of the United States Government* to learn what significant rulemaking activities the agency has planned. Follow up by checking the Uniform Calendar of Federal Regulations for a more complete although less descriptive list of the agency's plans. If there is something of interest, write or call the agency contact given for additional information. The Uniform Calendar appears in the *Federal Register* in April and October. Frequently, other government publications such as Congressional hearings can also be helpful in anticipating an agency's regulatory plans.

REFERENCES

1. Senator Leahy is quoted in Coleman, Barbara. *Through the Corriders of Power. A Citizen's Guide to Federal Rulemaking*. Washington, D.C.: OMB Watch. 1987, p. 9.

2. U.S. Congress. House. Committee on the Judiciary. *Publication of Gov-*

ernmental Rules and Regulations, Report to Accompany H.R. 6323. H. Rept. 74-280. Washington, D.C.: G.P.O., 1935. p. 1. (Serial Set 9886)

3. The embarrassing court case which provided the impetus for developing the *Federal Register* was Panama Refining Company v. Ryan (293 U.S. 388.

4. U.S. Office of Management and Budget. *Regulatory Program of the United States Government*. Washington, D.C., G.P.O., 1985- . (PrEx2.30:)

5. 53 FR 13604

6. U.S. Office of Management and Budget. *Information Collection Budget pf the United States Government*. Washington, D.C.: G.P.O., 1981/82- . (PrEx 2.29:)

7. U.S. Office of the Federal Register. *Document Drafting Book*. Washington, D.C.: G.P.O., 1986 (AE2.108:D65) provides insights into how agencies prepare regulatory documents.

8. U.S. Congress. Senate. Committee on Government Operations. *Study on Federal Regulations*. Committee Print. 95th Congress. 1st Session. Washington, D.C.: G.P.O., 1977, vol. 1, VIII.

9. Privacy Act documents are compiled annually in U.S. Office of the Federal Register. *Privacy Act Issuances*. Washington, D.C.: G.P.O., 1976- . (GS4.107/a:P939/2 and AE2.106/4:)

10. U.S. Office of the Federal Register. *Code of Federal Regulations. List of Sections Affected*, 1949-1963. Washington, D.C.: G.P.O., 1966 (GS 4.108:list/949-63) and *Code of Federal Regulations. List of CFR Sections Affected* 1964-1972. Washington, D.C.: G.P.O., 1980. 2 vol. (GS 4.108:list/964-72).

11. Presidential documents have been codified in U.S. President. *Codification of Presidential Proclamations and Executive Orders*. April 13, 1945-January 20, 1989. Washington. D.C.: Office of the Federal Register, 1989. (AE2.113:945-89)

12. 48 FR 27646-27672

13. For a helpful overview of how to keep informed and participate in agency regulatory activity see Coleman, pp. 81-95.

14. Unlike the "Parallel Tables" which are compiled from CFR authority notes, the CIS Index is restricted to names of laws mentioned in the CFR text.

Government Publications in Academic Science and Technology Libraries

Sarojini Balachandran

SUMMARY. There is a significant volume of scientific and technical documents, as opposed to report literature, available from federal and state government agencies. There is also a considerable number of government journals in the sciences containing research related information. Yet, there are not many studies available in library literature about the value of such materials to and their use by academic science and technology faculty in their teaching or research. The few surveys which have been conducted in the past point towards a low or minimal use of these documents. This, however, is not enough evidence to justify a generalization that scientific and technical documents fall under the low use category in academic libraries. Assuming that this is so, one needs to find out whether any programs like SDI by subject bibliographers can be instituted to augment user awareness. The article raises some pertinent questions relating to this topic, such as, how academic scientists become aware of the existence of these documents, what is their utility in academic teaching and research, how has the online and ondisc technology affected their use and finally, whether the publishing habits of academic scientists and technologists have any bearing on the library use patterns of these documents.

This article is devoted to raising some questions about the use in academic science and technology libraries of government publications as opposed to what are generically described as technical/report literature, regardless of whether such documents have been issued by federal or state governments. In spite of the volume of scientific and technical literature

Sarojini Balachandran is Head, Department of Science and Technology, Auburn University, Ralph Brown Draughon Library, Auburn, AL 36849-5606.

© 1991 by The Haworth Press, Inc. All rights reserved.

published through government agencies, one is hard pressed to find in library literature many studies relating to their use by academic scientists. Occasionally one finds references to use of documents by academic engineers and physicists such as the survey conducted at the University of Nebraska-Lincoln by Peter Hernon and Sara Lou Williams.[1] Here too, the document use patterns of scientists was part of an overall investigation of such use by all academic faculty. The Nebraska survey found that almost two thirds of the science faculty who responded had never used documents either for research or for teaching.

The use of government publications, on the other hand, by businessmen, economists and social scientists has been well documented.[2] One always comes across numerous instances of how, businessmen use the publications of the U.S. Department of Commerce relating to international trade, how economists use publications from the U.S. Bureau of Labor Statistics relating to employment, income, wages and prices, and how social scientists use a variety of statistical data available through the U.S. Bureau of the Census. All this, inspite of the fact that, in these fields, government is not the predominant publisher and that it has to share this distinction with private organizations like market research agencies, which collect and disseminate analogous information.

SCIENTIFIC AND TECHNICAL DOCUMENTS

The situation is more or less opposite in the field of science and technology, where government is acknowledged to be a major producer and contributor of research information. In the second edition of her comprehensive *Scientific and Technical Information Sources*,[3] Professor Ching-Chih Chen makes references to governmental organizations and contractors and their numerous publications, intended for use by scientists, engineers and other allied professionals. In fact, many of the agencies like the U.S. Department of Agriculture and U.S. National Aeronautics and Space Administration and "other respective parallel agencies are all major producers of scientific and technical research literature. Many of the significant indexing and abstracting tools in the field of science and technology are products of government agencies. . . . Although access to such information is generally considered a complex matter, there are numerous bibliographic tools that provide control over and access to unclassified and general government information."[4]

It has been conservatively estimated[5] that about 65 percent of the approximately 14,000 titles in the GPO sales program are scientific or technical in nature, with the percentage being even higher for the depository library program. It is pertinent, therefore, to question how many of these publications are used by academic science and technology professionals, how they become aware of their existence, how they are accessed and how important such publications are in their research and teaching and can some system be devised to improve and increase their use.

As indicated earlier, this article mainly deals with government documents in science and technology, as opposed to technical/report literature distributed through agencies like the National Technical Information Service. There are numerous articles relating to the use of materials in the latter category.[6] If the volume of scientific and technical documents belonging to the former category were not significant, one need not be concerned about issues relating to their use, utility, cost, bibliographic control and access. This, however, is not the case. Professor Chen's book cited earlier devotes an entire chapter just on government reference tools dealing with scientific and technical documents.[7] Other useful guides such as *A Guide to U.S. Government, Scientific and Technical Resources*[8] by Alluri and Robinson testify to the voluminous nature of such literature. Schwarzkopf, in his *Government Reference Serials*,[9] identifies and annotates numerous science and technology publications from federal agencies in the area of agriculture, biological sciences, computer science and data processing, telecommunications, earth and environmental sciences, energy, health and medicine, space science, oceanography and transportation. If one includes other non-reference type monographic and serial publications in science and technology from federal agencies, one will have no hesitation in concluding that there is a significant body of government literature in scientific areas whose use patterns in academic libraries may raise interesting issues.

GOVERNMENT SCIENCE JOURNALS

According to conventional wisdom, journal of periodical-type publications are more important in the area of science and technology, even as monographic or book-type publications are important in the field of humanities and social sciences. Significant results of scientific and technical research are published as articles in journals issued by federal agencies. The most recent government serials price list includes quite a number of scientific and technical periodicals. In a recent article entitled *A Checklist of Indexed Federal Periodicals*,[10] Gilligan and Hajdas examine the indexing access to periodicals. Beginning with a list of nearly 700 periodicals, the authors narrow the number down to 209. In this sample, government journals relating to science and technology amounted to nearly 30 percent, demonstrating the fact that the volume of scientific and technical research published through government journals is considerable. Yannarella and Alluri, in their compilation on *U.S. Government Scientific and Technical Periodicals*[11] have identified over 260 scientific journals containing research information. Problems relating to their selection and indexing coverage have been quite adequately dealt with in the library literature. It is understood that if these periodicals do not get much use, it is not because of a lack of indexing access. The questions relating to the nature and frequency of library use of these journals by academic scientists and the value and the utility of research related information available in these sources as compared to scholarly journals published by non-governmental institutions have not been analyzed significantly. Do they get substantial use in academic science and technology libraries? If not, why not? How do users get to know of their availability? Can efforts like SDI increase their use substantially?

STATE GOVERNMENT PUBLICATIONS

In addition to scientific and technical documents available through GPO or distributed directly by government agencies, state governments too publish a considerable volume of scientific and technical literature. One only has to glance through the subject index section of the *Monthly Checklist of State Government Publications* and the *State Publications Index* to realize how much scientific and technical research information is available in the state government documents, especially in the areas of agriculture, animal science, environment, geology, forestry and hydrology, to name only a few. In a recent study, Ford and Nakata examined the reference use of state government information in academic libraries.[12] Their survey found that the average use of state government publications by the teaching faculty was lower than that of graduate and undergraduate students, but higher than other categories of users such as college and university administrators, state and local government officials, business persons and other community patrons. It is not known from the survey what percent of the faculty use came from the science and technology department. It is interesting to learn from the survey that agricultural information, which was the only category closest to the sciences, received the lowest average points for use in reference situations. One wonders whether this low use indicator is due to a lack of awareness of the wealth of scientific information available in state government publications. It may also be that academic scientific and technical professionals have their own source of access to such information, other than conventional library channels. Or, maybe, such information is not very relevant to their research or teaching needs. It is important to find a satisfactory answer to these questions, especially in view of the recent trend towards transferring many of the federally-met obligations to the shoulders of the state governments, whose publication efforts may increase significantly because of this.

REPORT LITERATURE

Reference has been made earlier in this article about the existence of numerous articles on the use of technical/report literature, which by and large, constitute a major portion of federal government output in the area of science and technology. Saul and Mary Herner estimate[13] conservatively that the annual production of all unclassified U.S. government research literature, which in 1960 amounted to approximately 100,000 has currently increased by about 20 to 40 percent. Some of this research gets published ultimately in the form of conventional journal articles. It is said that this happens more in subject areas like nuclear science and technology, earth sciences, oceanography, biological sciences and medicine and less in areas like aeronautics, agriculture, energy, mathematics, missile technology and space science. While technical/report literature has quite a significant impact on academic and corporate scientific and technological research, it still suffers from quite a number of perceived inadequacies. Lack of professional evaluation by peers before the publication of these reports tends to diminish their value or utility in the eyes of some scientists. It is also said that some of the really significant scientific and technological findings are not included in many reports because their authors wish to maintain proprietory control over such information.

Many academic libraries do not acquire technical/report literature as a matter of course because of problems relating to cost, bibliographic control and access. All these issues affect the use of such literature in academic science and technology libraries. The question which comes to one's mind in this context is how much of these problems affecting the use of report literature are also common to scientific and technical government documents. As an added inconvenience, much of the report literature is available only on microformat, which often scares users in academic libraries, given the state of inadequate availability and poor maintenance of equipment relating to micro-readers and printers. Given also the recent trend to make available many GPO imprints only on a microformat, one wonders how much has this affected the acquisition and use of scientific and technical documents in academic libraries.

ONLINE TECHNOLOGIES

Reference has been made earlier about the availability of numerous abstracting and indexing services such as the *Energy Research Abstracts, U.S. Government Reports and Announcements Index, INIS Atomindex, Monthly Catalog of U.S. Government Publications Index*, National Regulatory Commission's *NRC Regulatory* and *Technical Reports, Scientific and Technical Aerospace Reports, Selected Water Resources Abstracts* and Defense Technical Information Center's *Technical Abstract Bulletin* and *Technical Abstract Bulletin Index*. The inconvenience, however, of identifying scientific and technical reports and documents has not been completely eliminated, mainly due to the time it takes to sift through these paper based resources. The on set of online and on-disc databases is said to have had a far-reaching impact in so far as it has decreased or virtually eliminated the time consuming aspect of any search.[14] For example, the recent availability of patent information on CD-ROM from the U.S. Patent Office in designated libraries has enormously increased the number of users of this material. Until a few years ago, the online databases were merely bibliographic in nature. The later development of many textual and numeric databases from federally funded programs like those available from the National Nuclear Data Center, National Library of Medicine, National Institute for Science and Technology and the National Agriculture Library's Text Digitization Project have accentuated and advanced the use of non-bibliographic materials quite significantly.[15] The question is how these developments have influenced, if at all, the use of government documents in science and technology libraries. An interesting example of digital technology being applied to augment the use of library materials is the Virginia Cooperative Extension Service's Public Information Systems Project.[16] Under this, an inter-active Video, tied to a microcomputer and CD-ROM is used in selected rural and urban shopping centers and library locations to access a variety of documents issued by the extension service relating to horticulture, health and nutrition. If successful, it is likely to be adapted by all land-grant universities whose extension services publish a variety of general science materials for use by the public.

LOCATION OF DOCUMENTS

The location and arrangement of library materials have a definite impact on their use. Government documents have been classified and arranged in libraries in a variety of ways. Some have used the sudoc classification and kept these documents in a separate section or division, quite distinct from other departments like the sciences, social sciences and humanities. Others have used the Dewey decimal system and interfiled documents with other library materials. If the academic scientists have to go to one section of the library for using government documents and another section for using non-governmental material, this is obviously an inconvenience. Finding the documents in the library's card catalog or online catalog may not necessarily be as easy as finding a monograph under an author/title search. It would be interesting to examine how these problems affect the use of documents in science and technology libraries. An argument has often been made in the past that the low or infrequent use of library materials by academic scientists was due to the fact that their research interests are so narrow or specific in nature. Whatever information they needed to pursue their special research was available to them through personal journal subscriptions, specialized mailing lists for preprints and reprints or through personal contacts within a narrow circle of peers. Hence they had neither the need for nor the time it took to obtain library information. This situation has changed drastically in recent years with the increasingly interdisciplinary nature of scientific research itself. Because of this development, for example, more engineers are looking for medical information in libraries to pursue their research in biotechnology. Information on materials engineering is required not only by engineers but also by physicists and others. This has had an impact on the use of science materials in academic libraries. The question is whether this trend has also effected the use patterns of science and technology documents in academic libraries.

PUBLISHING HABITS

It has been pointed out that the publishing habits of scientists are different from those of technologists.[17] While the scientist must publish in order to make a proprietory claim to his or her discoveries, the intent of a technologist is said to be not publication but the production of an artifact or creation of a process.[18] According to this view, a scientist produces material for use by a technologist, who then produces a process or an artifact.

The publication process for a scientist is mainly said to be a communication among a select group of peers in the field, while the technologist has a different audience, mostly a government agency. A scientist is therefore interested in the publication of a journal article, whereas a technical report is the primary means of communication for a technologist. For both the scientist as well as the technologist, a monograph is the least desirable means of communication because of the time it entails to produce the same, the time which is better spent on doing actual research. Do these distinctions and characteristics relating to the publishing habits of academic scientists and technologists have any bearing on the library use by them of available research literature, especially government documents, some of which are quite lengthy in nature?

CONCLUSION

To briefly summarize some of the questions raised in the foregoing: given the fact that the volume of government documents relating to science and technology (as distinct from technical/report literature) is significant, how do academic scientists and technologists use them, if at all? Is the suggestion put forward by one writer that such use is only marginal to be taken as accurate?[19] The experience of one medium sized college library would seem to indicate that it is so.[20] Can such an isolated experience be extrapolated to make it applicable to all academic libraries? Assuming the contrary that scientists and technologists do use government documents in academic libraries, what is the nature and frequency of their use? How do they become aware of what is available? What is their opinion as to the value or utility of such materials in their research and teaching? Would a sustained program of SDI by subject bibliographers result in the enhanced use of these documents? This writer's informal contacts with the science faculty who normally use the library indicated that most of them were not aware of what was available and showed some interest in learning about them through SDI. Some faculty did not feel a need for the documents while a few others were on selective mailing lists of government agencies. Use also depended on their area of research, for instance geologists and engineers used documents more than other groups in the science area. Some of this conforms to the findings in the Nebraska survey. However, more such surveys and additional evidence are needed to answer the questions posed here. The answers must be obtained first before any rational collection development programs relating to scientific and technical documents can be set in place, especially in the context of non depository libraries.

REFERENCES

1. Peter Hernon and Sara Lou Williams. "University Faculty and Federal Documents: Use Patterns." *Government Publications Review*, Vol.3 (1976), 93-108.

2. Peter Hernon. *Use of Government Publications by Social Scientists*. Norwood, N.J., Ablex Publishing. 1979 see also, Judith Rowe, "Expanding Social Science Reference Service to meet the Needs of Patrons More Adequately," *Library Trends*, Vol.30 (Winter 1982), 333.

3. Ching-Chih Chen. *Scientific and Technical Information Sources*. 2d ed. Cambridge, MA, MIT Press, 1987.

4. id. at 595-6.

5. Testimony of Ralph E. Kennickell, Public Printer of the United States before the U.S. House Committee on Science, Space and Technology, Washington D.C. July 15, 1987. P.5. (cited in *Government Information Quarterly*, Vol.5: no. *1* (1988), p. 43.

6. For an excellent summary of the use of technical report literature by the R & D Community, the manner in which the literature assists the community and an assessment of their value see, Charles R. McClure, "The Federal Technical Report Literature," *Government Information Quarterly*, Vol.5: no *1* (1988) 27-44.

7. Ching-Chih Chen, supra at 591-601.

8. Rao Alluri and Judith Robinson *A Guide to U.S. Government Scientific and Technical Resources*. Littleton, CO, Libraries Unlimited, 1983.

9. LeRoy C. Schwarzkopf. *Government Reference Serials* Englewood, CO, Libraries Unlimited, 1988. 149-231.

10. Judith Gilligan and Susan Hajdas. "A Checklist of Indexed Federal Periodicals." *Government Publications Review*, Vol. 13 (1986), 507-518.

11. Phillip A. Yannarella and Rao Alluri, Comp. *U.S. Government Scientific and Technical Periodicals*. Metuchen, N.J. Scarecrow Press, 1976.

12. Barbara J. Ford and Yuri Nakata. "Reference Use of State Government Information in Academic Libraries," *Government Publications Review*, Vol. 10 (1983), 189-199.

13. Saul Herner and Mary Herner. "The Unpublished Government Research Report," *Government Publications Review* Vol. 13 (1986), 97-104.

14. For a list of these databases, see, Diane Garner and Diane Smith, "Government Databases: A Sampler," *Government Publications Review*, Vol. 12 (1985), 143-154.

15. Ferne C. Allan and Wanda R. Ferrell, "Numeric Databases in Science and Technology," *Databases*, (June 1989), 50-58.

16. For more information on this project, see Mary Miller and Laurie Ruberg "Using Technology to Enhance Information Delivery: The Public Information System and Virginia's First Compact Disc," a paper presented at the conference of Southern Regional Extension Directors and Administrators, Jackson, MS, Sept. 13 1988.

17. Nan Lin, "A comparison between the Scientific Communication Model and the Mass Communication Model," *IEEE Transactions on Professional Communication*, Vol. PC15 (1972). 34-39.

18. C.D. Hurt. *Information Sources in Science and Technology*. Englewood, CO, Libraries Unlimited 1988. p.xi.

19. Terry Weech, "Use of Government Publication: A Selected Review of Literature," *Government Publications Review*, Vol.5: no *2* (1978). 177-184.

20. David W. Parish, "Utilization of a Government Publications Collection," *Government Publications Review*, Vol.5:no *2* (1978). 185-188.

Patents: Resources of Technical Information and Source of Library Service Opportunities

John H. Sulzer
Robert F. Rose

SUMMARY. Patents are invaluable sources of technological information, of importance not only to inventors, but also to the processes of economic development and technology transfer. Researching patents is an excellent means of tracking a business competitor, forecasting technological innovation, learning how to make and use a device or process, and finding answers to specific technical problems. Nevertheless, patents are under-used as sources of technical information. Many libraries, including the libraries of Penn State University, have established outreach programs to overcome that low use. Through the provision of such programs, libraries have the potential to be key players in the development of closer ties among universities, industries, and individual entrepreneurs. Locating patent information may not be an easy task, but it is not as complicated as many think. The development of computerized information systems has simplified the search process. Reference librarians, even non-documents librarians, can be of enormous assistance in leading researchers to patent information. However, they must be even more aware than usual of the need for confidentiality when providing patent reference service.

John H. Sulzer is Associate Documents Librarian, The Pennsylvania State University Libraries, C207 Pattee Library, University Park, PA 16802. Robert F. Rose is Head Librarian, Behrend College Library, The Pennsylvania State University at Erie Station Road, Erie, PA 16563-0902.

© 1991 by The Haworth Press, Inc. All rights reserved.

INTRODUCTION

In the United States, an inventor may be issued a patent for a period of seventeen years in exchange for publicly disclosing all of the details of the invention or process. When issued, a patent provides its owner with the right to exclude others from making or using the invention. The reason for this policy is simple. It encourages technological development by compiling a database of knowledge which will inspire and support further innovation. It is the disclosure of the details of the invention and the references to related technology which makes patent information so important to the researcher and engineer. Practically every industrialized nation in the world issues patents for the purpose of protecting its inventors and products, and to strengthen and expand its technological database.[1]

Business and industry in the United States today is increasingly competitive and faces growing challenges from abroad. In order to function profitably in our modern world economy, independent inventors, small business people, researchers at academic institutions, or scientists employed in industry, as well as the top corporations in the country, need to be aware of the vast collection of technical information available in patents.

THE IMPORTANCE OF PATENTS

In his volume on *Searching Patent Documents; For Patentability and Information*, Fred K. Carr points out that, "Many believe . . . patent literature has in recent years replaced the conventional scientific and trade journals as the most up-to-date source of information on technical progress in a number of areas of technology.[2] In fact, it has been estimated that 80 percent of the information contained in patents is not reported elsewhere in the technical literature.[3]

This is due to a number of reasons. Primary among these is that United States patent law requires that an invention may not have been described in a "printed publication" more than one year prior to application for a patent. Consequently, few inventors publish anything until they have been granted a patent. The need for protection is often seen to take precedence over dissemination of the information in professional publications, especially when potential profits are involved. Therefore, researching patents is an excellent means of discovering where a business or industrial competitor is concentrating research and development activity, and to forecast technological innovation.[4] Many consider patents of value only to scientists and technical researchers, "yet, to ignore totally the patent files is to overlook a potentially valuable source of competitor information."[5]

The most important characteristic of a patent, unlike other forms of technical literature, is its detail and completeness. Rather than giving a description of a solution within the context of a broad technical area, a patent is designed to describe the invention or process, teach how to make and use it, and show the best method for making it.[6]

Nevertheless, patents often are not recognized nor used as sources of technical information. Most people see patents only as legal documents. They usually do not think about searching patent literature until they are considering applying for one. Innovation and productivity are more often a result of building on old ideas than they are a result of sheer ingenuity. Familiarity with patent resources is thus becoming more and more essential. American engineering and business are unlikely to exploit technology effectively if they become detached from the basic content of technology, and do not exploit the knowledge that is contained in patent documents.[7]

USES OF PATENT LITERATURE

Although there are many uses for patent literature, the most important type of patent search in terms of innovation, business research, and economic development is what is generally known as a "state of the art search." Jacob Rabinow, a former engineer at the National Bureau of Standards, and a prolific inventor himself, believes that inventors, engineers, and scientists must have a comprehensive knowledge of the technical "art" of their disciplines in order to successfully develop new products. Rabinow explains that one must develop a knowledge of the art such that one can tease out the right ideas for doing something innovative.[8]

Creativeness and innovation depend upon thorough training in a discipline, its principles, and the structure of its knowledge. This, after all, is the basic reason for systems of patent disclosure. They provide a bank of technical information which is intended for the use of educated scientists, engineers, and inventors who can take the old ideas and progress to something new. A few hours in a patent library may reveal a number of solutions to any technical problem and may provide just the component which is needed to make a new product or process work. In addition, most of this information is in the public domain and free to anyone who wants to use it.[9]

A "state of the art search" can lead researchers to new ideas with which to feed their own inventiveness, and can save them from re-inventing the wheel and spending a lot of money doing it.

PATENTS, PATENTABILITY, AND THE PATENT PROCESS

A patent issued in the United States is literally a piece of property which can be owned, sold, borrowed against, leased, or willed to an heir if the patentee is concerned about living less than 17 years. It carefully delineates proprietary rights to a piece of intellectual real estate. A patent, in the language of the statute (Title 35, *United States Code*, section 101), provides the owner with the right to exclude all others from "making, using, or selling" an invention without license or consent for a period of 17 years. Any person who "invents or discovers any new and useful machine, manufacture, or composition of matter, or any new and useful improvements thereof, may obtain a patent."[10]

Each patent issued in the US has a title, a discrete number, and date of issue. The first page of any patent gives the name of the inventor or patentee, the name of the assignee if that is not the inventor, the application number, and the date of application. Additional information on the first page includes the US Classifications and the International Classifications under which the patent is categorized; the classes and subclasses which the patent examiners checked in their search for prior art to determine patentability; references to the related US and foreign patent documents which the examiners reviewed; the names of the examiners; and an abstract of the patent description. The rest of the patent consists of a detailed drawing of the invention or graphic illustration of the process, a detailed literary description of how the invention is constructed and how it functions, and the exclusive property claims.

There are five basic types of patents: general utility patents; design, or patents covering the ornamental shape of a product; plant, or those protecting asexually reproduced vegetation; reissues to correct errors in original patent documents; and statutory invention registration, a means of protecting the use of an invention without claiming exclusive rights. Utility patents are the ones with which most people are familiar and are the most important to our purposes here. They are generally broken down into chemical, or patents on chemicals and chemical compounds; electrical, or patents on electronics and electrical apparatus; and mechanical, or patents covering all types of machines and tools. They may cover anything from toys to a genetically engineered mouse.

METHODS OF ACCESS

Locating the proper patent may not be an easy task, but it is not as complicated and arcane as it might seem on the surface. If one has some specific information about a particular patent such as the name of the inventor or assignee, or the number of the patent and its country of issue, locating the document is not difficult.

However, librarians and researchers should develop a basic familiarity with at least the US Patent Classification System (USPCS), which dates back to the early 1800's. The US system consists of approximately 400 different subject categories or classes, and over 144,000 individual subclasses of invention into which the over five million US utility and design patents are organized. Because the US Patent and Trademark Office attempts to hold the number of patents in a given subclass to 200 or fewer, the system requires constant revision, so finding the appropriate class and subclass is the trick to locating the right patents.[11]

The USPCS is organized according to "proximate" or essential function. Simply put, this means that things will be grouped together which perform similar functions by applying similar natural laws to similar substances. Consequently, a cement mixer and a washing machine may be grouped in the same class. The structure of the USPCS is hierarchical, with each class covering a general area of technology, such as "Optics" in Class 350, and each subclass a given type of invention, such as "Stereo-viewers" in subclass 133 under Class 350. Each class and subclass has a specific number which is assigned to all the patents relevant to that category.

The USPCS has five main search tools which are published by the US Patent and Trademark Office. The *Index of Classifications* serves as a general subject index to the Manual of Classifications. The latter is the printed outline of the functional and descriptive titles which make up the USPCS. The *Manual* is used to locate the proper classes of invention in the technological area in which patents are being sought. A third source used in conjunction with the first two is the *Classification Definitions.* This is a form of dictionary that gives more extensive descriptions of the classes and subclasses found in the *Manual*, and cross references to classes that have been added or changed.

Except when working in the Public Search Room of the US Patent and Trademark Office in Alexandria, VA, which is the only patent library in the country where the patent documents are arranged on shelves by classification numbers, a researcher must compile a list of individual patent numbers in order to locate the documents. This is done by consulting the US Patent and Trademark Office *Official Gazette*, a weekly bulletin giving abstracts of newly issued patents, and the *Index of Patents*, which is published annually.

Fortunately, there are a number of computer systems which provide automated access to patents, and make patent searching much faster and much more effective. Probably the most comprehensive and up to the minute system for U.S. patents is the database of the U.S. Patent and Trademark Office itself. The *Classification and Search Support Information System (CASSIS)* is basically an online version of the USPCS. The user can search by patent number; class and subclass number; or by keywords in the *Index of Classifications, Manual of Classifications*, or the abstracts of the patents themselves for about the current eighteen months. *CASSIS* does not provide full text searching of patents, nor does it print out abstracts of patents. However, it does provide complete lists of patent numbers back to the first patent issued in any classification, and can list off company names and titles for some patents in the database, although these fields are not searchable.

There is also a compact disk version of *CASSIS*. *CASSIS/CD-ROM* is available at all Patent Depository Libraries and can be subscribed to for $300 a year from the Patent and Trademark Office. The CD-ROM version of CASSIS is much more sophisticated than its online counterpart and eventually will replace it altogether. *CASSIS/CD-ROM* is updated monthly and provides Boolean searching by keywords in the patent abstracts for about the last two years and in the patent titles back to 1969. One can also search by class and subclass numbers back to the first patent issued in 1790, by patent assignee, and patent number, and limit a search by state or country of the inventor's residence and by the year of issue. Like its online cousin, the CD version also offers searching capability in the *Manual of Classifications*. Both versions of *CASSIS* can be used free of charge at Patent Depository Libraries.

In addition to *CASSIS*, there are a large number of commercial services which have patent coverage among their data files.[12] They are more powerful and sophisticated than CASSIS and can do many things CASSIS cannot. Most offer some form of keyword and free text searching of the various fields on the first page of a patent, searching by patentee and assignee, and some means of locating later patents that cite a particular earlier patent document. They all offer printoffs of patent abstracts or extensive bibliographic data. One system, *LEXPAT*, provides word searching and retrieval of the entire text of US patents issued since 1975. Foreign patents can also be traced through these sources and most have some form of document delivery service which provides printed copies of patent documents. The "trade-offs" of using these services are their cost and the limitations of their coverage. They are intended to save the searcher time, not money, and none of them cover all utility patents before 1950.

The seven online services available in the U.S. which cover general utility patents exclusively are:

CLAIMS/U.S. PATENT FILES. IFI/Plenum Data Coporation. Vendor: DIALOG.

INPADOC. International Patent Documentation Center. Vendors: Pergamon; DIALOG.

INPI. Institut National de la Propriete Industrielle. Vendor: Questel.

LEXPAT. Mead Data Central. Vendor: Mead Data Central.

PATSEARCH. Pergamon Infoline, Inc. Vendors: Pergamon; BRS.

USPA. Derwent, Inc. Vendor: SDC/Orbit.

WPI/WORLD PATENTS INDEX. Derwent, Inc. Vendors: DIALOG; SDC/Orbit; Questel.[13]

PATENT DEPOSITORY LIBRARIES

There are 65 Patent Depository Libraries (PDLs) now located in 41 states. These depository libraries are all located in major metropolitan areas, centers of research, or at academic institutions. They all receive the Patent and Trademark Office publications, manuals, and indexes mentioned above, all have at least 20 years of patent backfiles, and all offer free access to *CASSIS* and *CASSIS/CD-ROM*. Most of these libraries also provide online searching services using one or more of the commercial systems. Information on the patent depository libraries can be obtained from the PDL Program Office by calling or writing to the U.S. Patent and Trademark Office, Patent Depository Library Program.

In addition to the Patent Depository Libraries, about 500 Federal Depository Libraries throughout the country receive the PTO *Official Gazette*. Many of them also have the *Manual of Classifications* and other US patent searching tools. Most Federal Depository Libraries receive the *Directory of Patent Depository Libraries* published by the PTO/PDL Program Office, which gives the location for each of the 65 PDLs and specific information about their staffs, patent holdings, services, and policies.[14]

A complete description of foreign patent services is not possible here, but there are a number of sources for this information which are available in most Patent Depository Libraries, and in many larger academic and public libraries. Two of these which should prove to be particularly useful to librarians and researchers are the book by Fred Carr mentioned above, and *Patent Information and Documentation in Western Europe: An Inventory of Services Available to the Public*. Carr's book covers US as well as foreign patent information and provides detailed information about the major patent offices around the world. The second source, by the European Communities, is a handbook giving detailed information on the patent offices and public services of 17 European countries; plus those of the United States, the USSR, and Japan; and three international patent organizations; the European Patent Office, the World Intellectual Property Organization, and the International Patent Documentation Center.

OUTREACH FOR PATENT SERVICES

Although a treasure trove of information, patents are often overlooked or bypassed by traditional library users as well as those doing applied research. The general lack of knowledge of patent resources and their relative inaccessibility result in this low use.

By creating an awareness of patents and providing access to the information they contain, libraries play an important role in the process of economic development and technology transfer. They can also provide key assistance to independent inventors – a somewhat endangered species these days.[15] While assistance to independent inventors and small business people may be considered by many to be primarily the responsibility of public libraries, many academic libraries also can serve the general public, and frequently act as a conduit of technical information between the research lab and the small business.

Through the provision of patent and other information services, academic libraries have the potential to be key players in the development of closer ties between universities and industries. Universities such as Purdue have developed "industrial associates" programs to coordinate the development of such ties.[16] Other universities, like Penn State, have developed cooperative partnerships or engineering research centers,[17] and other general types of research partnerships.[18] Such cooperative arrangements have been designed to speed up technology transfer and utlimately to enhance the competitive posture of U.S. industry.

Technology transfer, stated simply, applies to the process of converting research results into products or services that are patented or covered by licensing agreements.[19] In other words, it is "the process of moving ideas to the marketplace."[20] Effective technology transfer depends at least in part upon a "favorable and uniformly applied federal patent policy."[21] It was not until 1980 that a law went into effect delineating such a policy.

That law allowed universities to own the patents and new technologies which result from government-funded research undertaken at those institutions. Universities, in turn, have developed strategies to encourage technology transfer to the private sector.[22]

The U.S. Patent and Trademark Office has been a prime mover in the area of patent outreach services. It sponsors the Patent Depository Library Program, provides workshops on accessing patent information, has created "Project XL," a program to encourage young people to develop their problem-solving skills and their ability to think inventively,[23] and it publishes *AD LIBS*, a newsletter distributed to patent depository libraries. The Patent Office also cooperates in holding national and regional creative and inventive thinking conferences. The creation and subsidy of CASSIS, and its subsequent CD-ROM application, and their distribution to patent depository libraries was a major step forward in terms of patent outreach and the dissemination of patent information.

Most Patent Depository Libraries have also developed outreach programs to encourage the use of their patent collections. Two of the more creative approaches to patent outreach have been implemented at the University of Texas at Austin, and the State Library of Oregon.

UT Austin became a patent depository in 1983. Within a short time, use of their patent services had created an almost overwhelming drain on their reference services. To alleviate the pressure, they began development of an expert system which was installed in 1987. Menu-driven, the system is designed "to interpret both the user's skill/knowledge level and the general nature of the individual's patent search problem."[24] It also instructs users about patent access information tools, helps them to identify appropriate classes and sub-classes, and, via a gateway to CASSIS, provides a list of relevant patent numbers.[25]

The State Library of Oregon created the Oregon Patent Affiliates Network in late 1987. The network includes four academic libraries and two public libraries in addition to the state library. The State Library of Oregon is the official patent depository library and it provides the staff training for the affiliates, all of which have purchased the needed patent access tools. Users from around the state are referred to the affiliate libraries where they identify the classes and sub-classes in which they are interested. They can then submit further search requests to the state library, which provides CASSIS searches. Originally, the network planned to provide direct access to the state library's CASSIS/CD-ROM via telecommunication links. While technically feasible, the system was very cumbersome. The advent of inexpensive CASSIS/CD-ROM subscriptions now permits affiliates to install that service at their individual locations.

Users are allowed up to 25 free patents per month, which are delivered by telefacsimile or mail. The network has proved to be an effective means of expanding patent services to local areas throughout the state. It has also proved to be helpful in promoting economic development in those locations.[26]

THE PENN STATE CONNECTION: A PRELIMINARY APPROACH

The Pennsylvania State University describes itself as "one university, geographically dispersed." In addition to its main campus at University Park, it has twenty-two campuses scattered across the state. Most of those campuses offer lower division courses only. However, The Behrend College in Erie is a four-year and graduate college, the Capital College, near Harrisburg, is an upper division and graduate college, and the Great Valley Campus in southeastern Pennsylvania offers graduate level courses only. Regardless of the location, Penn State's 63,000 students have ready access to the extensive holdings of the Penn State Libraries' system—including patents—through their branch libraries.

The main library of Penn State is located at University Park and is a patent depository library. Efforts to increase patent accessibility for both university and non-university users are still in the developmental stages, but a number of activities have been initiated to promote patent service and access. These include course-related instruction, a workshop offered jointly with the U.S. Patent Office PDL Program Office, and mini-workshops held at the Behrend College Library. Efforts are being made to speed up the completion of CASSIS searches for dispersed locations, particularly the Great Valley Campus, through the Penn State Libraries' FAXNET system which links all dispersed libraries via telefacsimile.

One of the more interesting developments in terms of patent outreach services has been ties with the Pennsylvania Inventors' Association. The PIA was created in 1987, in cooperation with The Behrend College, to provide support for inventors—both novice and experienced—interested in having their inventions patented. Although organized specifically to support inventors in Northwest Pennsylvania, it now has members from around the state.

In addition to offering mini-workshops to the PIA, the Libraries have provided considerable computer searching support to the group. Although free CASSIS searches are offered to group members, few PIA members have taken advantage of this service. Instead, they have searches conducted through DIALOG'S CLAIMS database, preferring the immediacy of searches done locally and the keyword capabilities of DIALOG. Searches for PIA members comprised more than 40 percent of the online searches completed at the Behrend College Library in 1987-1988 and 20 percent of the total searches conducted in 1988-1989.

Beyond the fact that this service has been so enthusiastically received by PIA members, certain aspects of the search service deserve special note. First, there are no librarians at the Behrend College Library considered "experts" at searching patent databases. While thorough knowledge of search system protocols is essential, it is not necessary to be a government information or science librarian to provide effective service to users. Second, all users of the service understand that this is not an "official" or comprehensive search. It is, essentially, a preliminary search that provides an overview of the patents which currently exist for similar inventions. Third, all patent searching is by key word rather than by patent class, again emphasizing the preliminary nature of the searching. Fourth, since the PIA is headquartered at a University location, the surcharge usually assessed off campus users is waived, thus reducing the total cost by a significant degree.

Users of this service generally are very satisfied. Word of mouth is sufficiently good that non-PIA community users frequently inquire about the service. Those users are referred to the PIA for membership so they can enjoy the same discount cost structure as PIA members. Users have come from many areas of north central and northwest Pennsylvania and have even come from out-of-state to have patent searches run.

ETHICAL AND LEGAL CONSIDERATIONS

Confidentiality is an absolute necessity in the provision of patent reference service. Inventors trying to find out if their ideas are patentable may be reluctant to reveal to the reference librarian what those ideas are. Librarians should be aware that they may have to assure such users that their ideas will not be discussed outside the reference interview before they can even begin to provide the reference service.

Librarians must also be extremely careful that they do not proffer advice to the prospective patentee as to the likelihood of the idea being patentable. They can, and should, be able to inform users about the patent process and how to access the information provided in patents, and they should be able to assist users in finding that information. They must, however, be sure the user realizes that their assistance does not constitute an "official" or final patent search. This is especially important when dealing with novice inventors who frequently find the patent process confusing.

Although reference librarians, even non-documents librarians, can be of enormous assistance to patent researchers, their services are not a substitute for the advice of a good patent attorney. Although not a legal requirement, it is important to seek the advice of a patent agent of attorney when applying for a patent. Most applications are rejected on the first try because of the wording of the exclusive claims. An experienced patent attorney can help construct claims language which will be less likely to be rejected and more likely to protect the patent from being challenged or declared invalid after it is granted. Patent attorneys and agents throughout the country are listed in *Attorneys and Agents Registered to Practice Before the US Patent and Trademark Office* published by the US Patent and Trademark Office, and available in all patent depository libraries and many federal depository libraries.

REFERENCES

1. Sulzer, John H. "Patents: Literature for Competitive Ideas, Technology Innovation, Improvement of Productivity and Intellectual Protection." Paper presented at 42nd Meeting, Mechanical Failures Prevention Group, *Symposium on Technology Innovation – Key to International Competitiveness*, National Bureau of Standards, Gaithersburg, Maryland, September 15, 1987. Parts of this article are adapted and revised from the September 15, 1987, oral presentation.

2. Carr, Fred K. *Searching Patent Documents; for Patentability and Information*. Chapel Hill: Information, Inc., 1982, p.387.

3. Terragno, P. James. "Patents as Technical Literature." *IEEE Transactions on Professional Communication* PC-22:2, June 1979, p. 101. At a DIALOG sponsored workshop on INPADOC in Pittsburgh (June 1, 1989), DIALOG Senior Regional Representative Leslie Douglas reported similar results in an informal survey of DIALOG datafiles.

4. Canada. Statistics Canada. Science and Technology Statistics Division. *Patents as Indicators of Invention*. Ottowa: Minister of Supply and Services Canada, 1985, p.13.

5. Ojala, Marydee. "A Patently Obvious Source for Competitor Intelligence: The Patent Literature." *Database* August 1989, p.43.

6. Carr, op. cit., p. 12.

7. Sulzer, op. cit., passim.

8. Kanigel, Robert. "One Man's Mousetraps." *The New York Times Magazine*, May 17, 1987, pp. 48-53.

9. Keucken, John A. *Creativity, Invention and Progress*. Indianapolis: Howard W. Sams and Co., Inc., 1969, pp. 7&11.

10. U.S. Department of Commerce. Patent and Trademark Office. *General Information Concerning Patents: A Brief Introduction to Patent Matters*. Wash-

ington, D.C.: U.S. Government Printing Office, Revised, June 1, 1988, p. 3; 35 USC 101. Booklet available for sale from GPO, or by writing the Commissioner of Patents and Trademarks, Washington, D.C. 20231.

11. Brown, Eulalie W. "Patent Basics: History, Background, and Searching Fundamentals." *Government Information Quarterly*3/4:381-405, 1986, p.387.

12. Although somewhat dated, for an excellent article providing a comprehensive list of online databases containing patent information and a brief description of each see Kulp, Carol S. "Patent Databases: A survey of What is Available from DIALOG, Questel, SDC, Pergamon, and INPADOC." *Database*August 1984, pp. 56-72.

13. For an excellent comparison of these online patent searching tools see, Raduazo, Dorothy M. "A Review Article." *Government Publications Review* 13:277-286, 1986.

14. U.S. Department of Commerce. Patent and Trademark Office. *Directory of Patent Depository Libraries*, edited by James Arshem. 2d ed. Washington, D.C.: U.S. PTO, 1988.

15. Douglas, John H. "Whatever Happened to Independent Inventors?" *Science News* 110:4, July 24, 1976, pp. 60-61.

16. Worthy, Ward. "Purdue Program Enhances Academe/Industry Ties." *Chemical & Engineering News* 63:30 July 29, 1985, pp. 24,29.

17. Maugh, Thomas H. "Technology Centers Unite Industry and Academia." *High Technology* 5:10, October 1985, pp. 48-52.

18. For information on some of the types of partnerships being developed, see such articles as: Lundberg, Frank. "University-Industry Research Partnerships." *Journal of the Society of Research Administrators* 15:2, Fall 1983, pp. 35-38; Kuhlman, James A. "Industry, Universities, and the Technological Imperative." *Business & Economic Review* 32:4, Jul/Aug/Sep. 1986, pp. 15-19; and Main, Jeremy. "Business Goes to College for a Brain Gain." *Fortune* 115:6, March 16, 1987, pp. 80-89.

19. Donald R. Baldwin, "Technology transfer at the University of Washington." *Journal of the Society of Research Administrators* 17:4, Spring 1986, pp. 13-26.

20. Commonwealth of Pennsylvania. *Economic Development Partnership*. Discussion paper prepared for the Technology Transfer Task Force, Bryce Jordan, Chair. Harrisburg, PA: n.p., July 21, 1987.

21. Baldwin, op. cit., p. 14.

22. Ibid.

23. Information on Project XL can be obtained by writing the Commissioner of Patents and Trademarks, ATTN: PROJECT XL, Washington, D.C. 20231 or by phoning (703)557-1610.

24. Ardis, Susan. *Expert Patent System at the University of Texas Austin*. Presentation handout from the Patent & Trademark Office/Patent Depository Library Conference XII, Washington, D.C.: May 16-19, 1989.

25. Ibid.

26. Telephone conversation with Barbara O'Neill, Government Documents Librarian, Oregon State Library, Salem, OR, August 4, 1989.

The National Technical Information Service – Working to Strengthen U.S. Information Sources

Joseph F. Caponio
Dorothy Aukofer MacEoin

SUMMARY. The National Technical Information Service (NTIS) is a self-supporting agency of the U.S. Department of Commerce that actively collects, organizes, and distributes technical information generated by United States and foreign governments in all areas of science and technology. There are two million titles in the NTIS permanent archives, some of which date as far back as 1945, and last year NTIS added 63,000 new titles to its collection. The entire collection is available at any time – whether a report dates from 20 years ago or last month. In addition, NTIS provides government-generated computer software and computerized data files on both tape and diskette through its Federal Computer Products Center. To keep pace with technology transfer activities, the NTIS Center for the Utilization of Federal Technology licenses Federal inventions and makes them available to private industry and prepares and issues a number of publications, catalogs, and directories announcing Federal technologies and resources. In the area of foreign technology, NTIS has recently increased its holdings – up to a third of the reports entering the collection are now from foreign sources.

The idea that the world is now involved in an information revolution is no longer a matter of speculation. Every day the volume of information that needs to be dealt with increases, challenging those of us in information management and creating demands on our resources – not only for

---

Joseph F. Caponio is Director of the National Technical Information Service, Springfield, VA 22161. Dorothy Aukofer MacEoin is Editor of *NTIS NewsLine*.

© 1991 by The Haworth Press, Inc. All rights reserved.

cataloging and storing information, but also for getting the information to the people who need it. The U.S. government, as one of the world's most prolific information producers, is a rich source of information that is accurate, current, and of immeasurable value to industry and academia alike.

The National Technical Information Service (NTIS) is the only agency tasked with recording and storing, on a permanent basis, government-sponsored information, and for assuring that that information remains available to the general public. Although the task is monumental—particularly when confronted with today's tidal wave of information—NTIS is in the unique position of having 45 years experience in managing government information.

GETTING STARTED IN 1945

NTIS and its predecessor organizations date back to 1945 when President Harry S. Truman established what was then called the Publication Board.[1] The Board was charged with reviewing all government-generated scientific and technical documents and determining what could be released to the public. Later on, the Board's responsibilities expanded to include scientific and technical documents captured from the enemy during and at the end of World War II.[2] The Board's objectives were to organize declassified information so as to permit researchers, and especially industry, fast and easy access to information, and to notify the public and industry about what was available. The intent was to promote economic growth and development through the rapid dissemination of scientific and technical information.

Five years later Congress passed a law[3] that directed the Department of Commerce to operate a national clearinghouse to collect, store, and distribute scientific, technical, and engineering information. By 1970 the national clearinghouse was reestablished as the National Technical Information Service, and information in business and statistics was added to the collection.

Ever since its inception, NTIS has operated under some restrictions: by law, it must remain self-supporting by selling its products to users on a cost-recovery basis.[4] NTIS receives no Congressionally-appropriated funds for its basic archival and clearinghouse functions. And to complicate its collecting efforts, NTIS cannot require other government agencies to submit materials.

In spite of these restrictions, the scope of information NTIS carries has been expanding continually, and now includes all areas of science and technology, including, for example, medicine, health, business, computer sciences, ecology, natural sciences, and the "soft" sciences, such as psychology and sociology.

In 1980 NTIS added the Center for the Utilization of Federal Technology. This special NTIS program licenses Federal inventions and makes them available to private industry—often on an exclusive basis—and pays use fees to the Federal agencies that produced the inventions. In addition, the Center prepares and issues a number of publications, catalogs, and directories announcing Federal technologies and resources. The Center's activities emphasize technology transfer and the competitive position of the United States in international markets.

To handle the ever-increasing amounts of computerized information products, in 1988 NTIS formed the Federal Computer Products Center. The Center distributes computer software and computer datafiles on tape and diskette from more than 60 Federal agencies. Although it has been in existence just a short time, the Center has more than doubled its inventory and now handles over 1,400 datafiles and 1,700 software titles on both tape and diskette. The Center publishes *NTIS CenterLine*, a free quarterly newsletter that announces new material. (To subscribe, contact the NTIS Order Desk, Springfield, VA 22161, 703/487-4650, and ask for PR-838/NCD.)

PRIVATIZATION ISSUE RESOLVED

Throughout the years, there have been a number of attempts to have NTIS services taken over by private agencies. In 1987 and 1988 extensive hearings to examine the feasibility and ramifications of privatization were held. By mid-1988 Congress had resolved this recurring issue by passing two laws that prohibit contracting out NTIS services: the Omnibus Trade and Competitiveness Act of 1988[5] and the National Institute of Standards and Technology (NIST) Authorization Act for Fiscal Year 1989.[6]

The Authorization Act states: "The functions and activities of the Service [NTIS] . . . are permanent Federal functions to be carried out by the Secretary [of Commerce] through the Service and its employees, and shall not be transferred from the Service . . . without the express approval of the Congress." The Act also established NTIS as part of the newly-established Technology Administration of the U.S. Department of Commerce.

Furthermore, the new laws authorized NTIS to plan for "modernization" of its information-handling capabilities and services, provided for flexible use of contracts, grants, or cooperative agreements with the private sector, provided for stronger representation for industry in discussions of technology issues both here and abroad, established an Advisory Board, and called for an annual report[7] on fees, costs, and sales.

MODERNIZATION PLAN FOR NTIS

Foremost in the modernization plan is a concerted effort to improve NTIS electronic dissemination capabilities. The need for this was highlighted in the October 1988 report issued by the Congressional Office of Technology Assessment (OTA), *Informing the Nation–Federal Information Dissemination in an Electronic Age:*[8]

> NTIS appears to be ideally suited for the implementation of an electronic documents system. . . . Overall, an electronic NTIS should be able to increase the diversity and timeliness of NTIS (and related private vendor) offerings, increase the ability of NTIS (and private vendors) to match information products with potential users, and reduce the cost of NTIS products. An electronic NTIS should be better able to serve all users, but especially small and medium businesses and individual researchers.

The Authorization Act made it possible for NTIS to take positive steps to implement electronic dissemination plans as recommended in the OTA report. The impact this will have on NTIS and its customers was outlined in its annual report:

> Electronic dissemination of information is rapidly overtaking the more traditional media of paper and microfiche as the vehicle of choice for many users. Therefore, NTIS will make electronic dissemination a major focus over the next few years. In doing so, NTIS must become more knowledgeable about who its end users are and what kinds of information product they need. NTIS has traditionally placed great emphasis on involvement with intermediaries in the library community. Such involvement will continue even as end-users increase their use of personal computers to locate the information they need by themselves. This direct user involvement will increase dramatically in the next few years.

Modernization efforts already in place include production of portions of the NTIS Database on CD-ROM (in addition to online), diskette copying equipment to reduce order turnaround time, two-sided electronic printer systems for faster reproduction, expansion of the NTIS electronic ordering service called *QuickSERVICE* so that Deposit Account customers can dial in and check account balances, telephone facsimile order fulfillment service for customers who need rush documents, and an electronic telephone answering system. In addition, NTIS is currently evaluating a number of new technologies, in particular the optical disk, but also computer-assisted fiche cameras and film processing equipment, and bar-coding for inventory control.

Projected electronic dissemination activities include such items as increased use of CD-ROM and computer diskettes for selected portions of databases or subsets and for full-text information, direct computer-to-computer transfer of bibliographic datafiles and software, and increased use of electronic bulletin boards for time-sensitive information and for announcing new NTIS offerings.

NTIS AND THE INTERNATIONAL INFORMATION COMMUNITY

In addition to expanding technological efforts, NTIS actively participates in the international information community through special task forces and committees.

For example, NTIS is part of a joint U.S.-Japan Task Force established specifically to improve mutual access to international exchange of scientific and technical information. Dr. Joseph E. Clark, NTIS Deputy Director, is U.S. Chairman for this joint task force.

Task force goals include improving awareness of current scientific and technical information systems, increasing the quantity and quality of scientific and technical information and its translation, reducing impediments to the flow of information, and improving identification, collection, and dissemination of "grey" literature—those reports and research results that have not been formally published in established journals or technical literature.

WORKING WITH THE LIBRARY OF CONGRESS

In addition, this spring NTIS Director Joseph F. Caponio met with Winston Tabb, Head of Research at the Library of Congress to discuss coordinating information resources. Both agencies' representatives feel the best way to strengthen the United States' industrial, scientific, and technical information resource base is to coordinate their mutual efforts. To help accomplish this goal, two special task forces were established.

One task force will work in the area of technical report literature. Co-chairmen are Walter L. Finch, Associate Director, NTIS Program and

Product Management, and Joseph W. Price, Chief of the Science and Technology Division at the Library of Congress.

The second task force will cover translations and copyright issues and will be cochaired by David B. Shonyo, Director of the NTIS International Affairs Office, and Charlene Woody of the Library of Congress.

JOINT VENTURES WITH PRIVATE INDUSTRY

Another area covered by the Authorization Act that specifically affects NTIS – and an area that NTIS has acted on quickly – is the authorization for flexible use of contracts, grants, or cooperative agreements with academia and the private sector – in other words, joint ventures that allow enhancements to basic NTIS material. By fall of 1989 NTIS had signed joint venture agreements with 15 private firms.

The joint ventures of most interest to librarians include:

- *Simplified Searching* – NTIS and the BRS OnSite System have arranged for academic institutions to use the BRS/SEARCH software in conjunction with the NTIS Bibliographic Database. Through this arrangement academic customers do not need to purchase or create their own search software. BRS is a division of Maxwell Online, Inc., McLean, Virginia. (For more information contact Doria Beachell Grimes, Product Manager, Bibliographic Services, NTIS, Room 300-F, Springfield, VA 22161.)
- *R&D Alerts* – In this special program NTIS works with scientists and engineers at leading universities who preview new reports entering the NTIS collection to determine which ones may be most useful and valuable. These reports are then described in *R&D Alert* bulletins that NTIS distributes free of charge. Bulletins have already been published on Fiber Optics, Artificial Intelligence, and Telecommunications, and other subject areas are planned. To get copies of R&D Alerts that have already been published or to get on the mailing list to get future issues, contact Janet Geffner, Joint Ventures Program, NTIS, Room 207-F, Springfield, VA 22161.
- *Training Material* – W.G. Hunter and Associates of Northern Virginia publishes a nationwide newsletter directed to the training industry. Through arrangements with NTIS, each issue highlights some of the outstanding training material NTIS has collected from other government agencies. (To get this newsletter contact Dr. Darcia D. Bracken, NTIS Center for the Utilization of Federal Technology, Room 304-F, Springfield, VA 22161.)

NTIS AND FOREIGN TECHNOLOGY

More than a third of the reports currently entering the NTIS collection are from foreign sources, particularly from Japan. The services that follow are of particular interest for librarians.

The Japan Information Center of Science and Technology (JICST) File E Online Service covering 4,000 Japanese scientific and technical periodicals, technical reports, conference proceedings, and journal articles. Citations and abstracts for all JICST entries are in English. The database contains 600,000 citations, provides for online ordering of full texts, and is searchable on an ASCII terminal. NTIS can provide translation services for full-text documents. Additionally, there are five Japanese-language databases available through JICST. For more information contact Barbara Payne, NTIS Office of International Affairs, Room 306-F, Springfield, VA 22161.

Foreign Technology Abstract Newsletter – Published weekly, this newsletter covers reviews and syntheses of major research programs, activities of specific organizations and projects, and descriptions of new technologies, processes, and discoveries. Emphasis is on Western Europe and Japan, but coverage is also given to all other countries where important scientific and technologic developments are taking place. Information is collected from science and technology councillors stationed at U.S. Embassies, science officers of other U.S. Government agencies with overseas offices, and various experts visiting foreign scientific and technologic organizations on behalf of government agencies. For a free sample copy, contact the NTIS Office of International Affairs, Springfield, VA 22161 (703) 487-4819.

Directory of Japanese Technical Resources, 1989 Edition – This comprehensive reference work is published by NTIS under a mandate given by Congress in the Japanese Technical Literature Act of 1986. Coverage includes a section on Japanese online databases, features background articles on Japanese patent information as a research trend indicator, contains case studies of U.S. corporations in Japan, describes U.S. Government efforts to increase the flow of technical information between the U.S. and Japan, lists more than 300 significant Japanese technical documents translated by the U.S. Government that are available through NTIS or the National Translation Center, and provides a comprehensive listing of commercial services, government agencies, and libraries that collect, abstract, translate, or disseminate Japanese technical information. For more information contact the NTIS Order Desk, Springfield, VA 22161, 703/487-4650, and ask for free brochure PR-825/NCD.

NTIS SPECIAL PROGRAMS FOR LIBRARIANS

As brought out in the NTIS Annual Report, NTIS has traditionally placed great emphasis on involvement with intermediaries in the library community. Because librarians have always been and will continue to be a major force in helping NTIS achieve its objectives, NTIS has established a library liaison program, runs a free, annual user's conference, provides at-cost online training, publishes free search guides, and produces *NTIS NewsLine*, a free quarterly newsletter. (To subscribe to *NewsLine*, write to *NTIS NewsLine*, Room 2004-S, Springfield, VA 22161.)

LIBRARY LIAISON PROGRAM

The NTIS Library Liaison Network was established to provide open lines of communication between NTIS and the library community. The Network is made up of library groups, and members include, for example, chapters of the Special Library Association, the American Library Association, the Medical Library Association, the American Society of Information Specialists, university library groups, online user groups, and state library associations and groups. Membership includes international groups as well.

Benefits for Library Liaison groups include having a specific point of contact at NTIS, receipt of regular information updates and free promotional literature, and a voice in NTIS program and policy decisions. In addition, NTIS representatives visit a number of liaison groups each year to give programs or educational presentations, or simply to have an informal discussion or feedback session – at no cost to the liaison group. These visits not only allow NTIS to present current information, they also provide a forum for gathering ideas from the library community to take back to NTIS top management. If your group or chapter would like to join the NTIS Library Liaison Network, have a representative contact Sandra M. Rigby, NTIS, Room 1029-S, Springfield, VA 22161. There are no costs or fees involved.

NTIS ANNUAL CONFERENCE FOR INFORMATION SPECIALISTS

One of the most effective forums for exchanging information with the library community is the annual NTIS Conference. This conference is offered in spring every year, and provides an opportunity for information specialists to meet NTIS program managers, get updated information about NTIS products and services, and discuss future requirements and ideas. To receive advance notice about the next Users' Conference contact Verla Weaver, NTIS, Room 202-F, Springfield, VA 22161.

NTIS also provides at-cost online training for both the NTIS Bibliographic Database and the Federal Research in Progress Database (FEDRIP). Training is offered at a number of different locations throughout the United States. for more information contact Erieann Carroll, NTIS, Room 301-F, Springfield, VA 22161.

Free search guides are available for the NTIS Bibliographic Database and the Federal Research in Progress (FEDRIP) Database. Instructions on how to order these free guides follow the product descriptions given below.

A free newsletter, *Online Alert*, is also available. Write NTIS and ask for PR862.

NTIS DATABASES

The NTIS Bibliographic Database is available through a number of private vendors, and portions of it are available on CD-ROM. It covers NTIS titles dating back to 1964.

The Federal Research in Progress Database (FEDRIP) is an online listing of government research projects *still in progress*. It continues in part the database functions of the now defunct Smithsonian Scientific Information Exchange (SSIE). NTIS established FEDRIP in 1983 incorporating material from SSIE. The new database has proven to be so popular its usage has increased 100% in the last year alone. The file is reloaded monthly, and is available online through DIALOG. For additional information contact Doria Beachell Grimes, Product Manager, Bibliographic Databases, NTIS, Room 300-F, Springfield, VA 22161.

To order any of the following free search guides, contact the NTIS Order Desk, Springfield, VA 22161, (703) 487-4650. Please quote the number given when ordering.

NTIS Subject Category Descriptions: PR-832/NCD
Search Guide to the NTIS Bibliographic Database:

- on BRS: Request PR-831/NCD
- on DIALOG: Request PR-8929/NCD
- on ORBIT: Request PR-830/NCD
- on STN: Request PR-837/NCD

Search Guide to the Federal Research in Progress Database (FEDRIP):

- Request PR-847/NCD

For more information about what government information is available on CD-ROM, request *Locate Government R&D and Technology on CD-ROM*, PR-845/NCD.

Also available online is the Federal Applied Technology Database, which covers the information products of the NTIS Center for the Utilization of Federal Technology. There are more than 14,000 records in this database, which serves as a technology transfer resource linking U.S. companies with Federal laboratory technologies. It is available commercially through BRS Information Technologies. For more information, contact NTIS at the address above and request: *Federal Applied Technology Database User Guide*, PR-725/NCD.

In addition to all the above, NTIS assigns Standard Technical Report Numbers to agencies producing technical reports, handles subscriptions to periodicals from more than 80 government agencies, supplies Federal Information Processing Standards Publications, provides electronic media reproduction services for Federal agencies, and conducts seminars for private industry based on reports industry specialists have determined are most topical. Additional information on all of this is covered regularly in *NTIS NewsLine*.

In the 45 years NTIS has been the primary information source for government information, its basic mission has not changed – now, as then, its intent is to promote economic growth and development through the rapid dissemination of scientific and technical information. The way this mission is carried out, however, has changed dramatically to meet the increased demands the information revolution and new technology have thrust upon it. And as the information revolution evolves into the Information Age NTIS will continue to work on developing its resources, on keeping up with technology, and, most importantly, with getting that information to you, the end users.

NOTES

1. Executive Order 9568.
2. Executive Order 9604.
3. Public Law 776, 1950.
4. Title 15, U.S. Code 1151-7.
5. PL 100-418, signed August 23, 1988.
6. PL 100-519, signed October 24, 1988.

7. *Annual Report to the Congress From the Secretary of Commerce on the National Technical Information Service: Operations, Audit, and Modernization* (available from NTIS: order number PB89-166565NCD, $9).

8. *Informing the Nation – Federal Information Dissemination in an Electronic Age, United States Congress, Office of Technology Assessment, 1988*, p. 107 (available through NTIS as order number PR89-114243NCD, $16).

Free Information Brochures from NTIS

NTIS provides a number of free catalogs and brochures about its information products. To get copies of anything listed in this box contact NTIS. Please quote the "PR" number given when ordering.

Order from: NTIS Order Desk
Springfield, VA 22161
(703) 487-4650

For a free 32-page catalog that summarizes NTIS offerings, request the *NTIS Products and Services Catalog*, PR-827/NCD.

Products from the NTIS Center for the Utilization of Federal Technology are summarized in PR-801/NCD.

To subscribe to *CenterLine*, the free publication of the NTIS Federal Computer Products Center, request PR-838/NCD.

Also available: Directory of Computerized Data Files, PR-629/NCD; Catalog of Datafiles on Floppy Diskette, PR-771/NCD.

A brochure about the *Directory of Computer Software* is available as PR-261/NCD.

The Government Reports Announcements and Index (GRA&I) Journal is issued twice monthly, covers more than 2,500 entries each issue, and up to 63,000 R&D results annually. For a descriptive brochure request PR-195/NCD.

Government Reports Announcements and Index Journal—Annual Index covers all items announced annually by NTIS. It is indexed by keyword, author, sponsoring or performing organization, contract/grant and agency report/order numbers. Request free brochure PR-273/NCD.

Selected Research In Microfiche (SRIM) is a special NTIS service in which microfiche copies of all reports entering the NTIS system in specific subject areas are automatically sent to the subscriber within days of their announcement by NTIS. For details, send for a free copy of *A Guide to SRIM*, PR-271/NCD.

Abstract Newsletters are weekly summaries of new information products entering the NTIS system. They are broken down into 26 different subject areas and provide an easy, economical way to follow new activity in a specific subject field. Request PR-797/NCD.

Published Searches are bound, printed, annotated bibliographies showing what information is available on a specific subject from a single database (NTIS or one of 23 others). To get a free copy of the 132-page *Published Search Master Catalog* ask for PR-186/NCD.

To subscribe to *NewsLine*, write directly to NTIS NewsLine, Room 2004S, Springfield, VA 22161.

Vocabulary Mapping of Subject-Headings of Medical and Health-Related Government Documents at the University of Massachusetts Medical Center Library

Justine P. Honeyman

SUMMARY. The University of Massachusetts Medical Center Library is embarking on a project that will identify, integrate and map subject-heading vocabulary of medical and health-related government documents. The vocabulary will be derived from National Library of Medicine, Library of Congress, Government Printing Office and local subject-headings, and including acronyms, initialisms, SU DOC #s and jargon.

Using an application of the Massachusetts Institute of Technology's INSITE computer system, vocabulary will be stored and manipulated to produce a glossary and form a map or progression of terms towards available resources of information.

The background, methodology and discussion will be presented in the following manner:

- The University of Massachusetts Medical Center (UMMC) Library is a selective depository whose philosophy of acquisitions of docu-

Justine P. Honeyman is Government Documents Librarian, University of Massachusetts Medical Center Library, 55 Lake Avenue, North Worcester, MA 01655.

© 1991 by The Haworth Press, Inc. All rights reserved.

ments (and all materials) is based on a broad definition of health and related sciences, and the facility and community it serves.

- UMMC Library has taken several approaches towards providing better patron access.
- Methods of attempting to offer the patron better access to health-related information within the government documents can be pulled together into one software application, by mapping subject-heading vocabulary with agencies and their respective SU DOC #s.

SIGNIFICANCE

The University of Massachusetts Medical Center Library has been a Selective Government Documents Depository since 1972. The documents department houses over 55,000 publications and additions are made daily. They are housed separately and are not cataloged with other Library materials.

Government Documents are a rich resource of health-related information, and are heavily represented in publications from the Department of Health and Human Services and the United States Congress.[1]

The acquisition and selection of items is based on the community served by the depository. As the Medical Center has expanded, so has the scope of materials necessary to serve the patrons. The Medical Center considers all the elements that aid, assist and impinge on the well-being of an individual; research, health services, education, psychological and sociological aspects, agriculture, ecology, energy, environment and population. The individual's well being is also protected, guarded and insured by laws and their subsequent regulations on health and safety.

The health scientist, in particular, and the general public, at some level, are aware government agencies compile health data. Knowing which agency is in charge of what data is confusing because agencies are interrelated and coordinated with each other contractually. As one studies the documents and the subject areas they cover, it becomes clear that almost all federal agencies offer some sort of health-related information. The following is a sample of agencies that may be overlooked as a resource; i.e., Commerce – National Oceanic and Atmospheric Administration, Defense – U.S. Army Medical Research Institute of Infectious Diseases, Interior – Environmental Impact Statement, Justice – Community Drug Prevention.

Documents are underutilized for various reasons. Basically, the user is unfamiliar with the classification system and functions of federal departments and agencies as they are diverse and interdisciplinary.[2] The Government Printing Office recognizes the confusion caused by issuing agencies being interdisciplinary and publishes an item called SUBJECT BIBLIOGRAPHY, GP 3.22/2:nos., which covers a multitude of topics and is updated annually. An appraisal of a bibliography titled *Nursing and Nursing Care*, produces a list of titles, and SU DOC#s, from various issuing agencies pertinent to the topic. Included are agency initialisms where applicable.[3]

LIST OF TITLES AND ISSUING AGENCIES ON NURSING AND NURSING CARE

Nurses' Guide for Patients Undergoing Cancer Chemotherapy. HE20.3008:C 42/983. National Institutes of Health. (NIH)

Nursing and Related Care Homes as Reported from the: 1982 National Master Facility Inventory Survey. HE 20.6209:13/32. National Center for Health Statistics. (NCHS)

New Nurse in Industry: A Guide for the Newly Employed Occupational Health Nurse. National Institute for Occupational Safety and Health. (NIOSH) HE 20.7108:N 93.

Mental Illness in Nursing Homes: Agenda for Research. HE 20.8102:N 93. National Institute for Occupational Safety and Health. (NIOSH)

Preventing Fetal Alcohol Effects: A Practical Guide for Ob/Gyn Physicians and Nurses. HE 20.8308:F 43. National Institute on Alcohol Abuse and Alcoholism. (NIAAA)

Report to the President and Congress on the Status of Health Personnel in the United States. Vol. 1-2. HE 20.9302:H 34/v.1-2. Bureau of Health Professions. (BHP) Note: The Bureau of Health Professions carries a SU DOC # HE 20.6602: ALSO.

How to Select a Nursing Home. HE 22.208: N 93/980. Health Standards and Quality Bureau. (HSQB)

Dietetics, Nursing, Pharmacy, and Therapy Occupations. L 2.3/4/a:2250-8/986/87. Bureau of Labor Statistics.

Nursing Home Care: The Unfinished Agenda, An Information Paper. May 1986.Y 4.Ag4:S.prt.99-160. Special Committee on Aging.

Nurse Practitioners, Physician Assistants, and Certified Nurse-Midwives: A Policy Analysis. Y 3.T22/2:2 C82/2/case 37. Office of Technology Assessment (OTA).

SIGNIFICANCE

Books, manuals, guides and catalogs have been published to familiarize the patron with government documents search strategies. Within these guides are references to searching techniques via subject heading and/or the agency issuing types of information.[4] These guides are available to the patron, but becoming familiar with the publishing practices of the federal agencies in order to answer a specific question becomes a research task in itself.

Over the years, the debate to catalog and integrate documents into a library's collection has been discussed in various journals.[5-8] Government Documents at the UMMC Library are not integrated physically or within the card catalog, thus a point of access has been lost.

Vocabulary stems from various sources. The cataloging of materials, at UMMC Library, is done using National Library of Medicine subject-headings. Indexing and access to documents, through the *Monthly Catalog*[9] is done via Library of Congress subject-headings. The health professional uses jargon,[10] acronyms and initialisms[11] that should be considered and accommodated. The vocabulary of the health professional is exploding and is increasing rapidly with the even greater availability of online and print information produced by numerous bibliographic management systems.[12] The confusion for the patron must be recognized by the information scientist and rectified.

In 1977, Bernard M. Fry, Dean of Indiana University Graduate Library School, wrote, "Government publications comprise an information resource whose incorporation into the mainstream of library services should be a priority goal for both government and libraries".[13] This challenge has resulted in innovative library software being developed by documents librarians across the country.[14-20]

The UMMC Library has used various techniques, software, accessions lists, and guides, in addressing the problems encountered in accessing government documents. The Library can go a step further and apply the concept of vocabulary mapping to government documents through the incorporation of all access points-subject-headings, agencies SU DOC #s, acronyms, jargon, and initialisms.

The seeds for the execution of this project can be seen in the present programming and resultant print-outs and glossary produced using INSITE.[21] The flexibility of INSITE can accommodate mapping, similar to the type being accomplished by the National Library of Medicine. The NLM is developing a UNIFIED MEDICAL LANGUAGE SYSTEM (UMLS) which will integrate medical information terminology and direct the patron through the maze of vocabulary towards a logical inquiry. This will take the form of a software tool that can be used with various computer applications.[22]

UMMC Library mapping will be produced in printed format with later developments into a smaller software package.

The development and demonstration of mapped vocabulary will be discussed in the following sections.

PREVIOUS WORK–REPORT A

In the development of a technique to assist the patron in gathering information on a topic, levels of library skills should be considered and accommodated if it is to be most effective. This is a most important point and a challenge in the documents area as its philosophy is information for public consumption. Searching documents is not a commonly taught library skill, and access to them becomes an attempt to simplify a complex system.

The Medical Center utilizes INSITE, a facilities management system. First developed in 1970 by the Office of Facilities Management Systems at the Massachusetts Institute of Technology[23] it provides data bases for equipment, space payroll, accounting, etc., for both the school and the hospital. INSITE is designed to be a large data base system which allows for great flexibility in the storage and retrieval of data and the production of varied report formats. In 1984, the Library adapted this system to solve the problem of the Government Documents' inventory. The resulting adaptation has been used for the past six years to maintain shelflists and aid in patron access through the additions of subject-heading and glossary formats.[24]

To produce a documents data base, using INSITE, the entire collection is considered a single block of space and described by a number of fields. Presently, each document is described by seven fields or attributes (see Figure 1).

The data base may be accessed through any or all fields and in any order to produce a variety of printed formats.

FIGURE 1

FIELD	DATA	# SPACES	SAMPLE DOCUMENT
RAN K	SU DOC #	16	202:D84/24/75-84
RAN CLA	SU DOC #	6	HE20.8
RAN N	ISSUING AGENCY	32	HHS/NATL INSTITUTE
			ON DRUG ABUSE
RAN M	SUBJECT HEADING	16	DRUG ABUSE/TEENS
RAN AVA 1	DOCUMENT TITLE	96	USE OF LICIT &
AVA 2			ILLICIT DRUGS BY
AVA 3			AMERICA'S HIGH
AVA 4			SCHOOL STUDENTS.
AVA 5			1975-84.
AVA 6			AD
YEAR RECEIVED		2	01/01/1986
RAN CON	MICROFICHE	3	NO

Report A, accessing fields RAN M,RAN AVA 1-6, RAN CLA & RAN K,AND RAN N results in a subject-heading index.

DRUGS/TEENS	USE OF LICIT & ILLICIT DRUGS BY AMERICAS HIGH SCHOOL STUDENTS 1975-84	HE 20.8202: D84/24/75-84	HHS/NATL INSTITUTE ON DRUG ABUSE

PREVIOUS WORK – REPORTS B AND C

Report B, accessing fields RAN AVA 1-6, RAN M, RAN CLA and K, and RAN N results in a title index.

USE OF LICIT & ILLICIT DRUGS BY AMERICAS HIGH SCHOOL STUDENTS 1975-	DRUG ABUSE/ TEENS	HE 20.8202: D84/24/75-84	HHS/NATL INSTITUTE ON DRUG ABUSE

Report C, accessing all fields cites the type of format (NO, meaning format is paper; this explanation is in the preface of UMMC Library catalog), the year document was received and produces a SU DOC # index.

HE 20.8202 D84/24/75-84	HHS/NATL INSTITUTE ON DRUG ABUSE	DRUG ABUSE/ TEENS	USE OF LICIT & ILLICIT DRUGS BY AMERICAS HIGH SCHOOL STUDENTS

Formats can be programmed in various ways to produce information. The issuing agency may be listed in the first column and the titles published out of that agency may be listed in the next column; thus, familiarizing the patron with the type of publications produced by different agencies. For administrative purposes, titles may be listed according to the year they are received. All microfiche titles can be listed separately from titles in paper format for accounting and future space considerations.

The addition of a subject-heading index offers the patron an access point. The vocabulary was kept simple. A more effective access point was then developed due to the variations of vocabulary and jargon used by the health professional. A report of only subject-headings developed into a glossary; an early attempt at mapping subject headings was made by adding explanatory notes and directives.

e.g., allergy/(type)
/immunology
/research
/see also-NIAID (The acronym is found and expanded under appropriate alphabetical placement in glossary.)
NIAID/Natl Inst Allergy & Infect Dis

PREVIOUS WORK

In addition, a simple guide was devised that lists federal agencies and their initialisms, acronyms, and respective SU DOC #s, e.g., CID – Center for Infectious disease – HE.20.7800:,HMO Health Maintenance Organization – HE.9202:.

The card catalog at the UMMC Library is not an access point for government documents as they are not integrated within the cataloging system. The library has attempted to rectify the situation.

The Library uses the OCLC bibliographic system to catalog its books, serials, abstracts, monographs, reference and audiovisual materials. Beginning in January 1987, the Library contracted to receive monthly accessions lists in addition to catalog cards. Government documents appear in this monthly list because tapes of Government Printing Office bibliographic information are entered into OCLC.[25] The Library uses NLM subject-headings to catalog its materials. Integration is possible by requesting the accessions list be printed using both LC and NLM headings. A more complete integration is possible through manipulation of the OCLC data base by inserting an NLM subject-heading and SU DOC # in the appropriate tags.[26]

The development of various techniques to assist the patron through the complexities of government documents has acquired, along with it, vocabulary stemming from different bibliographic systems, NLM, LC, GPO, UMMC subject-headings including SU DOC #s, issuing agencies and their intitialisms and acronyms. These sources of vocabulary and the capabilities of INSITE can be combined to produce a mapping system to a government documents collection of health-related information.

MAPPING METHODOLOGY – PRINTOUT A

Government documents received for a five-year time span by this Library, will be analyzed, for their subject-heading designations. The five-year tenure is based on the Government Printing Office regulations that a selective depository need only maintain documents for that amount of time. Annually, those documents, that have been in the collection for five years and are not part of a series, may be discarded however, only after they are offered to other depositories and the regionals.

An expanded application of INSITE will analyze a document in the following manner:

(1) TITLE
(2) SU DOC #
(3) OCLC #
(4) NATIONAL LIBRARY OF MEDICINE SUBJECT-HEADING
(5) LIBRARY OF CONGRESS SUBJECT-HEADING
(6) GOVERNMENT PRINTING OFFICE MONTHLY CATALOG SUBJECT-HEADING
(7) UNIVERSITY OF MASSACHUSETTS MEDICAL CENTER LIBRARY LOCAL SUBJECT-HEADING
(8) OTHER SUBJECT-HEADINGS – those headings which appear on OCLC but do not fall under categories 4-7.
(9) ACRONYMS – health professional jargon
(10) INITIALISMS – issuing agencies
(11) SEE OTHER – The most informative SU DOC #s will be listed. The SU DOC # can be seen as a subject-heading.

Using the above worksheet format, the OCLC bibliographic system is searched for a complete document record. A record may contain both an *NLM* and *LC* heading, designations are also made as to the original cataloger, *GPO* or *OTHER* institutions. If an NLM heading is not found, one is traced and added to the local record using the appropriate tag. The *Monthly Catalog of United States Government Publications*, produced by the Government Printing Office, is searched for the subject-heading the document title was designated. These are usually LC but with slight variations. The worksheet is completed with the addition of related issuing agency initialisms and SU DOC#s, UMMC subject-heading, and acronyms when applicable.

The worksheet becomes a compilation of all previous techniques this Library has developed to assist the patron.

(1) TITLE: Nurse Practitioners, Physician Assistants & Certified Nurse Midwives: A Policy Analysis
(2) SU DOC #: Y3.T22/2: 2C82/2: Case 37
(3) OCLC #: 15153367
(4) NLM: Midwives, Nurse Practitioners, Primary Health Care
(5) LC: Nurse Practitioners, Physicians' Assistants
(6) GPO: Physicians' Assistants
(7) UMMC: Physicians' Assistants
(8) OTHER:
(9) ACRONYMS: HMO
(10) INITIALISMS: OTA, BHP, HCFA
(11) SEE OTHER: Y3.T22/2: HE 20.6610: HE20.9302: HE 22.2: HE 22.208: HE 20.20

Mapping: Reports may be programmed to alphabetically list subject-headings and their related components in any desired number and arrangements. For example, the entire analysis for the document may be printed as an in-house shelf-list and catalog. For the purposes of mapping and further analysis, items 4 through 11 may be printed resulting in the following visual demonstration, (Printout A).

MAPPING METHODOLOGY – PRINTOUT B

To refine the mapping, the subject-heading results (minus duplications) are reentered into the computer using a slightly simplified worksheet and program.

SUBJECTS : (1) Community Health Nursing
(2) Nurses/Visiting
(3) Visiting the sick
(4)
(5)
ACRONYMS :
INITIALISMS : HFCA BHP HSQB NCHS
SEE OTHER : HE 22.26/3: HE 20.6610: HE 20.9302: HE 20.6208:

General terms such as "Nursing," "United States," and "Nursing" that appeared in Printout A are not reentered as they will appear as a general term with reference points elsewhere.

Printout B comes closer to the final mapping strategy, further refinements can be made by eliminating irrelevant entries.

In Printout B, the first term will be indexed alphabetically and related terms follow as sub-categories. Those related terms will be inputted again. This time the sub-category becomes the initial indexed term, thus generating another printout, and cross-index.

The assessment procedure for verifying the cross-indexing of vocabulary will be done periodically. A simple data base will be established by entering each subject-heading term and printing out the list. This list will then be compared to vocabulary mapped in Printout B. Those terms which do not appear will be evaluated as to significance. Significance will be based on relevant usage versus terminology used infrequently. Once relevancy is determined, the subject-heading will be entered into the data base, with its related information, to ensure its appearance on Printout B.

CONCLUSION

The foremost goal of a library is to meet the information needs of the patrons. A technique was sought after to make the documents more accessible. In the past, in-house guides have proven to be effective. Even greater effectiveness can be accomplished through the mapping of vocabulary which in this case includes SU DOC #, issuing agencies, acronyms and initialisms. Printout B does achieve the goal of combining vocabularies.

The resultant mapping printouts may be used as a teaching tool and technique to lead the patron through a logical progression toward the desired information from this vast available resource called government documents.[27]

Printout A

NLM	LC	GPO	UMMC
Community Health Nursing	Community Health Nursing	Nursing United States	Nurses, Visiting
Mental Health, Nursing	Aged-Mental Health	Nursing Homes Mental Health	Mental Illness Nursing Homes
Midwives Nurse Practitioners Primary Health Care	Nurse Practitioners Physicians' Assistants	Physicians' Assistants	Physicians' Assistants
Nursing Homes	Nursing Homes	Nursing Homes	Aged, Nursing Homes
Occupational Health Nurse	Nursing, Industrial Hygiene	Nursing	Nurses / Occupational Safety

Other	Acronyms	Initialisms	See Other
		HCFA	HE 22.26/3:
Visiting the sick		BHP	HE 20.6610: HE 20.9302:
		HSQB	
		NCHS	HE 20.6208:
		NIMH	HE 20.8102:
		HCFA	HE 22.18:
		Select Committee on Aging	Y 4.Ag 4/2:
		OTA	Y 3.T 22/2:
		BHP	HE 20.6610: HE 20.9302:
	HMO	HCFA	HE 22.2:
		PHS	HE 20.20:
		HSQB	HE 22.208:
		HSQB	HE 22.202:
Gerontology		HCFA	HE 22.18:
		AOA	HE 23.3001:
		NIA	HE 20.3851:
		Select Committee on Aging	Y 4.Ag 4/2:
		NIOSH	HE 20.7101:
Nursing, Expanded roles		BHP	HE 20.6610: HE 20.9302:
		Labor	L 2.3/4/a:

Printout B

SUBJECT-HEADINGS	ACRONYMS
Aged, Mental Health Mental Health, Nursing Mental Illness, Nursing	
Aged, Nursing Homes Gerontology Nursing Homes	
Community Health Nursing Nurses, Visiting Visiting the sick	
Nurse Practitioners Physicians' Assistants Primary Health Care	HMO
Nursing, Expanded roles Nursing, Industrial roles Nursing, Occupational safety Occupational Health Nurse	

INITIALISMS	SEE OTHER (SU DOC #)
NIMH	HE 20.8102:
HCFA	HE 22.18:
Select Committee on Aging	Y 4.Ag 4/2:
Select Committee on Aging	Y 4.Ag 4/2:
AOA	HE 23.3001:
NIA	HE 20.3851:
HCFA	HE 22.18:
HSQB	HE 22.208:
HCFA	HE 22.26/3:
BHP	HE 20.6610:
	HE 20.9302:
HSQB	
NCHS	HE 20.6208:
BHP	HE 20.6610:
HCFA	HE 22.2:
PHS	HE 22.20:
HSQB	HE 22.208:
OTA	Y 3.T 22/2:
NIOSH	HE 20.7101:
BHP	HE 20.6610:
	HE 20.9302
Labor	L 2.3/4/a:

REFERENCES

1. Rips RE. The reference use of government publications. Drexel Library Quarterly. 1965 Oct.; 1:3-18.

2. Whilbeck GW, Hernon P. The attitudes of librarians toward the servicing and use of government publications; A survey of federal depositories in four mid-western states. Government Publications Review. 1977 1:183-99.

3. Government Printing Office. Subject Bibliography-Nurses and Nursing Care. Washington: Superintendent of Documents, May 19, 1987. Subject Bibliography; No. SB-019). (GP 3.22/2:019/987).

4. Sears JL, Moody MK. Using Government Publications, Vol. 1: Searching by Subjects and Agencies. Phoenix, Arizona: Oryx Press, 1985:5-33.

5. Bowden VM, Swannen, S. Implementing change: The Installation of an Integrated Library System at UTHSCSA. Bull Med Libr Assoc 1985 July; 73(3):271-7

6. Nakata Y. From Press to People Collecting and Using U.S. Government Publications. Chicago, American Library Association 1979:31-37.

7. Pressen C. Organization of a separate government documents collection, University of Waterloo—A case history. Government Publications Review 1975 2:167-76.

8. Ryoo HB. Managing an integrated depository documents collection. Government Information Quarterly. 1985 2(3):299-313.

9. Government Printing Office. Monthly Catalog of United States Government Publications. Washington: Superintendent of Documents, 1951-1999 (GP 3.8:).

10. Fenske RE, Fortney LM. The use of jargon in medical school libraries. Bull Med Libr Assoc 1986 January; 74(1):12-15.

11. Lovinger KF. The Federal Government Subject Guide. London: McFarland & Company, Inc., Publishers, 1987:1-22.

12. Library of Congress, Cataloging Distribution Service. Multiple Thesauri in Online Library Bibliographic Systems. Washington: Government Printing Office, 1987. 3-5 (LC 30.2:M91)

13. Fry BM. Government Publications and the Library Implications for Change. Based on a speech delivered, May 1977, before the Federal Publishing, Printing and Information Policy Institute, American University.

14 Gillham V. Government documents at the University of Guelph. Government Information Quarterly 1984 1 (1):75-81.

15. Kiser CB. Automated shelflist at George Mason University. Administrative Notes, Washington: Government Printing Office 1986 7(18):3-4 (GP 3.16/3-2: 7/13)

16. Mooney MT. Automating the U.S. Depository items numbers file. Administrative Notes, Washington: Government Printing Office 1986 7(18):3-4 (GP 3.16/3-2: 7/18)

17. Morton B. Implementing an automated shelflist for a selective depository collection. Government Publications Review 1982 9:323-44.

18. Peay WJ, Florance V, Epstein WC, Thelin AM. Medoc: An index for the health sciences. Government Information Quarterly 1985 2(2):193-205.

19. Presser C. CODOC: A computer-based processing and retrieval system for government documents. College & Research Libraries 1978 39:94-8.

20. Smith KF. Robot at the reference desk? College and Research Libraries 1986 47(5):486-488.

21. Honeyman JP, Starzyk AR. Confluent Streams: The Production of An Inhouse Government Documents Catalog Using a Facilities Management System (INSITE). Administrative Notes, Washington: Government Printing Office 1987 8(9):3 (GP 3.16/3-2:8/9).

22. National Library of Medicine News. Washington: Government Printing Office, 1987:5-6 (HE 20.3619:42/4,5).

23. INSITE, Office of Facilities Management Systems, Massachusetts Institute of Technology.

24. Honeyman JP, Starzyk AR. Enter: INSITE— A facilities management database becomes an indexed government documents catalog. (In preparation for publication.)

25. Library of Congress, Cataloging Distribution Service. MARC Distribution Service 1987. Washington: Government Printing Office, 1987:6 (LC 30.28:987)

26. Honeyman JP, Phelps J. Integration of government documents with catalogued materials through an accessions list. (In preparation for publication.)

27. Reynolds CJ. Discovering the Government Documents Collection in Libraries. Reference and Adult Services Division of the American Library Association, 1978 14 (Spring):228-31.

Availability and Mutilation of U.S. Geological Survey Publications: An Analytic Study

Patrick Ragains

SUMMARY. A study was undertaken at Montana State University Libraries to determine if missing and mutilation rates differed between monographs in the general collection and U.S. Geological Survey publications. Prior to this investigation, it was assumed that there might be a higher rate of items missing from the collection of U.S. Geological Survey publications than from the general collection and that there would be a greater incidence of mutilation among the U.S.G.S. materials. Items were chosen according to a random sample and the resulting data analyzed using a Chi-square test for significance at the .05 level. Contrary to the investigator's initial assumptions, it was found that U.S.G.S. *Bulletins* and *Professional Papers* were not mutilated more often than monographs in the general collection, and that there is no statistically significant difference in rates of availability. Additional evidence encountered in the course of the study suggests that the U.S.G.S. publications may be used much less frequently than other library materials. Recommendations are made for further research concerning use and accessibility. The methodology used in this investigation is potentially applicable to many other types of collection studies.

Montana State University Libraries presently has in excess of 482,000 books and bound periodicals in its collection, including extensive holdings of the publications of the United States Geological Survey dating back to the survey's beginnings at the end of the nineteenth century. The library has been a federal depository since 1907. Two well-known series of U.S.G.S. publications are the *Bulletins* and *Professional Papers*, both

---

Patrick Ragains is Assistant Professor and Government Information Specialist, Montana State University Libraries, Bozeman MT 59717.

© 1991 by The Haworth Press, Inc. All rights reserved.

of which are outlets for authoritative geoscience research covering the United States and its territories, as well as other parts of the world, the moon, and other planets. These series are profusely illustrated with maps, photographs, charts, and tables, with the maps and charts often inserted in pockets attached to the inside back cover. Because of the illustrative content of these publications, it was assumed that the U.S.G.S. *Bulletins* and *Professional Papers* would be more vulnerable to mutilation than those items in the library collection with fewer illustrations. User complaints of charts and maps missing from U.S.G.S. publications at MSU Libraries (and reports of entire publications being missing) have added weight to this assumption, even to the point that some librarians have feared that these important resources might be destroyed. This study was begun in order to investigate these concerns.

SELECTED LOSS, AVAILABILITY, AND DETERIORATION STUDIES

Many studies of loss and availability of materials in other libraries have been published, with both types commonly relying upon sample surveys. The authors of most loss studies have sought to establish accurate loss rates by meticulous and repeated searches for missing items.[1] Availability studies usually rely upon reports of user success (usually gathered from completed questionnaires) in locating specific titles.[2] Once the data has been collected and compiled, reasons for non-availability (i.e., item not acquired, in circulation, library error, user error) can be analyzed using a branching technique such as the one developed by Kantor.[3]

Several studies of mutilation and deterioration of library materials exist, the most detailed being a survey in the Yale University Library system which spanned over three years and was supported by grants from the National Endowment for the Humanities and the Andrew W. Mellon Foundation.[4] Over 36,500 books were eventually examined in this survey, which provided the Yale Libraries with a large amount of reliable information about the condition of its collections. Another investigator sampled periodicals for mutilation, combining that data with instances of mutilation as reported by users, or found during either shelfreading or binding preparation.[5]

The one known study of shelf availability of government publications is an unpublished report to the University of Arizona Librarian by Claudia Bakula, a master's candidate in library science and administrative intern at the time of the investigation.[6] This was an enumerative study, meaning it described specific characteristics based on a sample from one group of items. Bakula examined availability of documents that had been barcoded and entered on the library's online catalog. The frame of the study was the library's depository collection, an open stack area segregated from the main collection and shelved by Superintendent of Documents classification. From a sample of one hundred items, only two items were not located at or near the proper shelf location, in any preshelving location, or checked out. In addition to establishing a missing rate, Bakula sought to identify agency, subject, and physical characteristics of missing publications, but this proved impossible due to the small results. Bakula's use of sampling and choice of a search procedure that would closely replicate the user's experience served as models for the present investigation.

DESIGN OF THE STUDY

The present investigation is, by contrast, an analytic study, comparing attributes of the general collection and a subset of U.S. Geological Survey publications. Comparative data was taken from a sample of monographs from the main stacks in the Renne Library (Montana State University's main library). There were several reasons for this choice. First, the U.S.G.S. publications to be sampled are monographic series housed in the Renne Library's open stacks under Library of Congress classification, and it was considered desirable to compare these with like materials in the overall library collection. Periodicals are generally thought to be mutilated more often than monographs, and it was assumed that more valid information would result if these materials were excluded. Separate stack locations (Documents, Special Collections, Archives, Reference and storage) and a branch Creative Arts Library were also excluded due to differing circulation policies and other variables possibly affecting access.

In addition to identifying the frame of the study, it was necessary to develop a satisfactory method for collecting and analyzing the data. Both the general library collection and the subset of Geological Survey publications were too large for every item to be examined, so sampling was considered to be a desirable alternative. Statistical consultants advised the investigator to select a sample size based on a "best guess" for missing and mutilation rates.[7] From an estimate that missing and mutilation rates might be as high as fifty percent, a sample size of one hundred each from both the general collection and the Geological Survey publications would have a ninety-five percent chance of detecting a ten percent or greater difference in the incidence of the target characteristics in each group. The sample data would be analyzed using a Chi-square test for significance at the .05 level.

Digits chosen from a random number table governed the selection of items in the sample.[8] From five-digit groupings in the table, the first three digits in a chosen group were used to select the general stack books using the library shelflist and U.S.G.S. publications from a group of check-in cards, which are the library's primary records for these materials. For general stack books, a shelflist drawer was selected according to the first two random digits and, after measuring into the drawer the number of inches indicated by the third digit, a shelflist card was chosen, and its call number noted.[9] If the chosen card was either for a serial or a book in a stack area excluded from the study, then the next card for an item belonging to the study frame was selected from the drawer. For U.S.G.S. publications, the first digit was used to count into the set of check-in cards, with the second two digits indicating the number of items to count into the card selected. Fifty items were chosen from each series, for a total sample of one hundred Geological Survey publications.

Each book chosen in the survey was searched on the shelf and, if needed, in sorting locations and circulation records. Books in the sample were searched only once, with the intent of duplicating users' experiences as closely as possible. This regimen for data collection tests the availability of items known to be in the library's collection, and therefore differs from Kantor's research design, which relied upon reports of user success in finding titles not necessarily known to be held by the library. Each book found was examined for deliberate mutilation either by marking in any part of the item or removal of illustrative material. Also, each item was checked against at least one bibliographic authority that provided sufficient detail to determine if all of its illustrative matter was intact.[10] On the scales for assigning numeric values according to the degree of mutilation detected, books which were not marked at all were assigned a value of "1," those with marking, but all printed matter still intact and readable were scored as "2," and books with markings which had destroyed some printed matter were scored as "3." Likewise, books with all illustrative matter intact were scored as "1," those with some illustrative matter missing were scored "2," and books with all of the plates or illustrations missing were assigned a value of "3." Recording the number of circulations for each book would have been desireable, but proved impossible due to incomplete circulation histories for many items.

PRESENTATION AND ANALYSIS OF THE DATA

The data collected in the study are presented in Figure I, followed by analysis of availability and mutilation factors. In two cases, the data has been condensed from the categories that were examined. Since none of the books examined were mutilated at Level 3 (indicating the book was either marked in such a manner that some printed matter had been destroyed or with all of its illustrative matter removed), it was possible to list only the data for books which were mutilated at Level 2.

The data in Figure I was analyzed to detect any significant differences between monographs in the main collection and U.S.G.S. publications. In order to meet the test of significance, at least ninety-five out of one hundred additional trials would need to yield the same basic results; this can also be referred to as a test for significance at the .05 level. Figures II, III, and IV present the design and results of Chi-square tests for differences in availability, mutilation by marking, and removal of illustrations.

Since the resulting Chi-square value of .59215 is smaller than the critical value of 3.84, we do not reject the hypothesis that there is no significant difference in availability of the group of U.S.G.S. *Bulletins* and *Professional Papers* and the second group, comprised of monographs in the main stacks. It may be reasonably concluded that any difference in availability does not exceed ten percent.

The Chi-square value of 10.396 is greater than the critical value of 3.84, requiring the hypothesis of no difference to be rejected. In other words, it cannot be stated that there is no significant difference in mutilation by marking between the two groups. The incidence of marking is greater in the general stack sample than among the U.S.G.S. publications, and that the difference is probably ten percent or greater.

Here the value of 1.189 is smaller than the critical value. The null hypothesis, that there is no significant difference in mutilation by removal of illustrative matter between the U.S.G.S. publications and monographs in the main stacks, is therefore not rejected. It can be concluded with ninety-five percent certainty that any difference between the two collections in removal of illustrative content does not exceed ten percent.

CONCLUSIONS

Statistical analysis of the data collected for this study did not validate the prior assumptions about the condition of MSU's holdings of U.S. Geological Survey *Bulletins* and *Professional Papers*. Concerns about mutilation and theft were found to be either incorrect or perhaps exaggerated. There is no evidence that special security measures, such as removal of plates to a locked storage area, are necessary to protect publications in the two series from mutilation. It could be that perceptions of widespread

Figure I: Availability and mutilation	U.S.G.S.	Main Stacks
AVAILABILITY		
n=	100	100
on shelf	98	90
preshelving (sorting shelf, truck)	0	0
checked out	0	5
not traceable	2	5
PHYSICAL CONDITION		
n=	98	90
marking - Level 2: marked, but no printed matter destroyed	1	13
illustrative matter - Level 2: some illustrations missing	3	0

Figure II: Availability

N= 200 df= 1

	U.S.G.S.	Main stacks
Available or traceable	98	95
Not traceable	2	5

Chi-square= .59215 Critical value= 3.84

Figure III: Mutilation by marking

N= 188 df= 1

	U.S.G.S.	Main Stacks
Level I: Free of marks	97	77
Level II: Marked/ not destroyed	1	13

Chi-square= 10.396 Critical value= 3.84

phi= .235

Figure IV: Mutilation by removal of illustrative matter

N= 188 df= 1

	U.S.G.S.	Main stacks
Level I: all ill. intact	95	90
Level II: some ill. missing	3	0

Chi-square= 1.189 Critical value= 3.84

mutilation resulted from knowledge of isolated cases or a concentration of mutilation in a small subset of the Geological Survey publications, such as those concerned with locations in Montana and its neighboring states. In the former case, options for addressing specific instances of mutilation could easily be identified (seeking replacement via the *Needs & Offers* list or the out-of-print market).

Different problems might be posed by the discovery of higher mutilation rates among U.S.G.S. publications dealing with nearby geographic areas. Although it was not possible to confidently record the number of checkouts for items in the sample, those assigned to collect the data in this study noted greater numbers of circulations for monographs at large than for the U.S.G.S. items. Such scant evidence of use was unexpected, as Montana State University has graduated over 560 geologists at the baccalaureate and master's levels since 1957. When such anecdotal information is considered in tandem with the hard data on mutilation, it raises questions about the accessibility and usefulness of the collections. Possibly, low rates of use are due to lower levels of bibliographic access. Holdings records for the U.S.G.S. publications are maintained out of the library's public areas, and are certainly less likely to be consulted by users (or for them) than are the card and online catalogs. In the future, an investigation into the use of information by the university's geology faculty and students would appear worthwhile. If the library's U.S.G.S. holdings are not being used, one might call into question the advisability of maintaining a comprehensive collection of the agency's publications (two other academic libraries in the state, a school of mines and a regional depository, have equivalent collections of U.S.G.S. publications).

Finally, it bears mentioning that this type of study has wide applicability for examining many types of problems associated with library collections. It would be easy to follow up on the present study, for example, by constructing a research design to examine citation patterns in geological research. Attributes of large collections can be effectively studied with fairly small samples. Further, sample sizes and confidence levels for statistical tests can be easily changed to meet the varying degrees of accuracy which might be considered necessary to support changes in collection management practices. Such investments of time and effort as are expended to investigate potential problems of library collections are well-spent, considering the benefit of collections and services that are more relevant and accessible to users.

NOTES

1. Greenwood, Larry and Harlley McKean. "Effective Measurement are Reduction of Book Loss in an Academic Library." *Journal of Academic Librarianship* 11 (November 1985): 275-283; Pinzelik, Barbara P. "Monitoring Book Losses in an Academic Library." *Library & Archival Security* 64 (Winter 1984): 112.

2. Mansbridge, John. "Availability Studies in Libraries." *Library and Information Science Research* 8 (1986):299-314.

3. Kantor, Paul B. "The Library as an Information Utility in the University Context: Evaluation and Measurement of Services." *Journal of the American Society for Information Science* 27 (1976): 100-112.

4. Walker, Gay, Jane Greenfield, John Fox, and Jeffrey S. Simonoff. "The Yale Survey: A Large-Scale Study of Book Deterioration in the Yale University Library." *College & Research Libraries* 46 (March 1985): 111-132.

5. Sleep, Esther L. "Periodical Vandalism: A Chronic Condition?" *Canadian Library Journal* 39 (February 1982): 39-42.

6. Bakula, Claudia. *Missing Government Documents: A Research Study*. (Graduate Library School, University of Arizona, Tucson. 1984) Photocopy.

7. Jeffrey D. Banfield, Assistant Professor of Statistics at Montana State University, and Chip Todd, a graduate assistant in statistics at the university, served as statistical consultants in developing the sampling methodology.

8. Snedecor, George W. *Statistical Methods: Applied to Experiments in Agriculture and Biology*. (Ames, Iowa: Iowa State College Press, 1956): 10-13.

9. Acknowledgements are due to Elaine Nienhouse, Associate Professor and Reference Librarian at Ferris State University, Michigan. Nienhouse served as the investigator's assistant in this and other phases of the project, selecting items from the library shelflist, supervising the search process, and examining many of the sample pieces.

10. The bibliographic authorities used were physical descriptions from readily available cataloging records (via the library's online catalog, the Western Library Network, and, for many U.S.G.S. publications, GPO cataloging via a commercial CDR-CM product), or lists of illustrations in the books themselves.

GPO Cataloging Records in the Online Catalog: Implications for the Reference Librarian

Thomas Kinney
Gary Cornwell

SUMMARY. Reference staff at many libraries are facing a sudden and dramatic change in the size and composition of their library's online catalog as a result of loading large files of Government Printing Office (GPO) retrospective cataloging records. While these records provide a much-needed increase in access to federal documents, they have special characteristics which make them difficult to work with. This article is intended to provide reference librarians with the basic "GPO cataloging record literacy" they need to deal successfully with the load of these records into an online catalog, and also to explore some of the specific implications of such a load for reference service.

INTRODUCTION

Historically, United States federal government documents have represented one of the most valuable yet underutilized collections in the library.

Thomas Kinney is Assistant Head, Library Systems Office, University of Florida Libraries, Gainesville, FL 32611. Gary Cornwell is Assistant Chair, Documents Department, University of Florida Libraries, Gainesville, FL 32611.

© 1991 by The Haworth Press, Inc. All rights reserved.

Although reference librarians are aware that government documents contain a wealth of information, lack of comprehensive bibliographic access has inhibited their use. Quality indexes such as the *American Statistics Index* (*ASI*) and *CIS* provide access for knowledgeable users, but the fact that most libraries do not catalog their federal documents has been an insurmountable obstacle in promoting their widespread use. However, with the recent proliferation of online systems and the availability of machine-readable cataloging for many U.S. government documents, libraries have begun to integrate cataloging records for government documents into their local online catalogs.

The addition of Government Printing Office (GPO) cataloging records typically results in sudden and dramatic changes in the size and composition of a library's online catalog. GPO record loading is much more complex than the usual retrospective conversion project due to the special characteristics of the GPO retrospective file. This article is intended to provide reference librarians with the basic "GPO catalog record literacy" they need to deal successfully with the load of these records into an online catalog, and also to explore some of the specific implications of such a load for reference service.

BACKGROUND

A full appreciation of what it means to load the GPO retrospective file into a local online catalog requires a fairly detailed understanding of some federal documents "lore" that is generally not well understood outside government document circles. At the risk of boring the more knowledgeable, this section reviews some of the basic and not-so basic concepts of federal documents librarianship. An understanding of the concepts covered in this section is assumed in subsequent sections.

Basic Characteristics of the *Monthly Catalog*

By law, the Superintendent of Documents is required to prepare a catalog of government publications listing the documents printed during the previous month, where they are available, and how much they cost. The GPO has implemented this directive through the production of the *Monthly Catalog*. While the *Monthly Catalog* serves as the primary access point to government publications, it is important to note that not every publication listed in the *Monthly Catalog* is available for selection by depository libraries. Documents not distributed as part of the Depository Library Program are referred to as *non-depository* documents. There are several thousand non-depository publications listed in the *Monthly Catalog* each year.

Even though the non-depository documents listed in the *Monthly Catalog* are not available for selection through the GPO, there are a variety of ways in which a library can obtain them. For example, subscriptions are available from the CIS Corporation to non-depository statistical publications indexed in *ASI*. Libraries may also receive material through the Library of Congress Documents Expediting Project. Additionally, the Readex Corporation offers a subscription to all non-depository publications listed in the *Monthly Catalog*.

With the exception of Regional Depositories which receive all depository publications distributed by the GPO, depository libraries select which categories of publications they receive from the GPO through *item number* profiling. Each year depository libraries are given the opportunity to evaluate and update their item number profile with the GPO to reflect the current information needs of their library. They are able to delete items from their selection profile at any time during the year.

An important feature of the item number is that it is the only element of the *Monthly Catalog* listing for which the format of a document distributed by the GPO may be determined (i.e., paper or microfiche). Virtually all cataloging done by the GPO is for the paper version of a document. However, much of what is actually distributed to depository libraries is microfiche.

The Superintendent of Documents Call Number

The GPO assigns Superintendent of Document (SuDoc) call numbers to all publications listed in the *Monthly Catalog*. Depository libraries are under no obligation to use this number in classifying their documents. However, since the SuDoc number is readily available, most depository libraries use it to some extent in classifying their publications.

Over the years, the basic philosophy of the SuDoc number has remained essentially unchanged. It is an alphanumeric call number based on the Superintendent of Documents classification scheme. This scheme is based on the principle of provenance, so that all publications of a particular government agency are grouped together. A SuDoc number is made up of a SuDoc stem number, which identifies the agency and series to which the document belongs, plus some type of extension to differentiate the individual item from others in the series. For monographs this extension is typically a cutter number; for numbered series, the number within the series; for annuals, the year of the publications; and for periodicals, the volume and number of the issue. *T1.2:M58* is a typical SuDoc number.

"*T1*" indicates that the publication was issued by the Secretary of the Treasury. "*.2*" indicates that this publication has been classified a General Publication, and the *M58* is the cutter number for the monograph *Middle Eastern Multinational Financial Institutions*.

Each time there is reorganization within the government, the SuDoc number for a series can change radically. The *Digest of Education Statistics* is the standard statistical source in most libraries. Yet since 1962, reorganization within the federal government has resulted in the title being classed 6 different ways: *FS5.210:10024*, *HE5.210:10024*, *HE5.98:date*, *HE19.315:date*, *ED1.113:date*, and *ED1.326:date*. As discussed below, different libraries may choose different options in dealing with these call number changes.

Major changes in SuDoc classification can also result from changes in philosophy or rule interpretation at the GPO. The most recent and vivid example of this relates to recurring titles within series. One such title is *Fertility of American Women*, an annual publication which is part of the Current Population Reports, Series P-20. Traditionally, the GPO assigned a call number to this publication following the *series numbering* rather than incorporation the *year of publication* into the call number. For example, the 1983 edition of *Fertility of American Women* is number 395 in the P-20 series and has the SuDoc call number C3.186:P-20/395. This practice is consistent with the usual way recurring titles are shelved, bound, referenced and checked-in.

However, the GPO has recently begun to "class-out" recurring titles from numbered series by giving them unique call numbers. For example, the 1984 edition of *Fertility of American Women* has the call number C3.186/10:984. This reclassification does not reflect any change in the publication itself, just in the GPO choice of call number. The serial is still part of the series and will continue to be referenced that way in most bibliographies. It should be noted that libraries are under no obligation to follow the GPO change in call number. They may choose to ignore the new call number and continue to shelve this title with other numbers in the P-20 series. Another option is to change the call number of all previous issues to the new call number so that all issues of *Fertility of American Women* are shelved together.

Guidelines for Depository Libraries

Libraries which participate in the Depository Library Program are required to follow specific guidelines. The guideline which probably has the most significance for the online catalog is the requirement that each depository library maintains piece level check-in records for all depository materials. Additionally, the library is expected to maintain these check-in records in a timely fashion. Ideally the library would receive, process, check-in, and shelve all depository material within 24 hours of receipt.

Depository libraries are encouraged by the GPO to frequently evaluate and weed their collections. Documents held for more than 5 years may, with the permission of the Regional Depository Library, be withdrawn. During the weeding process, depository library staff must keep in mind that their depository collection was established to serve an entire congressional district. Consequently, the collection should reflect the information needs of all citizens in the district and not just the primary clientele of the library.

MACHINE-READABLE CATALOGING FOR FEDERAL DOCUMENTS: THE GPO RETROSPECTIVE FILE

For federal documents as for any collection, the greater the number of machine-readable cataloging records already available, the easier (i.e., less expensive) it is for an individual library to add cataloging records for that collection to its online catalog. As it turns out, machine-readable cataloging does exist for a large subset of federal documents, namely all (or virtually all) documents listed in the *Monthly Catalog* starting with the July, 1976, issue. Not only is this cataloging available via widely-used bibliographic utilities (including OCLC and RLIN), but libraries may also purchase subsets of these records corresponding to their holdings from several vendors.

The reason such an extensive file of machine-readable cataloging exists for this set of materials is that the GPO started using OCLC records as the basis for producing the *Monthly Catalog* beginning with the July, 1976, issue. Beginning with this issue, each listing of a document in the *Monthly Catalog* has been derived from a separate machine-readable cataloging record created by the GPO using OCLC. The GPO retrospective file is simply the collection of all of these records from July, 1976, to the present. A library may use the same item number profile it uses to select publications from the GPO to select cataloging records which reflect the library's depository document holdings.

Understanding the primary reason the GPO created these cataloging records—to produce the *Monthly Catalog*, not to catalog the GPO's own collection of documents or to provide a cataloging service for depository libraries—is the key to grasping both the potential benefits and the problems associated with the GPO retrospective file.

THE GPO RETROSPECTIVE FILE: PROBLEMS AND SPECIAL CHARACTERISTICS

The GPO retrospective file is currently available on tape—the format currently best suited to loading into local systems—from the Library of Congress as well as several commercial vendors. There have historically been a number of problems with the GPO retrospective records that have made them difficult to integrate into local online library catalogs. Judy Myers' landmark article "The Government Printing Office Cataloging Records: Opportunities and Problems"[1] provides a detailed discussion of these problems and lays out a proposal for their resolution. In this section, we review these problems and discuss the progress that one vendor—Marcive—has made in addressing these problems.

As the result of an extensive project undertaken by Marcive in conjunction with the libraries at Texas A&M University, Louisiana State University, and Rice University, the GPO retrospective file currently available from Marcive is by far the most extensively "cleaned up" version of this file available. This project is referred to in this article simply as the "Marcive project." Several publications describing this project in more detail are currently in progress, including an article by Laura Tull of Texas A&M.[2]

Note: This discussion represents the authors' understanding of the GPO retrospective file as available from the Library of Congress and Marcive as of September, 1989. Libraries planning for the load of the GPO retrospective records should be sure to obtain up-to-date information on the GPO file as available from these or any other vendors, and not rely solely on secondary sources of information.

Document Format Identification and Description

The *Monthly Catalog* listing for a document almost always describes the paper version of a document, even though the GPO may distribute the document in microfiche. This means that many records in the GPO retrospective file do not describe documents in the format that they were distributed. The Marcive project did not attempt to correct this problem.

Even though a GPO catalog record may not describe the actual format of a document as it was distributed, the record will at least identify the actual format through the item number. For example, the item number for *The Code of Federal Regulations* distributed in paper is 0572-B; the same title distributed in microfiche has the item number 0572-C. The *Monthly Catalog* listing for a document distributed in microfiche will include the word "microfiche" following the item number, making it possible to easily identify documents distributed in microfiche. Unfortunately, it is not uncommon for the "microfiche" designation to be missing in both the *Monthly Catalog* listing and the corresponding record in the retrospective file. Many of these errors are corrected in the lists of corrections included periodically in the *Monthly Catalog*, but many are not. These errors have not been corrected in the LC file; corrections included in the *Monthly Catalog* have been incorporated into the Marcive file.

Duplicate and "Availability" Records

That the GPO retrospective file is "full of duplicate records" is a complaint frequently voiced about GPO cataloging. This generalization barely hints at the actual complexity of the GPO retrospective file. Since the file from LC contains one record corresponding to each *Monthly Catalog* entry, it necessarily contains multiple records for any document which has had multiple *Monthly Catalog* listings.

The three main types of documents for which such multiple listings occur—multipart monographs, annuals and other less-frequently issued serials, and periodicals—are discussed below. We have used Myers' term "availability record" to distinguish between the different types of multiple records present in the GPO retrospective file. She introduced this term to differentiate the multiple records for monographs issued in parts and for annuals and other less-frequently issued serials—created as a result of the GPO's need to list the availability of individual parts or issues in the *Monthly Catalog*—from true cataloging records.[3]

Multipart Monographs

For single part monographs (and multipart monographs for which all parts are listed in the same issue of the *Monthly Catalog*), only one listing appears in the *Monthly Catalog*. This listing, and the corresponding catalog record from which the listing was derived, describe the document as a whole. In contrast, when the different parts of a multipart monographs are listed in different issues of the *Monthly Catalog*, the GPO retrospective file does not contain a single catalog record describing the monograph as a whole—instead there will be a set of separate availability records, each of which describes a different part (or set of parts). Typically, each of these multiple records contains the same OCLC number, since they have all been derived from the same "template" record entered by the GPO on OCLC.

Annuals and Other Less Frequently Issued Serials

In contrast to periodicals, each annual volume of a publication such a the *Statistical Abstract of the United States* is listed separately in the *Monthly Catalog*. The *Monthly Catalog* listing will typically include information on both the serial as a whole (such as the frequency of issue) and the particular volume (such as the actual month and year the volume was issued). The corresponding GPO cataloging record is really an availability record for one particular volume, not a true cataloging record describing the serial as a whole. As a result, most annuals and other less-frequently issued serials listed in the *Monthly Catalog* are represented in the GPO retrospective file by a set of availability records. As with multipart monographs, these records usually have the same OCLC number, since they have typically been derived from the same "template" record on OCLC.

A particularly confusing set of records may be present in the retrospective file when the GPO has changed the way a recurring title within a numbered series is listed in the *Monthly Catalog*. The GPO may catalog the title as a monograph in some years, but as a serial in others. The title *Characteristics of Households and Persons Receiving Selected Noncash Benefits*, for example, is represented by some records in the retrospective file as a numbered monograph within the P-60 series and by other records as an open-ended annual report.

Periodicals

Individual issues of periodicals (defined by the GPO as serials that are issued more than three times each year) are typically not listed separately in the *Monthly Catalog*. Instead, the periodical as a whole is listed once each year in a special issue of the *Monthly Catalog* called the "Periodicals Supplement." (Prior to 1985, this issue was called the "Serials Supplement." Even at that time, however, it contained listings only for periodicals (and a select group of monographic series titles), not for annuals and other less-frequently issued serials).

Unlike multipart monographs and less frequently-issued serials, each of the multiple records included in the GPO retrospective file for periodicals is a true cataloging record which does describe the periodical as a whole. Not only do all of the records for one periodical title typically have the same OCLC number, but they are often nearly identical (depending on what changes may have occurred from year to year in issuing agency, SuDoc number, price, and so on).

Multiple Records and the Marcive Project

One of the most ambitious parts of the Marcive project has been the elimination of these various types of multiple records from the retrospective file. Each set of availability records for multipart monographs has been consolidated into a single "composite" catalog record which describes the monograph as a whole. Availability records for individual volumes of serials have been eliminated and replaced with true cataloging records which describe each serial as a whole. Duplicate records for periodicals have been eliminated from the file, and the single remaining record for each periodical title has been reviewed for accuracy and completeness.

Authority Control

Since the GPO has participated in the Name Authority Cooperative Project (NACO) since 1981, *name headings* in GPO cataloging records created since then should be consistent with the Library of Congress Name Authority File. GPO cataloging records created from 1976 through 1980, however, include a significant number of name headings which are not represented in this file, either as valid headings or as cross-references. (Some of these headings are in correct AACR2 form, but have not yet been established by LC or a NACO participant. Others contain misspellings or other irregularities, or are in a form which has not been incorporated as a cross-reference in the LC Name Authority File). *Subject headings* in earlier GPO cataloging records have frequently been mis-tagged; many subject headings which had actually been established by LC were tagged as locally assigned, whereas some headings assigned locally by the GPO were tagged as LC headings. *Series names* also present problems. While GPO has been contributing series names to the LC Name Authority File since 1986, LC and the GPO have over the years frequently established different forms of name for the same series.

Many name and subject headings in the Marcive file have been changed to match the heading established by LC through computer matching of headings in the GPO retrospective file with the most current versions of the LC Name and Subject Authority Files. Marcive project participants reviewed all name and subject headings which failed to match the LC files, revising them where necessary to reflect current LC practice. Problems with the tagging of subject headings have been corrected. While the Marcive participants have reviewed many series headings for consistency and spelling, no attempt has been made to bring these headings into conformity with series names established by LC.

Missing and Mis-Tagged Numbers

In many early GPO cataloging records, numbers or codes which are important as access points, as descriptive information, or as parameters in record selection and processing are missing or "mis-tagged." This is due largely to the fact that several special MARC tags for government document numbers had not yet been established when the GPO first began cataloging on OCLC. Item numbers, GPO stock numbers, contract numbers, and technical report numbers often appear in general note fields. Many SuDoc numbers are tagged as local call numbers and sometimes additionally as general notes. Approximately 7,000 records lack OCLC numbers. There are also some records which lack a SuDoc number.

Marcive project participants have added the missing OCLC and SuDoc numbers to the file. Correctly tagged fields have been added for "mis-tagged" item numbers, SuDoc numbers, stock numbers, and technical report numbers.

SuDoc Number Changes for Serials

Serial publications distributed by the GPO undergo fairly frequent SuDoc number changes due to changes in the issuing agency. Since depository libraries typically check-in and shelve documents by SuDoc number, a complete record of a serial title's SuDoc number changes is a useful tool for providing access to the title. Most *Monthly Catalog* listings for serials (and the corresponding cataloging records in the retrospective file as available from LC) do not include a complete record of the title's SuDoc number changes. The Marcive project participants have reviewed and where necessary completed the record of SuDoc number changes for the single record included in the Marcive record for each serial (including periodicals).

Other Problems

As is to be expected in any large cataloging operation, GPO cataloging records contain a variety of miscellaneous errors. In terms of implications for access to government documents, the most significant errors are missing or incorrect item numbers and incorrect SuDoc numbers. Other errors include misspellings, errors in filing indicators (MARC codes which indicate the number of characters that should be "skipped" in indexing), errors in SuDoc numbers, and so on.

The GPO publishes correction lists periodically in the *Monthly Catalog*. These corrections are not reflected in the GPO retrospective file as distributed by LC. All of the corrections which have appeared in the *Monthly Catalog* have been keyed into the Marcive retrospective file. Many misspellings and other errors have been corrected as part of the editing and review process for resolving the multiple record problem (see above). The Marcive project participants have also reviewed all title headings for misspellings.

IMPLICATIONS FOR THE REFERENCE LIBRARIAN

The load of the GPO cataloging records into a library's online catalog will of course have a tremendous impact on the library's Documents Department. However, since the reference librarian is often the first point of contact for library users, the loading of the GPO file will have a significant impact on reference staff as well. In this section, some of the problems that loading the GPO file will present to reference staff are explored. While reference librarians will need to understand these issues in order to accurately interpret the library's online catalog to library users, this will also help them to participate more fully in the all-important planning process that should precede the actual load of the records.

Coverage

Since the GPO retrospective file begins with the July, 1976, issue of the *Monthly Catalog*, the records loaded into a library's online catalog from this file will not reflect the library's earlier documents holdings (which may be extensive). At the present time, there is no tape product that contains cataloging records for earlier publications. However, since many libraries have cataloged some pre-1976 documents online, the potential does exist for such a product in the future.[4]

With the many options available for obtaining non-depository documents, a library may well decide to load GPO cataloging records for these publications. For example, many libraries receive non-depository publications through the Readex Corporation. These documents are currently available in microfiche and can be shelved by SuDoc number. However, prior to 1980, this material was available in microprint only. Since multiple documents may appear on the same microprint card, pre-1980 publications cannot be filed by SuDoc number. The access point for this material is the *Monthly Catalog* entry number.

Access Points

Because of the relationship between the GPO retrospective file and the *Monthly Catalog*, each record in the file includes a *Monthly Catalog* entry number. The entry number is simply the last two digits of the year followed by an accession number. For example, the 500th document to appear in the 1989 *Monthly Catalog* will have the *Monthly Catalog* entry number 89-00500. This number is important for two reasons. First, as discussed above, pre-1980 Readex material is only accessible by this number. Secondly, commercial indexes such as *ASI* typically include this number in bibliographic citations. Many patrons will mistake the *Monthly Catalog* entry number for the SuDoc call number. Online catalog access by *Monthly Catalog* entry number will allow the reference librarian quick access to the corresponding bibliographic record and the correct call number.

In order to make full use of online catalog records for government documents, reference librarians need to become familiar with several other numbers and codes which are unique to government documents. The most important of these is the SuDoc call number. Issuing agency, series, and sometimes even title can be determined from the call number. Unfortunately, the SuDoc number can also serve as a source of confusion. Because it is an alphanumeric call number (and often includes a cutter number) it closely resembles a Library of Congress call number. For example, *T1.2:M58* is the SuDoc call number for *Middle Eastern Multinational Financial Institutions*, while *T12.M57* is the *LC call number* for the *Missouri Directory of Manufacturing and Mining*. The similarity between these call numbers is not only potentially confusing for library patrons, but also to library staff.

Processing of Ongoing Document Receipts

While the library may purchase and load the tapes from July, 1976, through the most current issue of the *Monthly Catalog*, it is also important to plan for the ongoing cataloging of newly received documents. As discussed above, libraries participating in the Depository Library Program are committed to creating timely, piece level check-in records for all depository documents. One option that a library has for cataloging new document receipts is to buy monthly tapes that correspond to ongoing issues of the *Monthly Catalog*. Unfortunately, full cataloging records are not available—either on tape or online—for many depository documents at the time they are received. There is currently a 6 month or so average time lag between the distribution of a document and the availability of the cataloging record for that document on tape.[5] This delay in bibliographic access is unacceptable both from a practical standpoint and by guidelines established by the GPO. (At the time of this writing, the GPO is developing a new cataloging tape product which is expected to decrease this lag time and also to make the GPO cataloging records generally more usable).[6]

Another option is for libraries to individually catalog each document received. This approach is used by many libraries and generally provides timely bibliographic access to the material. However, for libraries receiving a large percentage of material available from the GPO this is an extremely expensive alternative. From the standpoint of the reference librarian, this approach frequently provides the fastest and most complete access to this material.

Depending on the sophistication of the local online catalog, a library may choose to create brief temporary online records for new documents. These records may then be replaced by complete bibliographic records when they become available. While this approach does provide timely check in, it requires a large investment of staff time creating records that will eventually be deleted from the database. More importantly for the reference librarian, the bibliographic access provided by such brief records is typically limited to author, title and series.

A final alternative is for new receipts to be recorded in some file independent of the online catalog, such as a card catalog or microcomputer file in the Documents Department. From the point of view of the reference librarian, this approach severely limits access to new documents. With this approach, the online file reflects neither the entire retrospective documents collection nor current receipts.

Increased Demands

Upon loading a file of the GPO retrospective cataloging records, a library with a large uncataloged federal documents collection will likely experience a significant increase in the size of its online catalog. At the University of Florida Libraries, for example, the GPO retrospective file is scheduled for loading in the Fall of 1989. At that time, government document records are expected to represent about 13% of the titles in the online database. To put this figure in perspective, this percentage of titles is the same as that for the entire central science library. UF Libraries reference staff are expecting a significant increase in the number of reference questions relating to this material. Libraries which have loaded large GPO files estimate increases of 200 to 300 percent in the number of government document related reference questions.[7] Both the Documents Department and other reference staff must be prepared to handle this increase.

If the library adds their holdings for this material to a national database they can also expect an increase in the number of interlibrary loan request received. In June, 1987, the University of Florida Libraries had their holdings set in OCLC for the entire GPO retrospective file. As a Regional Depository the UF Libraries received about 10 out-of-state ILL requests for government documents each month. After holdings were set on OCLC, this number jumped to about 130 per month. This increase necessitated a revision of the Library's ILL lending policy.

Format

Virtually all of the records in the GPO retrospective file describe the paper version of a document. Apart from the item number code itself, the word "microfiche" following the item number is the only indication in the *Monthly Catalog* that a document was distributed in microfiche. Additionally, because selected titles in a series may or may not have been converted to microfiche, this designation is often in error. In order to determine the format of a document library staff and users will have to closely examine the online record. Ironically, once the format has been determined, there is a possibility that it will be wrong anyway.

Additional problems may occur if the item number field is used to assign the holding location. At the University of Florida, the word "microfiche" in the item number field is being used as one of the determinants for assigning holding in the online catalog. For example, EPA Draft Environmental Impact Statements have the item number 0431-I-55 (microfiche) and are distributed to depository libraries in microfiche. Data load specifications call for the occurrence of the word "microfiche" in the item number field to cause this series to load into the online catalog with the holding location of *Main Library, Documents (microfiche)*. Incorrect holding locations in the online catalog resulting from incorrect data in the item number field can lead to confused and disgruntled patrons and staff. Awareness of this problem by reference staff can help to avoid potential problems.

Serials and Other Multipart Monographs

Reference librarians need to know how the problem of multiple records for serials has been addressed. They need to know what type of multiple records are present in the file obtained from the vendor, what type of elimination or modification of multiple records has been performed locally as part of the load process, and what (if any) post-load modification is planned to transform volume specific availability records into true cataloging records.

Reference librarians need to understand how SuDoc number changes for serials are reflected in the online catalog. Does the cataloging record for each serial title include a complete record of SuDoc number changes? Are the holdings for each SuDoc number reflected accurately in the online catalog for serial titles with holdings shelved under several different SuDoc numbers?

Reference staff will also need to know what types of records may have been loaded for recurring titles within numbered series. If availability records have been eliminated (as with the Marcive file), issue-specific information for individual volumes (such as the *Monthly Catalog* entry number and series number) may also have been lost. Some recurring titles may be represented by a set of records describing several volumes as separate monographs, plus a set of serial availability records.

As with serials, reference librarians need to know what availability records for multipart monographs are present in the file obtained from the vendor, how these records may have been eliminated or modified locally, and what plans are in place for post-load modification of these records.

Catalog Maintenance Issues

In any load of GPO retrospective records there will inevitably be some missing records, as well as some records loaded for documents which are not in fact part of the library's collection. There are various reasons why this may occur. Some documents listed in the *Monthly Catalog* as depository were actually never distributed. The library may lack some records (or receive some records in error) due to missing or erroneous item numbers in the GPO retrospective records. If the reference staff finds a large number of missing records or records for documents not in the collection, the possibility of an error in local processing or in profiling with the vendor should be investigated. The most important thing is that some mechanism be available for resolving these problems in a timely manner.

In order to prepare for potential authority problems after the load of GPO retrospective records into a local online catalog, reference librarians must have a clear understanding of what types of authority processing has been done on the file, either by the vendor or locally as part of the load process. A library which loads an unprocessed subset of the GPO retrospective file is bound to experience serious problems with name headings in pre-AACR2 form and incorrectly tagged and out-of-date subject headings. Even the load of a "highly processed" file such as that currently available from Marcive may introduce inconsistencies between series headings in the GPO records and series headings for documents previously cataloged by the library using LC series authority.

In addition to potential authority conflicts, libraries which have cataloged some government documents prior to the load of GPO retrospective records will likely experience some problems with duplicate records. Even the usually reliable approach of checking for OCLC number matches will fail to prevent the load of some duplicate records, since duplicate records for some documents have been created by LC and GPO on OCLC. Reference librarians need to make sure that some mechanism is in place for identifying and resolving these duplicates.

A depository library's federal documents collection is intended to be highly dynamic, continually changing in response to the changing information needs of the citizens of the congressional district served by the collection. In order to adapt to these changing needs, depository libraries are encouraged to weed their collections continually. A well-managed depository library may also be expected to make significant changes to its item number profile on an annual basis. It is important that the online catalog accurately reflect the dynamic nature of the collection.

CONCLUSION

Reference staff have long been accustomed to dealing with the problems and subtleties of the catalog, whether card, microfiche, or online. Variability in the quality of retrospectively converted machine-readable cataloging records is only one of a host of factors that reference librarians must take into account when dealing with the online catalog. The special characteristics of the GPO cataloging records make their integration into local online systems one of the most challenging retrospective conversion projects that a library may undertake. Consideration of the specific implications for reference staff discussed here should help enure that the project is a success.

REFERENCES

1. Judy E. Myers, "The Government Printing Office Cataloging Records: Opportunities and Problems," *Government Information Quarterly* 2 (1985):27-56. Articles dealing with the GPO retrospective file from additional perspectives include Carolyn C. Jamison's "Loading the GPO Tapes – What Does It Really Mean?" (*Government Publications Review* 13 (1986): 549-559), which addresses the details of tape processing, and Jan Swanbeck's "Federal Documents in the

Online Catalog: Problems, Options, and the Future" (*Government Information Quarterly* 2 (1985):187-192), in which she discusses the loading of GPO records into local systems in the context of overall planning for enhanced bibliographic access to government documents.

2. Forthcoming in *Technicalities*.

3. Myers, pp. 36-37.

4. Carol Turner and Ann Latta, *Current Approaches to Improving Access to Government Documents* (Washington, D.C.: Association of Research Libraries, Office of Management Studies, 1987), p. 39.

5. Margaret T. Mooney, "GPO Cataloging: Is It a Viable Current Access Tool for U.S. Documents?" *Government Publications Review* 16 (1989):259-270, p. 268.

6. "GPO to Produce Improved Cataloging Tapes," *Administrative Notes* 10 (1989):1.

7. Based on discussions with Joseph McClane, Chief, Inspection Team, United States Government Printing Office.

Computerized Access to Government Publications at Colorado State University Libraries

Douglas J. Ernest
Fred C. Schmidt

SUMMARY. The quality of reference assistance for library users seeking information from government publications has recently been called into question. Concurrently, advances in electronic technology offer means to substantially improve access to government information. Colorado State University Libraries has several computer systems available to access its documents collection, which is separately shelved. These systems include RLIN, CARL, NOTIS, and a number of CD-ROM products. Use of each system is examined, and examples of reference inquiries are given. In general, practice at Colorado State indicates that availability of electronic systems does improve access to government publications and enables reference staff to successfully negotiate documents queries. Fragmentation and privatization of government files, however, threaten to undo the gains thus achieved.

INTRODUCTION

Often in both academic and public libraries publications of the U.S. federal government and other governments are shelved and classified separately from non-governmental publications. The result has been difficult access and less use of government publications than their value warrants. This situation extends not only to library users but also to documents and reference librarians, whose ability to adequately assist the public in use of government documents has been called into question in a series of recent

Douglas J. Ernest and Fred C. Schmidt are Social Sciences/Humanities Librarian and Head, Government Documents Department, respectively, at Colorado State University Libraries, Fort Collins, CO 80523.

© 1991 by The Haworth Press, Inc. All rights reserved.

studies. The advent of electronic technology now offers substantial hope in overcoming the barriers to documents access. Colorado State University Libraries (CSUL) has access to government publications through a variety of electronic media, ranging from national bibliographic utilities to local CD-ROM work stations. This article will examine the CSUL reference experience with documents access. The following literature review will first place that experience in context.

LITERATURE REVIEW

Only recently has attention focused on the reference aspects of documents collections. In 1985 Moody published a useful survey of the literature.[1] She found that it was not until the 1970s that the literature showed a trend toward discussion of documents reference as opposed to the acquisition and organizations of collections. One of the more important articles written during the early 1980s was by Zink.[2] He feared an impending crisis in documents reference work, one created by the multitude of commercially produced documents indices, each with its own thesauri, and the increased use of microfiche as a preferred depository format. He advocated that documents librarians work to alleviate the frustrations of users and familiarize themselves with proper storage of microformats. In retrospect, Zink's article is of importance for its recognition that documents users were frustrated by access that was dependent upon a bewildering variety of print indices, each with its own strengths and limitations. In 1988 Moody once again examined the arena of documents reference, elucidating issues of importance for the near future.[3] Among these she included use of new technology; proliferation of formats, indices, and access points; quality of reference service; and integration of government documents into the rest of the library structure.

By far the most comprehensive work on documents reference has been by Hernon and McClure, sometimes as individuals and other times as coauthors.[4] Using unobtrusive testing techniques in which librarians were unaware that they were being studied, Hernon and McClure found that the general performance of documents reference staff was not good. Findings indicated that reference personnel answered correctly only about 55% of the questions administered, were unfamiliar with the content of basic reference sources, spent minimal time with individual library users, conducted superficial reference interviews, seldom referred users to other information agencies, and were sometimes abrasive.[5] Hernon and McClure confined their earlier work to documents reference personnel in academic libraries, but a study they conducted in 1986 that included public libraries and general reference staff found no substantial differences, other than the fact that general reference personnel performed more poorly in answering documents questions than did their documents colleagues.[6] Yet another study indicated that librarians performed even more inadequately when asked to identify publications of the National Technical Information Service (NTIS). The correct answer fill rate was only about 42 percent.[7] Although one might quarrel with Hernon and McClure's techniques, their studies unmistakably indicated problems with documents reference service.

Concurrent with the increased attention focused upon documents reference has been an interest in the role that automation can play in documents. In an article published in 1982 McClure noted that the subject had scarcely been broached and went on to discuss applications of OCLC and online searching. He noted that most documents departments had no computer terminals and suggested strategies for acquiring the new technology.[8] Interestingly, that same year Hernon edited a book dealing with the "new technology and documents librarianship," but none of the articles dealt substantially with reference work; discussion instead centered upon processing applications.[9] OCLC was the first bibliographic utility to go online on a national basis; articles by Walbridge outlined the use of OCLC in a documents context.[10] She noted that OCLC contains records from the *Monthly Catalog* from 1976 on and therefore is useful for identifying vague or incomplete bibliographic citations. The fact that government publications were integrated on OCLC often led users to documents collections to find items they would not have been aware of otherwise. Two other articles focused on online searching as a means to access government publications. The first, by Futato, included brief descriptions of documents databases and discussed procedures for implementing online searching.[11] Two years later Byerly detailed the uses of online searching for documents; these included bibliographic verification and ready reference searches.[12]

Three other authors took a more global view of computer applications in documents collections. In 1987 Wilkinson discussed barriers to use of U.S. government publications and found that despite an increased tendency by federal agencies to provide information in electronic formats, documents departments were unprepared to cope with the computer era; a study done in 1983-1984 indicated that only 12 percent of depository libraries had their own terminal.[13] Also in 1987 Tyckoson examined appropriate technologies for government information, discussing paper, microform, and electronic formats. Among the latter he gave brief note to online searching of commercial databases, use of bibliographic utilities such as OCLC, and the purchase of optical technology products mounted on microcomputers.[14] Finally, Hernon drew together the literature dealing with depository libraries and the electronic age in a review article that also suggested additional topics needing research.[15]

Over the last several years, then, the quality of documents reference service has been a topic of concern, as has the application of electronic technology to improve user access to government publications. The two have seldom been examined in conjunction, however. How can electronic technology be used on a daily basis to assist library users, and what effect does it have on the quality of reference service offered?

RLIN

CSUL's experience with accession to government publications via the Research Libraries Information Network (RLIN) database has been discussed in detail elsewhere, so only a summary will be attempted here.[16] The General Reference Desk received an RLIN terminal in 1984, and 1986 saw the installation of terminals at the Science and Documents reference desks. The documents collection at CSUL is arranged by Superintendent of Documents (SuDoc) classification and shelved separately from the rest of the collection in an area some distance from the General Reference desk. Moreover, documents were not included in the card catalog, located near the Reference Desk. Hence, during those times when the Documents desk is not staffed and responsibility for documents reference falls upon General Reference staff, access to documents information historically has not been easy. Staff had to rely on the *Monthly Catalog of United States Governments Publications* and John L. Andriot's *Guide to U.S. Government Publications* for subject access and SuDoc call numbers. Use of RLIN has simplified documents access considerably. Government Printing Office (GPO) tapes dating back to 1976 have been loaded on RLIN, which provides such a variety of access points that the *Monthly Catalog* is no longer needed and was removed from the area.

RLIN has separate files for books, serials, and maps, all of interest to documents users. Terminals can be set individually to search more than one file simultaneously. Among the access points or "indexes," are personal name (PN), title phrase (TP), title word (TW), corporate/conference name phrase (CP),corporate/conference word (CW), and Library of Congress subject headings (SP). Once an item is located on the database, it can be displayed in one of several formats; the long (LON) format includes the SuDoc's call number. Other valuable features include the combination of terms or indexes through the use of Boolean operators, right hand truncation, and the "also" (ALS) command, which allows one to narrow a search result by language, publication date, or institution. By entering DCGD, the institutional code for GPO records, one can narrow a search result to only those items published by the GPO.[17]

Examples of the value of RLIN as a documents finding aid are not wanting. One student was seeking information on the Legislative Reorganization Act of 1970. Rather than use a print resource, such as the *Congressional Information Service* (CIS), the librarian turned to the computer. A search of the title *Legislative Reorganization Act* uncovered thirteen entries, including some for the acts of 1946 and 1967. One entry included the public law number for the act of 1970, enabling the student to consult the *Statutes at Large* with greater ease, while another entry represented a Congressional hearing on the 1970 legislation. Since the hearing predated the 1976 GPO tapes, it lacked a SuDocs call number, so the *Monthly Catalog* had to be consulted. This transaction began at the General Reference Desk, so the user was armed with useful information about government publication even before entering the Documents collection.

Another user was attempting to locate a proceeding that dealt with wetland assessment. The terms "wetland" and "assessment" were searched simultaneously as corporate entry keywords. Two entries were found, including one with a DCGD identifier. This was a surprise to all concerned, as the user had no indication that this particular proceeding might be associated with the federal government. The bibliographic information, including the SuDocs call number, was printed and given to the user. In this instance, RLIN revealed a federal government publication that almost certainly would have been overlooked otherwise, for it was not listed in the card catalog and few would have guessed that it might be in Documents.

As a land grant institution, Colorado State University has academic programs in agriculture, forestry, water engineering, agricultural economics, and natural resources that spark heavy demand for publications of federal land agencies such as the National Park Service, the Forest Service, the Bureau of Land Management (BLM), and the Bureau of Reclamation (BR). Many of these publications are specialized and fugitive in nature; recognizing this problem the Documents Department makes special efforts to collect these publications and, in 1978, received a Higher Education Act Title II-C grant to catalog and classify them by SuDoc number. Over 10,000 titles were cataloged and loaded first into OCLC and later into RLIN.[18] As an example, a search of the subject "Routt National Forest" limited to CSUL's identifier revealed twelve documents published from 1961 to 1980 and cataloged under Title II-C auspices. They dealt with subjects such as environmental impact statements, timber sales, and dwarf mistletoe. Without RLIN and the Title II-C project, library users would have almost no access to these publications.

CARL

The Colorado Alliance of Research Libraries (CARL) was incorporated in 1978 and at present has six members: the University of Colorado at Boulder, the University of Denver, the University of Northern Colorado, the Colorado School of Mines, Auraria, and the Denver Public Library. CARL's most important project is its Public Access Catalog (PAC), an online catalog with separate files showing holdings for each institution. Records for PAC are taken from OCLC among other sources.[19] The CARL PAC has taken a different direction from RLIN. Rather than being structured around the traditional author, title, and Library of Congress subject headings, PAC assumes that the user has no preconceived notions about an online catalog and therefore allows for natural language inputting and modification of results as the search session evolves. Thus the user can search one or more key words and further modify with additional key words as the search progresses.[20] Access points include "word," "name" (including corporate name), and "browse." Browsing can be done by title, call number, and series. PAC is menu driven and enables even unsophisticated searchers to use Boolean techniques without the need for elaborate explanation. Since the initial inception of the database two separate files have been added that access government publications. The first includes documents, primarily federal, housed at the University of Colorado, Boulder and the Denver Public Library. Both institutions are regional depositories and began contributing records to PAC in about 1986; in turn CARL began subscribing to the GPO MARC tapes.[21] The second file, brought up more recently, includes Colorado state publications from the collection of the State Library.

CSUL acquired dial-up access to PAC in September, 1988. At present there are two PAC terminals available to library users and each of the reference stations, including Documents, can link to PAC via a gateway accessed through NOTIS terminals. Logon instructions accompany the public terminals; despite the fact that logon is complicated, most users master the task without difficulty. About one-fourth of logon attempts are unsuccessful because all ports are busy or there are telecommunications difficulties. More bothersome is the fact that, unless activity is maintained, PAC will dump dial-up users after a couple of minutes. This makes it difficult for reference staff to use PAC at times when traffic is heavy; engaged in assisting users, the librarian returns to the NOTIS/PAC terminal to find that he/she has been logged off in the interim.

Although we have made no studies, casual observation indicates that most CSUL users who access PAC select a file that represents the online catalog of one of the CARL members rather than turning to the Government Publications or Colorado state files. Users often become conscious of the government files only when directed to them by a librarian.

An excellent example occurred when an undergraduate approached the General Reference Desk and asked for assistance in locating government publications dealing with abortion. She was directed to a PAC terminal and shown how to access the Government Publications file and search the work "abortion." Thirty-two items having "abortion" or "abortions" in the entry were retrieved. The user wrote down several titles and their SuDocs call numbers and proceeded to the Documents shelving area. The same type of search could have been performed on RLIN by the librarian, but the user would have been only a passive onlooker. Her introduction to PAC allowed her to perform the search herself and to learn a new and painless way to access government publications. Had she wished, she could also have searched the Colorado State Publications file and found a report on induced abortions by the Colorado Department of Health. On another occasion the documents reference librarian turned to PAC to answer a question at a time when the RLIN terminal was temporarily down. A student was seeking any U.S. Forest Service or National Park Service publication dealing with visitor perception of the visual quality of a natural landscape. A word search on the Government Publications file employing "visual" and "perception" retrieved a Forest Service publication entitled "Visual Vulnerability of the Landscape: Control of Visual Quality" that answered the student's question. The PAC record also indicated that the publication had a bibliography that would presumably lead to additional sources.

A final example dramatically underscores how electronic technology can ease access to government publications. In one of their unobtrusive reference studies Hernon and McClure found that only 23.1 percent of the librarians queried were able to identify three especially difficult government publications.[22] If the librarians tested had access to RLIN, they would have found all three titles readily, even without prior knowledge that they were government publications. Similarly, two of the three can be retrieved easily on CARL, although the user at present has to take the initiative to search the Government Publications file.[23]

MARCIVE GPO TAPE LOAD INTO NOTIS

For the majority of depository libraries that have maintained separate uncataloged federal government publication collections, the loading of GPO tapes into local online catalogs promises to substantially increase use of government publications. The Watson and Heim study at Illinois demonstrated the premise that where government publications are given integrated equal access in a central bibliographic file (card catalog and/or online catalog), use of government publications equals that of general library materials.[24]

Norton has reported that loading only one year of the GPO tapes into Brigham Young's NOTIS online catalog resulted in a 40 percent increase in the use of its government publications collection.[25]

CSUL's NOTIS online catalog became active in September 1988. A commitment has been made to integrate GPO's post 1976 *Monthly Catalog* tapes into its NOTIS online catalog in the fall of 1989, using tapes supplied by MARCIVE, Inc. This vendor, in conjunction with Rice, Louisiana State and Texas A&M Universities, has enhanced the original GPO tapes by elimination of duplicate records, making numerous corrections in the MARC fields and restoration of missing data in the records. Retrieval of GPO records in NOTIS can be made by author, title, subject and keyword-Boolean searches. The GPO tapes are being loaded successfully into other online catalog systems. The point here is that optimum use of GPO records can be achieved by integration into the main public access catalog. To illustrate the desirability of such integration, one can look at the situation at CARL. GPO records are currently loaded into a separate file and can be accessed through a menu command. Notwithstanding, due to request by some of its largest member libraries, CARL plans to load the GPO tapes into individual library databases to enable these libraries to provide optimum access of these records to their users.

GPO records are also available for dialup searching through various database vendors such as DIALOG and BRS. This option will become less attractive to users at institutions with online systems capable of keyword-Boolean searches, but will remain a desirable option to users lacking such a system or requiring only occasional searches.

CD-ROM TECHNOLOGY

CD-ROM technology has begun to provide users with an ever-increasing variety of government indexing and abstracting services and full-text databases. Acquisition of such databases as GPO records, National Technical Information Service (NTIS), ERIC, Selected Water Resources Abstracts (SWRA), AGRICOLA, MEDLINE, Congressional Masterfile, and others has provided users with cost-free search capabilities not previously possible with printed indexes. Acquisition of full text databases on CD-ROM format databases such as HYDRODATA (streamflow records, peak records, water quality records) and CLIMATDATA (temperature, precipitation, hourly precipitation, etc.) has enabled CSUL to remove several hundred linear feet of *Climatological Data for* [*states*] and *Water Resources Data for* [*states*] from the main documents collection. The amount of time saved by researchers of these full-text CD-ROM data disks has been quite dramatic. Hydrologists using this system at CSUL have estimated that they have saved anywhere from one week to two months of searching time when compared to using the paper-based data. CD-ROM products are just beginning to be included in the depository distribution system. All depository libraries have received the Census Bureau's census test disc no. 2, which contains data from the 1982 Census of Agriculture and the 1982 Census of Business. GPO plans to distribute the 1987 Economic and Agricultural Census on CD-ROM and the 1990 population census on 20 to 30 disks. The acquisition of in-house CD-ROM publishing capability by GPO is a strong indication of the direction toward which GPO is heading.

This new medium is not without drawbacks. The major limitation of CD-ROM for reference use is the one-station, one-user situation. At CSUL, users often need to wait in line or sign up to use certain heavily-used data bases. CSUL plans to alleviate this problem by establishing a local area network (LAN), and using multiple processors with stacker units. Users will then be able to use extensive screen menus to determine the database they wish to access. Other options being considered for future application include loading heavily-used databases on CSUL's main online public access catalog (NOTIS) as separate files.

Another significant limitation of the use of CD-ROM technology has been the need for investment in sophisticated retrieval hardware. For example, to retrieve full-text data at a reasonable speed, institutions could acquire IBM/IBM-compatible PCs equipped with 80286+ processors, 20 to 40+ mb hard disk drives, math co-processors, EGA/VGA monitors, single or multiple disk CD-ROM drives and quiet, high-speed printers. Such user station configurations can easily cost five thousand dollars or more.

User acceptance of the CD-ROM technology is so great that often the printed versions of these databases are little used. For example, since databases such as ERIC, Hydrodata, Climatedata, NTIS and others have been received in CD-ROM format, their equivalent print indexes have been virtually ignored, even though they may be shelved only a few feet away from the work stations, and may have, in some cases, additional access points.

Other limitations of CD-ROM technology experienced by CSUL and other institutions include the existence of multiple types of software used by vendors to retrieve data from the various databases. This lack of standardization has forced reference staffs to devote much more time for one-on-one training of users, thus placing a severe strain on staff time for other reference service.

Despite these limitations, CD-ROM technology has proven to be a powerful tool in providing retrieval of large masses of government information in a timely manner, and will be extensively used by the federal government to disseminate large masses of information such as census data through the depository system.[26]

CONCLUSION

As early as 1983 McClure and Hernon indicated that bibliographic integration of a government publications collection could occur without physical integration.[27] To date the CSUL experience substantiates that such is the case. Certainly the ability of reference personnel to answer reference queries with documents sources has vastly improved. When the MARCIVE GPO tape load into NOTIS is completed, bibliographic integration will take another giant step forward. In a few years the time may be at hand when, as one enthusiast foresees, library users will sit down at a single computer work station that will allow access to all government publications, federal and non-federal, using a simple set of search commands.[28]

The future may not be so rosy, however; cautionary voices are being raised. In 1987 Hernon noted that the rise of desktop publishing and the availability of government files from a mix of commercial and government sources in a variety of electronic configurations can lead to fragmentation of government information and lack of bibliographic control.[29] Equally alarming, Kranich has pointed out that the privatization of federal government computer files is leading to dramatically increased costs and consequent more limited access by users who are less affluent.[30] The specter arises that information produced at taxpayer expense may become most readily accessible to the wealthy and powerful. It is ironic that, even as technology is making government publications more accessible than ever to library users and enabling reference librarians to utilize documents collections in ways that were impossible before, market forces and the nature of electronic media may combine to continue or even exacerbate the separate nature of government publications. Documents librarians and their colleagues will have to be alert to ensure that technology and access to documents equate.

REFERENCES

1. Moody, Marilyn, "Twenty-five Years of Government Information: Changes in Reference Service Attitudes," *RQ* 25 (1):39-45 (Fall 1985).
2. Zink, Steven D., "The Impending Crisis in Government Publications Reference Service," *Microform Review* 11 (2):106-111 (Spring 1982).
3. Moody, Marilyn, Critical Issues in Government Information Reference Service, *RQ* 27 (4):479-483 (Summer 1988).
4. Their earlier work is summarized in Peter Hernon and Charles R. McClure, *Public Access to Government Information: Issues, Trends, and Strategies* (Norwood, N.J.: Ablex Publishing Corporation, 1984) and Charles R. McClure and Peter Hernon, *Improving the Quality of Reference Service for Government Publications* (Chicago:American Library Association, 1983).
5. Hernon, Peter, "The Unrecognized Crisis: Library Reference Service at the Crossroads," *Government Information Quarterly* 3 (4):329-332 (1986).
6. Hernon, Peter and Charles R. McClure, "Unobtrusive Reference Testing: the 55 Percent Rule," *Library* Journal 111 (7):37-41 (April 15, 1986).
7. Hernon, Peter and Charles R. McClure, "The Quality of Academic and Public Library Reference Service Provided for NTIS Products and Services: Unobtrusive Test Results," *Government Information Quarterly* 3 (2):117-132 (1986).
8. McClure, Charles R., "Technology in Government Document Collections: Current Status, Impacts, and Prospects," *Government Publications Review* 9 (4):255-276 (July/August 1982).
9. Hernon, Peter, ed., *New Technology and Documents Librarianship* (Westport, CT: Meckler Publishing, 1983).
10. Walbridge, Sharon, "OCLC and Government Documents Collections," *Government Publications Review* 9 (4):277-287 (July/August 1982); Sharon Walbridge, OCLC and Improved Access to Government Documents, *Illinois Libraries* 68 (5):329 332 (May 1986).
11. Futato, Linda, "Online Bibliographic Database Searching for Government Documents Collections," *Government Publications Review* 9 (4):311-322 (July/August 1982).
12. Byerly, Greg, "Online Searching: Just Another Tool for Document Librarians," *Government Publications Review* 11 (3):203-210 (May/June 1984).
13. Wilkinson, Patrick J., "Political, Technological, and Institutional Barriers to U.S. Government Information," *RQ* 26 (4):425-433 (Summer 1987).
14. Tyckoson, David A., "Appropriate Technologies for Government Information," *RQ* 27 (1):33-38 (Fall 1987).

15. Hernon, Peter, "Depository Library Collections and Services in an Electronic Age: A Review of the Literature," *Government Information Quarterly* 4 (4):383-397 (1987).

16. Ernest, Douglas J., "Accessing Federal Government Publications with RLIN," *Government Publication Review* 15 (3):237-244 (May/June 1988).

17. For a detailed description of RLIN reference searching, see Arturo A. Flores, "A User Friendly Guide to RLIN for Friendly Users," *Legal Reference Services Quarterly* 5 (4):43-56 (Winter 1985/86).

18. Copeland, Nora S., Fred C. Schmidt, and James Stickman, "Fugitive U.S. Government Publications: Elements of Procurement and Bibliographic Control," *Government Publications Review* 12(3):227-237 (May/June 1985); Ernest, Accessing Federal Government Publications with RLIN, p. 241.

19. Shaw, Ward, "Cooperative Academic Library Networks: the CARL Experience," *The Southeastern Librarian* 38(2):53-56 (Summer 1988).

20. Rice-Jones, Judith. "An Interview with Ward Shaw and Patricia Culkin: Designers of CARL PAC," *Colorado Libraries* 11 (1):5-12 (March 1985).

21. Koppel, Ted, "Government Publications Access at C.A.R.L.—Issues and Processes," paper presented at the annual meeting of the Special Libraries Association, Denver, Colorado, June 15, 1988.

22. Hernon and McClure, "Unobtrusive Reference Testing . . . ," p. 39.

23. The three titles are: United States, Federal Aviation Administration, *Air Traffic Control Staffing Standard System* (Washington, D.C.: Department of Transportation, Federal Aviation Administration, 1975); Roger K. Salaman and E.C. Hettinger, *Policy Implications of Information Technology* (Washington, D.C.: U.S. Department of Commerce, National Telecommunications Administration, 1984); and *Computer-Based National Information Systems: Technology and Public Policy Issues* (Washington, D.C.: Congress of the U.S., Office of Technology Assessment, 1981.)

24. Watson, Paula E. and Kathleen M. Heim, "Patterns of Access and Circulation in a Depository Documents Collection Under Full Bibliographic Control," *Government Publications Review* 11(4):269-292 (July/August 1984).

25. Norton, Beverly, (Federal Documents Librarian, Brigham Young University), Personal Communication, July 12, 1989.

26. Sanchez, Lisa, "Dissemination of United States Federal Government Information on CD-ROM, an Issues Primer," *Government Publications Review* 16(2):133-144 (March/April 1989).

27. McClure and Hernon, *Improving the Quality of Reference Service. . . .* pp. 140-141.

28. Purcell, Royal, "Future Computerized Use of Government Publications," *Library Software Review* 8 (1):16-18 (January/February 1989).

29. Hernon, "Depository Library Collections and Services in an Electronic Age . . . ," pp. 383, 393.

30. Kranich, Nancy C., "Information Drought: Next Crisis for the American Farmer?" *Library Journal* 114 (11):22-27 (June 15, 1989).